Upward Call
How to Draw Closer to God

by

J. Scott Wilson

"Upward Call"

Cover photo: It tells the story of a man very alone, searching for something greater, something outside of himself and outside of the world. Then he is drawn to a distant voice calling him upward, "Seek My face."

Bible references are from the RSV and the NASB unless otherwise noted.

"Upward Call"

The Parish Press
Keller, Texas

ISBN: 978-0-9896267-7-4

Library of Congress Control Number: 2021923158

Printed in the United States of America

"Upward Call"

Brethren, I do not regard myself as having laid hold of it yet; but one thing I do, forgetting what lies behind and reaching forward to what lies ahead, I press on toward the goal for the prize of the upward call of God in Christ Jesus
(Paul of Tarsus, Phil. 3:13–14).

"Upward Call"

Editors

Edit911
William J. Summey Jr, Ph.D.
Belmont University College of
Theology and Christian Ministry

Lana W. Wilson B.A., M.Ed., LPC

Cover Design

Murry Whiteman
Graphic Artist

"Upward Call"

Acknowledgments

I begin by thanking God for the privilege of undertaking this project. I learned so very much.

To my dear wife, Lana, who remains by my side through all our life together. And a special thanks for her remarkable assistance in editing this book.

To our dear children, Mary and her husband Jonathon, John, Steven, and Rob, for whom I remain grateful, and the wonderful parenting and Christian spiritual guidance they have bestowed upon our twelve grandchildren.

To Bishop Keith and Joann Ackerman for the guidance they have offered and the hard work they have done to bring this book into reality.

To all the clergy of the Anglican Diocese of Fort Worth, the bishops, priests, and deacons who together have braved the recent tumultuous years, remaining faithful.

To Bishop Fanuel Magangani, the nuns of Saint Mary's Convent, and the clergy of the Diocese of Northern Malawi with whom we have been blessed to share our lives and ministries over the last several years.

To the men of the Robson Ranch Saturday Morning Men's Bible Study group with whom I have been blessed to journey in our fellowship and study over the last several years.

"Upward Call"

Canon. J. Scott Wilson, SSC was ordained priest in the Episcopal Diocese of Dallas in 1977, and served in Dallas, Ft Worth, Oklahoma and Pennsylvania.

In serving on both the parish and diocesan level, Canon Wilson has spent considerable time ministering to teenagers in the greater church, seeking to awaken them to a living relationship with God through Jesus Christ. The many retreats and conferences he conducted among teens and adults led to invitations for ministry to South Africa, Tanzania, and, more recently, Malawi, where he has worked primarily with clergy.

For his continued work on repeated trips among the clergy and nuns of the Diocese of Northern Malawi, he was named in 2017 as Honorary Canon of Saint Peter's Cathedral, Likoma Island.

Though Cn. Wilson's undergraduate work and early years professionally were in engineering, he earned both the standard degree in seminary and a later Masters of Theology in Biblical Studies.

His love for evangelism motivated a study of Spanish in Guatemala in order to start a Hispanic congregation in his parish church. He also developed an evangelism seminar, TELET, that he has conducted in many parish churches and on the diocesan level, training lay people and clergy in sharing their faith in Christ with others.

At one weekend conference Cn. Wilson conducted, he met his darling wife, Lana. They married in 1999. Together they have four children and twelve grandchildren. Lana, a retired licensed professional counselor, has accompanied him on many of his adventures. Canon Wilson and Lana live in Denton, Texas. In his free time, he enjoys sports and travel.

"Upward Call"

Foreword

In a world filled with strong opinions and partisan realities, Father J. Scott Wilson in his excellent book, "Upward Call" has transcended external conflicts and presented to the People of God a book that can unite a person within his or her very soul, by giving us very practical ways to walk with the Lord. Writing a book about the Spiritual life in today's world runs the risks of several polarizations: anecdotalism (all about the author) to intellectualism (all about concepts) and external examples (look at your felt experience) to introspective examples (what are you thinking?). Fr. Wilson does a remarkable job of taking the two extremes, and weaving together a seamless story — a story of walking with Jesus Christ.

In classical Ascetical Theology, we are presented with terms that help immensely those who are on a serious spiritual journey. In many modern books on the spiritual there is either an avoidance or ignorance of classical Spirituality which can result in having a book that is easily forgotten, and not particularly useful for a book study or a class. Fr. Wilson has produced a book that results in being drawn ever closer to Christ in both a classical and contemporary way, by confronting and explaining, without being slavishly wedded to one way versus another.

Simply put, this book is a love story about a relationship with Jesus Christ, and the goal is for others to discover that being with Jesus is more than (1) having happy thoughts about Jesus and (2) going to church every Sunday. And now, you as a reader, must walk with the author chapter by chapter in a pilgrimage to and with Jesus Christ our Lord and Savior.

The Right Reverend Keith L. Ackerman, SSC
Eighth Bishop of Quincy
President of The Parish Press

"Upward Call"

Introduction

Human beings are made of body, mind and spirit. We endeavor admirably to take care of our physical bodies and spend large portions of our lives filling our minds with knowledge and understanding, but our spirits are woefully neglected. The spirit of the Christian is the only part that lasts forever.

Christians know this truth and are instructed throughout the New Testament to make training up of their spiritual lives their highest priority. "Seek first His kingdom" (Matt. 6:33), Jesus said. "Pursue after peace with all men, and after the sanctification without which no one will see the Lord" (Heb. 12:14). As Jesus told the rich, young ruler, "Go and sell your possessions and give to the poor, and you shall have treasure in heaven" (Matt. 19:21). With these and many more teachings, we are directed to prepare for the eternity awaiting us, over and above what we do here on earth.

The lure the immediate things of this world have to offer tend to drown out the call of God. Our Lord is always calling us to the higher, eternal things. And we must remember, we have but one lifetime to hear the right voice, make the greater choice, and pursue the higher, eternal things.

C. S. Lewis is credited with giving us a good perspective: "Aim at Heaven and you will get the Earth 'thrown in'; aim at Earth and you will get neither."[1] He is telling us to seek heaven first, and righteousness in God and all the truly good things earth has to offer will be ours as well. Seek instead the ambitions offered us by this world, and, in the end, we will have neither. Our spiritual lives are to be our highest priority, for this is where we find union with God,

---

[1] C. S. Lewis, *The Joyful Christian* (New York: Touchstone, 1977) "Hope," p. 138.

"Upward Call"

who loves us more than we can imagine and longer than we can ever imagine — forever.

This book takes the reader on a course toward Heaven. It provides a roadmap to build up our spirit over and above the things of this world. It shows us how to seek first His kingdom and answer the upward call of God.

Upward Call
How to Draw Closer to God

"Upward Call"

Table of Contents

"Upward Call"

Beginning a New Life with God

In churches across the world, many people claim an affiliation with the Christian faith, yet have little concept of a living Lord with whom they may have a loving relationship. They believe there is a God and believe they really ought to go to church, do charitable things, and avoid sin. But walking with Jesus Christ is much more, and there is much He wants to show us. Similarly, many others claim belief in God and Jesus Christ, yet choose not to attend a church for one reason or another. Consequently, for them, too, their Christian faith is little more than some kind of moral system that warns them from sinning. What all these souls may have never experienced is drawing closer to God and enjoying Him daily. He truly wants a relationship with us, and the things we can discover from our Lord fill our lives with purpose, love, wonder, adventure, peace, warmth, and joy. This is the "upward call" of God (Phil. 3:14).

I went to my spiritual mentor many years ago because I had a problem; I just did not know what it was. Though I thought at the time I was in pretty good shape spiritually, I must have sensed a lacking somewhere in me. At any rate, I managed to convey this need to him, and he recommended some books — the classics, he called them. Politely, he said this is what he read (or reread) when he was feeling that way. When I began reading one of these, *The Dark Night of the Soul*,[2] it struck me so deeply. The author was describing people who had a level of faith and, through this faith, offered up their prayers. I was thinking, "Yes, yes, this is me," when he next referred to these people as "beginners." I was stunned; I accepted the charge humbly. I was humbled, relieved, and excited

---

[2] St. John of the Cross (1542–1591), *The Dark Night of the Soul* (Doubleday: An Image Book, 1959).

all at the same time. There really was more. Reading some of the other works my mentor recommended made it increasingly clear to me: there really was a whole new realm of love, prayer, and excitement to engage in as I grow closer to God. I sense that my life would never be the same; the "upward call" of God was now securely planted in my heart.

Returning to my earlier years as a newly ordained priest in my twenties, I assisted in a large church of over a thousand members. I made it my project to promote attendance at a weekend renewal conference. The conference had proven very effective with several members. The senior lay leader of the parish, whom I barely knew, agreed to attend this conference and surprised me a few days later by stopping by my office unannounced. Standing in front of my desk, he explained that he had served as Senior Warden twice over his several years at this church, Junior Warden three times, head of the Ushers Guild a number of years, and chaired the "Every Member Canvas" four times. He always believed that by taking on these responsibilities, he had been a good Christian. "I realize now," he said, "all I have ever been was a good churchman. Now, I am a Christian!" In other words, "Now I get it!" Then he left my office. I could not have been more pleased. He was a classic case of a long-standing church member who had come closer to the Lord and heard the "upward call."

Drawing close to our Lord is all about having a relationship with Him, and there is only one foundation upon which this is acceptable: He is Lord, and we are His blessed children; He is shepherd, and we are His sheep.

I was born and raised with a very different attitude about my life, namely that I was in charge of it. I believed that if any good was going to come of my life and if I was going to wind up, in the end, having enjoyed it, it was up to me to make it so. I was in charge. My happiness, well-being, and sense of accomplishment was the focus of my greatest endeavors. This viewpoint is normal for most all human beings. Consequently, making Jesus our Lord and looking to Him as our shepherd will require an essential change.

"Unless you repent, you will all likewise perish," Jesus said (Luke 13:5). *Repent* is the keyword. It means to turn one's life around. Repentance does not mean, as many suspect, getting down on one's knees and sorrowfully begging forgiveness for one's most grievous sins (though this could hardly hurt!). Instead, it means consciously surrendering to God's chief control of the use and direction of one's entire being — body, soul, and mind. It is turning one's life from self-service to God's service. When God encountered Paul on the road to Damascus (Acts 9), the flash of light around him left him stunned, and he fell to the ground. Jesus then spoke to him audibly, "I am Jesus whom you are persecuting, but rise, and enter the city, and it shall be told you what you must do" (vv. 5–6). Paul made no protest but entered the city, was soon baptized, and began living his life for God. His life's purpose underwent a diametrically opposite change.

Paul had repented. From what a person thought he understood to be the right way to live, repentant, he now had committed himself to a completely different way. He chose a lifestyle where God was His Lord. Paul pretty much had his mind changed for him. But from that point on, he became a leading representative of the nascent Christian belief.

The decision to repent usually requires, for one thing, humility. *Pride* is a term often used to describe our state as an unconverted person; it describes the nature of our being since birth. Pride means I believe in myself, but repenting means I am letting go and letting God take charge of my life. Therefore, letting go — an act of humility — is necessarily associated with repentance.

3

When I was still a young priest, I visited a church member, Sarah, who was hospitalized. Pride was clearly an issue with Sarah because she always wanted me to know that even though I was her priest, she had been in the church many more years than I; and therefore, she knew a lot more than I. I began explaining that we needed to give our lives to the Lord and let Him guide us through this life.

"I know," she protested. Then, she explained that she would "get her life together" and give it to Him.

I responded, "Sarah, look at yourself. You are 52 years old, in the hospital, diabetic, alcoholic, and with many family problems. Yet, this is what you've accomplished so far with your life." I explained, "God does not want us to get our lives together and then give them to Him. He wants our life just as it is now; He wants to come in and help us get our lives together." Her silence told me I had hit home. But pride being what it was with her, she said nothing further to me about this — and never did. Several weeks later when she was out of the hospital and back at the church for a Bible Study class I was leading, she stood up and directed an impassioned plea to those present: "Ladies, you must understand, we don't get our lives together ourselves. We have to turn them over to God just as they are and let Him take over." Silently, internally, I jumped with joy. "There is joy in the presence of the angels of God over one sinner who repents" (Luke 15:10). I soon left that church to accept a position elsewhere. But when she died several years later, I was notified that she had requested that I participate in her funeral, which I did.

Repentance can also spring from the troubling awareness that we are sinners needing forgiveness. Of course, we cannot stop sinning on our own. It takes a rescue from God to deliver any of us from the sinful side of life that haunts us. We do this with a prayer, which may be simple to say, but deep to our core in meaning. Jason was such a person. Jason was a teenager heading to college but wanted to benefit from one more session at the Diocesan Summer Camp. He was a particularly quiet and pensive young man, and it was hard to ascertain what was really bothering him. I gathered that he was relatively intelligent. After getting together a number of times at his request, he still wanted to meet once more. The questions continued about Jesus, Satan, evil power, and the temptation in the wilderness. Each question and answer were followed by a period of pensive silence. I could not tell where this was going, but I sensed that we were beginning to circle the wagons. Finally, staring at me with deep concern, he asked, "How can I stop sinning so much?" The question showed me clearly that he was plagued with conflict and had been trying hard to lead a proper life apart from darkness, doubt, and fear. I asked Jason, "Have you ever asked Christ into your life?" No, he hadn't. I gave Jason a short lesson on why and how we accept Christ into our lives. I explained that when He is sincerely invited into a person's life, Jesus promises to come. Jason prayed, and his life was changed in a beautiful way.

When we ask Christ to come into our life, we are surrendering our life to Him. Paul writes, "I have been crucified with Christ; and it is no longer I who live, but Christ lives in me; and the life which I now live in the flesh I live by faith in the Son of God, who loved me and gave Himself up for me" (Gal. 2:20). First of all, baptism is a kind of death. "Do you not know that all of us who have been baptized into Christ Jesus have been baptized into His death?" (Rom. 6:3). But what has died? Paul explains that his "old self" was put to death. It is not right to say that my will has died because my will is more alive now than ever. But I no longer have the same will I had before, which was entirely self-oriented, my "old self." Now, I am invigorated with God's will. For indeed, an important part of me has been transformed. Now I find myself wanting His will to be done. In the Garden of Gethsemane, the night before Jesus dies, He prays,

"My Father, if it is possible, let this cup pass from Me; yet not as I will, but as Thou will" (Matt. 26:39). He does not relish the pain and suffering soon to be experienced, but His time in prayer enables Him to fulfill His Father's will for Him. So, with Christ coming into our lives, there is a significant transformation of the will: from my old will, which has been put to death, to my new will enlivened and guided by God.

This truth can be further explained with the insight of Oswald Chambers, who says that the words, "it is no longer I who live, but Christ lives in me," refer to the "breaking and collapse of my independence." This truth is because one's own choosing breaks the individual independence from God we are born with. Henceforth, the Christian no longer follows his own ideas, but chooses "absolute loyalty to Jesus."[3]

"I have been crucified in Christ." The old "I" no longer lives, but now the new "I," which subsists on faith in the living Lord. Human beings want independence, but they also want love and a good life. God is the only source of true love and a truly full life, and the desire for independence must be sacrificed for the life and love that come from God.

---

[3] Oswald Chambers, *My Utmost for His Highest* (Grand Rapids: Discovery House Publishers, 1992), November 3.

We Must Seek God

There are two interesting parables in the Gospel of Matthew that help us understand seeking and finding Jesus.

The kingdom of heaven is like treasure hidden in the field; which a man found and hid; and from joy over it he goes and sells all that he has, and buys that field.

Again, the kingdom of heaven is like a merchant seeking fine pearls, and upon finding one pearl of great value, he went and sold all that he had, and bought it.

(Matt. 13:44–46)

The kingdom of heaven is the realm in which God is Lord, and His people are His subjects, whom He deeply loves. The kingdom is not geographical; it is relational. It exists wherever and whenever people are in a relationship with God as their Lord. Therefore, it is described here as something of great joy and value, which it is.

Interestingly, the two parables are coupled together; they describe the two different ways people come to discover a relationship with God. In the first, the man is not looking for the kingdom. He just finds it. This experience is something like Paul's experience. Paul isn't seeking God; rather, he seeks to fulfill a badly mistaken notion of what God wants: he seeks to destroy Christianity. But having found the treasure — or the treasure finding him — he sells out all he has to obtain it. Paul sacrifices his former life, reputation, and probably most of his possessions to live as a messenger for Jesus.

Most of us are more like the merchant of the second parable: we are seeking. What we are seeking, we may not really know. But there is a yearning, a hunger we sense deep inside that has not yet been fulfilled. We have not found fulfillment through the accomplishment of a goal, success in business, satisfaction from the admiration of others, accumulation of wealth, excellence in skills, talents, nor athletic achievement, nor even in the love of another person. The merchant is seeking fine pearls and, in his search, finds a pearl of such outstanding, excellent value that he too sacrifices all that he has to obtain it. The pearls he already owns represent things that give some value to the life he lives. The merchant is seeking because the fulfillment of life he hopes for has not yet been found, not until he discovers the pearl of great value. The treasure and the pearl of great value are the kingdom of heaven — the incomparably fulfilling relationship we can have with God through Jesus Christ. This relationship fulfills life, and there is nothing that can replace it. Even in the church, many people inherently know they are yet to discover something that provides greater value for them in this life. So, whether consciously or unconsciously, they search.

Having an understanding of these things, St Augustine, the fourth-century Bishop from Hippo (Algeria), described the human condition in this way: "You have made us for Yourself and our hearts are restless until they find their rest in Thee."[4] Blaise Pascal, the 17th-century French philosopher and theologian, added this to Augustine's observation, "There is a God-shaped vacuum in the heart of every man, and only God can fill it."[5]

These truisms explain the reason the human soul undergoes the search. God creates the human soul for Himself. Until God is found, the restless yearning for fulfillment drives us into the search. Blessed are they who undergo the search, for they shall be satisfied! (See Matt. 5:6.)

The price of obtaining the kingdom as described in these parables is worthy of discussion. In both cases, the man has just the right

---

[4] St. Augustine (Bishop of Hippo) *Confessions* (Hackett Publishing, 2006) p. 18.
[5] Pascal is credited with this summarization, the literal comment can be found in Blaise Pascal, *Pensees (New York, Penquin Books, 1966) p. 75.*

amount to obtain what he wants. Notice it takes "all that he had" to make the purchase. There is not too little, nor is there too much. The seller does not say to the merchant, "You have overpaid for the pearl; here is your change." No, it takes everything the merchant has to close the deal. And yet, no seller says what is offered is not enough. In both cases, "all that he had" was the right amount. This amount is intended because, as the Bible says, "You will seek Yahweh your God, and you will find Him if you search for Him with all your heart and all your soul" (Deut. 4:29). All your heart and soul is the price the merchant is willing to pay; this is what is meant by "all that he had." It is not all our possessions, for God could care less for our possessions. It is all our heart and soul — the fullness of our emotional and personal heartfelt endeavor. God wants us to truly want Him. And if we do search for Him in this way, He promises that we will find Him. "Yahweh (God's Name) searches all hearts, and understands every intent of the thoughts. If you seek Him, He will let you find Him" (I Chron. 28:9).

None of us is perfect in our words, deeds, nor especially in our thoughts. Therefore, seeking Him becomes a continuing endeavor. In fact, as long as we remain in this lifetime, we will always be seeking Him. There is no "arrival," even though God's fulfillment begins immediately. Seeking is a lifelong state, one could say. But as our heart continues toward Him, God comes running toward us, just as the father did when he saw the Prodigal Son returning home. God loves us and longs to be with us, even more than we love Him. And He shows this in that as we begin to approach Him sincerely, He comes "running" to us.

My own conversion was quite dramatic. Prior, I always thought of God and Jesus as historical figures — persons who had come at a certain point in history, did what they did, and left when they were through. They did not know me from Adam (excuse the pun). The morning after my "conversion," when I discovered that God truly knows and wants me, I quickly found a Bible and began reading passages that leapt out at me as if they were written specifically for me. I was amazed and began applying them in my new prayer life: "Whatever you ask in prayer, you will receive, if you have faith" (Matt. 21:22). Like the parent wanting to win the heart of a newly adopted child, God granted me everything for which I prayed for weeks. He called me. I began coming toward Him, and He came running to me. My heart was filled with joy, peace, and, above all, excitement. A great adventure in my life had begun.

Jesus says, "And I tell you, ask, and it will be given you; seek, and you will find; knock, and it will be opened to you. For every one who asks receives, and he who seeks finds, and to him who knocks it will be opened" (Luke 11:9–10). To properly understand the Greek use of the verbs, it must read, "Ask and keep on asking, seek and keep on seeking, knock and keep on knocking." In other words, as willing servants and children of our Lord, we affix ourselves in the position of constantly asking, seeking, and knocking and with our heart thus turned "Godward." He responds willingly.

How to Draw Closer to God

We Obey God

It was my own father who once asked the good question: "How do we love God?" He had always heard that we are supposed to love God, but, honestly, he didn't. He loved his wife and children, but he felt no love for God. He appreciated God and all He had done, but the only "love" my father understood was the warm, desiring kind that one feels. And no, he did not feel that kind of affection for God.

The love we read about in the Bible is not a love that is felt; it is an act of will. It can later generate into something genuinely feel, but, at the root, Christian love is an act of will. Love is choosing to make someone else the object of our interests, focus, energy, and endeavor. "Love thy neighbor as thyself." We certainly love ourselves in this fashion, even when we are not too happy with who we are. We spend a great deal of time and energy on our well-being, trying to make ourselves happy. The deeper meaning of Christian love will be addressed later, but seeking God or journeying to Him, regardless of whether it is instigated by a love of self or a love of God, generates love for Him. It pleases Him. So, at the heart of the matter, we can ask, "How does one go about loving God?"

God's "Love Language"

Each of us has what is sometimes called a "love language." I certainly have one: if you want to win my love, you will give me chocolate ice cream (with brownie chunks in it)! Tickets to a football game also work well. On the other hand, my wife could care less for tickets to a football game, a hockey game, a baseball game, etc., but bring her a lovely bouquet of roses, and she lights up like a beautiful rose herself. My granddaughter, who has no interest in any of the above, would smile ear to ear if we bought her a princess outfit. Each of us has a love language, and so does God. He is enough like us —

11

or we are enough like Him — that He, too, has a love language. He even has the wherewithal to tell us what it is: "If you love Me, you will keep My commandments" (John 14:15). In this way, God sees that we love Him by our willful choosing (not forced) to keep His commandments.

Thus, undertaking a renewed commitment to follow His commandments is a vital place to begin our journey to God. But which commandments? All of them. Most of us are pretty familiar with the Ten Commandments; they're considered fairly basic. And of course, there are the Big Two:

You shall love the Lord your God with all your heart, and with all your soul, and with all your mind. This is the great and first commandment. And a second is like it, You shall love your neighbor as yourself. On these two commandments hang all the law and the prophets (Matt. 22:37–40).

The Sermon on the Mount (Matt. 5–7) provides a great deal of Jesus' teachings and commandments. A careful itemization of this short passage will provide over forty precepts such as:

- things to do — "Turn to him the other cheek."

- things not to do — Don't "look on a woman to lust for her."

- things to be — "You are the salt of the earth."

- things to think — "Do not be anxious."

Some of these laws can be quite challenging: "But I say to you, love your enemies and pray for those who persecute you" (Matt. 5:44).

Every book in the New Testament includes, implicitly or explicitly, directions that serve as commandments from our Lord. To love Him means keeping these commandments. It is not so much the "big" commandments that we must keep. Instead, we please and love Him by keeping even the "smallest" of them. It is the simple, willful choice of keeping a commandment, small as it may be, as a means of loving God that speaks directly to His love language and, indeed, pleases Him.

I found this truth about the love language interesting to me in the following story. One young lady was disturbed that her parents and many church members spoke enthusiastically of a personal experience with God that galvanized their relationship with Him. Their walk with the Lord was rooted in this experience, and it was the basis for the testimony they shared with others. Though these personal experiences with God were exciting to hear about, they increasingly bothered her that nothing of the kind had ever happened to her. She waited and waited, but no experience with God came to pass. This drought went on for some time when, in frustration, she simply made up her mind she was going to begin "acting like a Christian, doing the things a converted Christian would do." Amazingly, she immediately found, in her newly committed behavior, the very warmth of God moving in her heart, for which she had been longing.

Obedience Is Something We Learn
Obedience to God is a growing thing. First, we learn to be obedient to God. Then, building upon what we learned, we work at it throughout our lifetime. The Bible says even Jesus "learned obedience from the things He suffered ..." (Heb. 5:8). We learn by doing the things God shows us, in our conscience or through scripture. It seems He gives us small things to do for Him, and when we do them, He entrusts us with more significant things. Instead of reserving Saturday afternoons for a football game, for example, we mow the neighbor's lawn or offer to make a run to the grocery store for the widow in our church. We "learn" obedience in this way.

13

"Upward Call"

In the parable of the talents, Jesus rewards the servant to whom He had entrusted five talents, five talents more, saying, "Well done, good and faithful slave; you were faithful with a few things, I will put you in charge of many things, enter into the joy of your master" (Matt. 25:21). As we prove we are willing to obey Him in small matters, He entrusts us with more significant matters. And every step forward brings us more into the "joy of the master." Obedience to God becomes an incredible journey.

Did the people of the Bible do a commendable job of keeping God's commandments? No, in fact, it might surprise you to note how many of "God's people" failed Him quite often. The most classic example involved God's "chosen" people, the Hebrews. They were oppressed and enslaved in Egypt and cried out to God to rescue them. He did. God sent Moses to deliver His people from Egypt. The rescue of the people at the Red Sea (symbolic of baptism) was the most significant and formative event in the history of the Hebrew people. Freed now from the clutches of Pharaoh, they were led into the wilderness where they learned to trust God, obey Him, and follow Him. When He brought them to the entrance of the Promised Land (symbolic of heaven), they balked. They did not listen to the words of God to go in, conquer, and inhabit the land. Instead, they listened to the naysayers who warned that the current inhabitants — the Canaanites — were too big and powerful, and the Hebrews would be conquered and killed. Naturally, their decision not to trust God angered Him, and, as a consequence, He sent them back into the wilderness for forty more years of education. Time and time again, God spoke to the people of Israel,

> *See, I have set before you this day life and good, death and*
> *evil. If you obey the commandments of the LORD your God*
> *which I command you this day, by loving the LORD your God,*
> *by walking in his ways, and by keeping his commandments*

and his statutes and his ordinances, then you shall live and multiply, and the LORD your God will bless you in the land which you are entering to take possession of it. But if your heart turns away, and you will not hear, but are drawn away to worship other gods and serve them, I declare to you this day, that you shall perish; you shall not live long in the land which you are going over the Jordan to enter and possess it (Deut. 30:15–18).

Stunted Growth

I have known many, many Christians in the church who seemed stuck in their journey toward God. I suspect it has something to do with not obeying God's commandments. For example, I have heard people say, "I'll never forgive so-and-so for what he did." Jesus said, "If you forgive men for their transgressions, your heavenly Father will also forgive you. But if you do not forgive men, then your Father will not forgive your transgressions" (Matt. 6:14–15). This is a commandment. Absolute forgiveness "from the heart" is paramount to our Lord. He expects unequivocal obedience in everything He teaches us.

I knew a teenager who asked for a contribution toward the mission trip she wanted to take with her church youth group. But she was not hesitant to let it be known that she "hates" her parents. I told her I could not contribute to her trip, because God cannot use her when she refuses to "honor her father and mother" — an important commandment. She went on the trip anyway, but was laid up in bed with an illness from the first to the last day of the trip and did not participate in any mission trip activities.

Do people say things like, "Okay, I will love my enemy, but only if he changes his way first!" or "I'll forgive my brother-in-law, but only if he apologizes"? When we belong to Jesus Christ, who teaches us always to love, forgive, and never seek revenge, we do these things regardless of the reception the people give us — we do them unconditionally. If we seek to grow, we must do what He says. We must "keep His commandments." And many of His commandments involve how we engage and treat other people.

We are motivated to obey His directions first of all, because He loves us when we do not deserve His love. "God demonstrates His own love toward us, in that while we were yet sinners, Christ died for us" (Rom. 5:8). He forgives us when we do not deserve forgiveness. Christ is our example; He forgave those crucifying Him even while nailing Him to the cross. Secondly, by choosing to follow His commandments in this way and practice unconditional love toward others, we are being His sons and daughters, which means we are acting out of His character that resides within us. We are reflections of His nature; we are His light in this world. "I say to you, love your enemies, and pray for those who persecute you; in order that you may be sons of your Father who is in heaven" (Matt. 5:44–45). These things are important. It is not a question of whether our neighbor or our enemy deserves our kindness. It is a question of what would please the Lord, and whether God deserves my loving my neighbor. He has paid a very high price to rescue me from sin and win me as His son. Put another way, it is not a question of whether my neighbor deserves my magnanimity. It is a question of whether Jesus deserves my obedience. If we respond to our enemy in the same kind as he did us, we choose to be like him, sons of this world. Jesus said that though his followers remain in this world, they are not *of* this world; they are sons *of* the Kingdom of God. And being different is what makes them His light in this world.

The commandments of our Lord, when we follow them, will influence us and mold us into His likeness. It is not the other way around; we do not evaluate or judge the worthiness of His law based on our situation in life. Instead, his law judges us, and by this, I mean it shows us where we need to transform ourselves into sons and daughters of His kingdom. We read the Bible and meditate on His teaching so that we can carry out His will and become like Him. It is about developing within us the character of Christ.

We are created in the image of God (Gen. 1:27), but we lose this image because of sin through Adam and Eve. Christ's death on the cross makes it possible for us to regain the image. Now, with His help, we are rebuilding it within us. So, the more we show loving-kindness to others — not because they earn it, but because our Lord commands it — the more we are being transformed into the character of Christ.

Consequently, taking on the cloak of living our lives for God and following His commandments becomes a great adventure. Each encounter where others mistreat us and each encounter where we can sacrifice for others is an opportunity to choose to act out the character of Christ within us. And each opportunity affords us the chance to grow more strongly and purely into His character and image.

I want to draw this matter to a close with a reflection of the parable Jesus used to end the Sermon on the Mount:

> *Every one then who hears these words of mine and does them will be like a wise man who built his house upon the rock; and the rain fell, and the floods came, and the winds blew and beat upon that house, but it did not fall, because it had been founded on the rock. And every one who hears these words of mine and does not do them will be like a foolish man who built his house upon the sand; and the rain fell, and the floods came, and the winds blew and beat against that house, and it fell; and great was the fall of it (Matt. 7:24– 27).*

Here are two men. One has a house that survives, because it is built on a solid foundation, a rock. The other has a destroyed house, because it was built on a shifty and unreliable foundation, sand. We begin by looking at the three things they have in common: they each hear the words of Jesus (in the Sermon on the Mount), they each build a house, and each of their houses was subjected to the mighty storms of life. What makes the first man wise, and thus different from the second man, is not that he just hears the words of Jesus — all the teachings and precepts in the Sermon on the Mount — but he *does* them. Look at the words carefully. He listens to the teachings of Jesus and, unlike the foolish man, applies each of the teachings to his own life. He asks himself what these things mean, how to apply them, and then does them as an act of loving and serving the Lord. This approach is what a wise man does. When the "storms" of life do come, as indeed they do for all of us, his life — every aspect of it — built like a house on the foundation rock of Jesus, survives the storms, and continues to succeed. Many hear and give the teachings of Jesus a polite nod, but then go off and do whatever they want. The house they build on sand eventually falls.

What if I Fail?
Even the most serious commitment to keeping our Lord's commandments will be met with the inevitable: we will drop the ball. We will err, we will sin, we will do things repeatedly that displease our Lord. Though our hearts may be in the right place, our old, self-loving nature will fail us readily.

There is a good story among the desert monks in the early centuries of the Christian faith. One of the monastery's brothers is being brought up on charges, because he has committed some offense that could have him removed from the community. The quiet, elderly senior monk shows up at the trial carrying a wicker basket with fine sand running through the dry reeds onto the floor. "What are you doing, Father?" they ask. He responds that his many sins pour forth from him daily as the grains of sand do from this basket. Silenced by his humility, they forgive the offending brother and let him stay.

Paul writes that "all have sinned and fallen short of the glory of God" (Rom. 3:23). And then he later writes about himself,

> I do not understand my own actions. For I do not do what I want, but I do the very thing I hate. ... For I know that nothing good dwells within me, that is, in my flesh. I can will what is right, but I cannot do it. For I do not do the good I want, but the evil I do not want is what I do. (Rom. 7:15,18,19).

Many think this was Paul talking about the life he had before he was converted. That was not at all the case. He would not have said this before he got converted, because he was doing what he wanted. He was laying out his own cause and following his own course.

As we draw closer to God, we don't find ourselves being less sinful, but more. This truth is because the closer we come to Him, His "light" exposes more and more the significant presence of sin in us. It is a rule that the nearer we come to the Light, the more clearly we see our sins pouring from us as grains of sand from a loosely woven wick basket.

Built into the fabric of God's commandments is the solution. We confess our sins honestly to Him, and He pours out His grace to cover them. As sin increases, the grace of God abounds all the more (Rom. 5:20). The more and more we realize and are saddened by the abundance of our failures, the more and more we are grateful for the covering of these sins through God's grace.

Pittsburgh, Pennsylvania, is just west of the Allegheny Mountains and regularly clouds and moisture back up against the range and settle over the city. There seems to be an endless cycle of rain, hard freeze, thaw, and more rain throughout the long winter months. The hard freeze in the cracks of the road swell and crumble the pavement. This cycle plays havoc on the roads and highways throughout the area. One must tip his hat to the Department of Transportation, working at length to repair these roads. The result of the weather is an enormous number of potholes, and some of them have grown wide and deep. It is not unusual to see drivers alongside the road changing their tires after inadvertently crashing into one of these potholes. Of the many potholes created, some are small and shallow, some are wider, and some are deep, which jar the drivers numb when accidentally hit. The solution is that when the road crews get to them, they pour into each one enough asphalt to fill the hole and return the road to a smooth surface. Some holes take a little asphalt, and some take a lot, but, whatever the size, no matter how offensively large they grow, they get whatever amount of asphalt is needed — this a good image of God's grace. The sins in our lives are like those potholes. Some are small, and some are quite large, and God's grace abounds all the more to fill whatever is lacking. The more we sin, the more grace abounds. The resulting path to God, by His intention, is fully amended and set right so that we may joyfully and hopefully resume our journey to Him.

To benefit from His grace, we must confess our sins. We confess to God or another person, as the Bible urges us to do. And the confession must be sincere.

I led a retreat for another church in Oklahoma, and a woman came to me to make a confession. She confessed several "little" things and then got around to telling me the thing that bothered her the most. Several years ago, she and her husband had a big fight and separated for a time. During that time, she got involved with another man. "Do you see that little (six-year-old) boy that's been running around the church today?" she asked tearfully. He's the result of that mistake. Though she loved the little boy very much, he was also a constant reminder of her betrayal. So, she confessed this. I listened, I understood, I sympathized, and then I told her God forgives her. Next, I asked her if she realized she may never confess this sin again. She looked at me quizzically (I suspected she had confessed this many times already). If you confess it again, you are implicitly telling God His forgiveness was not good enough for your sin, was inadequate, and needs to be repeated. She may not confess this particular sin again, because it *was* forgiven. He paid the price; His crucifixion was enough. A stake had been put in the ground to mark this point in her life; she was forgiven and set free to go forward fully forgiven, free to pursue our Lord and live her life in Him, because this was the gift and blessing of God's forgiveness. Her joy was impassioned. It was a sin to go back. She was free to go forward in every way.

Confession needs to be sincere. We call it "contrition" when a sinner confesses sincerely. "Remorse" is what we call it when the confessor is less than genuinely sorry. For example, he could be sorry only that he is caught or sorry that consequences inconvenience him. These feelings are not a genuine confession.

On the other hand, when we are genuinely sorry that our sin hurts other people and God, and we intend to do whatever is in our power to remedy the problem, this is genuine contrition. Sincere confession happens when (a) we admit we sinned, (b) we are truly sorry for the harm we caused, (c) and we sincerely intend to remedy the problem. For example, we run into our neighbor's car and not only apologize, but we also pay for every last dime of the repair. Together this is contrition and makes the ground for a sincere confession. (Not to complicate the matter, but if we realize that our confession is not contrite and not sincere, though we wish it were, we can confess this and ask His assistance!)

21

"Upward Call"

For God to be this generous with His grace is truly remarkable. Considering what He wishes to accomplish in each of our lives (our perfect union with Him), it could be suggested that He take a firmer hand against His many wayward followers — threatening them with dire consequences. But this is not His approach. Instead, he has chosen the most gracious approach imaginable: to send His Son to die on the cross to atone for all our sins and then be readily available with a truckload of grace to cover all our subsequent failings. All for the asking! The only imaginable, responsible reaction to what He has done must be profound gratitude and sincere yearning to give to Him everything He could want. That we should find in ourselves this deeply heartfelt appreciation is God's intention.

In one of Jesus' parables on the subject, He tells of a slave whose king had loaned him 170 million dollars (the current equivalent of 10,000 talents of silver). (What king would loan a slave that much?!) When the king calls for the loan to be settled, the slave falls on the ground, prostrates himself before the king, and begs for more time to pay, promising, "I will repay you everything!" The king feels compassion for him, releases him, and forgives him the entire debt (Matt. 18:26,27). The purpose of the humongous (and un-repayable) amount of debt is probably to show us the debt we owe God for our sins against Him — an un-repayable amount!

God knows that our commitment to keep His commandments and draw near to Him will be met with failure. Therefore, confession and forgiveness are built into the commandments as the means to deal with these inevitable failures. We are commanded to confess our sins. There is another good side to this: our humility. When I do what God wants of me, I am pleased; when I fail, I confess but am very humbled and displeased. When I do what He wants, I am pleased and encouraged that He has given me the grace to live a life worthy of Him. When I fail, I am humbled yet grateful for His endless grace, and reminded that He is the "author and perfecter" of my journey to Him and complete transformation into his image. He gets all the credit. This humility is necessary for my growth. The point is that both — the good commendation for obedience and the humility of failure — are necessary. He lets me stumble often for this reason. As long as I get back up, resume the journey, and remain grateful, all will be well.

Not All Laws
We love God by keeping His commandments. "Which commandments?" It was said previously, "all of them," but this is not exactly true. While we keep most everything directed to us in the New Testament, there are several laws and commandments in the Old Testament that we do not keep. There are numerous dietary laws, for example, commanding the Hebrew people not to eat: eagles, vultures, kites, falcons, and buzzards. Mice, lizards, and crocodiles are included in the taboo list, as well. I mention these because I am about to have lunch and never want to eat any of these anyway. However, shrimp and bacon are on the restricted list, and I am glad I needn't follow laws about these. While keeping the dietary laws is a big thing among Orthodox Judaism even today, the Book of Mark reads, "Thus He (Jesus) declared all foods clean" (7:19) and voids a whole host of dietary laws. What Jesus voids are the laws of the Mosaic Covenant, which are put in place in the time of Moses (beginning in the Book of Exodus). The laws in the earlier covenant in the Book of Genesis allows eating a broad selection of foods. The Lord said to Noah, "Every moving thing that is alive shall be food for you: I give all to you, as I gave the green plant" (Gen. 9:3).

There are chapters of laws governing the detailed and exact construction of the tabernacle where the people worshiped God. Laws covering buildings, instruments, utensils, oils, and incense to be used in the tabernacle are spelled out. These, too, are repealed.

Lastly, the criminal laws commanding us to stone persons who use the Lord's name in vain are likewise repealed.

While these and many related laws are voided to us, the principles behind each of these laws still carry some weight and should be considered. For instance, the presence of dietary laws teaches us that God considers it our moral responsibility to take care of our bodies. The detailed laws governing the construction of their worship centers and the practice of worship lay before us quite clearly that worshiping God is very important to Him. While some people may balk at having to dress right and travel to church on Sunday, these efforts contribute to the appropriate and spiritually healthy practice of making a sacrifice of thanksgiving to God. God, who has made a tremendous sacrifice for us, is thanked and rewarded by our weekly worship of Him. "He who offers a sacrifice of thanksgiving honors Me" (Ps. 50:23).

Lastly, while we do not hold to the same practices of criminal punishment stipulated in the Old Testament, the responsibility of assuring that proper justice is carried out remains a principle of God's will and law for our human society today.

We Pray for Assistance
God is the "author and perfecter" of our faith (Heb. 12:2). He gets us started, guides us along the way, and brings us to the point of perfection in Him. Therefore, we need Him every step of the way. For this reason, we pray about this whole matter of keeping His commandments. Daily or constant prayer is most appropriate for asking God to transform us into a renewed understanding. It is a prayer that not only will we remain faithful to Him, but that He will have His way with us. The Lord's Prayer includes these things: "Thy will be done (with me) ... give us our daily bread ... deliver us from evil." Also, there are many portions of Psalm 119 (The Psalms are the Bible's prayer book) that are beneficial prayers for this purpose:

24

"Deal with Thy servant according to Thy loving-kindness, and teach me Thy statutes. I am Thy servant; give me understanding, that I may know Thy testimonies" (vv. 124–125).

We Pray

Our prayer life is not a part of our relationship with our Lord; it *is* our relationship with our Lord. I know this is a bold statement, but I join with others who consider it true. We relate to God just as we relate to other people. We talk with them. If we are going to seek after God and enter a relationship with Him, we have to talk with Him as well. Our relationship is characterized by the depth, quantity, sincerity, and breadth of our prayers.

When I conduct pre-marital or marital counseling, we talk about the different expectations men and women typically have for their married life. Perhaps it is no surprise that surveys indicate the top five things women inherently want from their husbands and the top five things that men inherently want from their wives are all different![6] What makes for a good marriage is a husband devoted to fulfilling her wants while she industriously seeks to fulfill his. But, of course, they each first have to learn what the other wants before providing it. They have to learn because, to a great degree, the other's wants are natural for neither one of them.

One of the top expectations for women is conversation. Wives need this. She marries this good-looking guy, because she imagines she will spend hours conversing with him, and it will be delightful. So, it often goes like this: She says one day, "Dear, we need to talk." The husband says what seems to him the most logical response imaginable, "About what?" Then she says, with a tinge of frustration, "I don't know, we just need to talk!" He is puzzled because, in a typical man's mind, a conversation is a human

---

[6] Willard F. Harley Jr., *His Needs, Her Needs* (Ada, MI, Revell, 2001).

apparatus designed for the exchange of needful information: "I'll pick up the kids. You stop by the grocery store." "Check." But to women, a conversation is a whole lot more. It is how they feel intimacy and love. Sitting down at the table or on the sofa in the living room talking about who-knows-what, each one sharing their thoughts and aspirations, and listening attentively to the other is near paradise. Add some candlelight, and no telling what you'll get out of it!

Okay, hold onto this image (without the candlelight), and you're on the path to understanding something about God. He likes conversation; it is important to Him. Prayer is a conversation, and this is how we conduct our relationship with Him. The topics can be of a great many kinds. We will talk later about different types of prayer, but, in general, the topics can be matters that trouble us, matters we need guidance with, matters we need His intervention on, matters that just need sorting out, and a whole host of compliments, honors, and thanksgivings we want to send His way. Mostly, we want to learn to depend on Him, enjoy Him, understand Him, get guidance from Him, and thank Him. Jean-Pierre de Caussade, an eighteenth-century French spiritual director, said, "God loves to see us like little children in His presence,"[7] as in right now while we are praying to Him. St Teresa of Avila, a sixteenth-century abbess from Spain, said, "See, He is only waiting for us to look at Him."[8]

Our prayer with God is our relationship with Him. The more we learn how to pray and the more we learn *to* pray, the more this relationship will develop. And I say emphatically that there is no

---

[7] Jean-Pierre de Caussade, *Abandonment to Divine Providence* (Joseph Pich, 2013) Ch 11, Letters Book 4, letter 7.

[8] Saint Teresa of Avila, *The Way of Perfection* (MobileReference, 2010), Ch. 26.

more enjoyable, valuable, and lasting relationship anywhere than this one with Him who has perfect love for us.

The Languages of Prayer

There are three languages we use in prayer. The first is written prayers. One advantage of written prayer is that several people can join together ("liturgical prayer"). We know that Jesus used memorized "written" prayer a lot since most faithful Jews in that day did. He gives us such a prayer, the Lord's Prayer, which some Christians who have a developed prayer life may recite as many as two or three times each day. Written prayer also gets us beyond the limitation of thoughts of our limited minds. I am glad to pray about and say to God a lot of things, but they are things that would never on their own have found a way into my simple mind!

One such prayer, which I like and say every morning, is a prayer listed "for the Renewal of Life":

> *O God, the King eternal, whose light divides the day from the night and turns the shadow of death into the morning: Drive far from us all wrong desires, incline our hearts to keep your law, and guide our feet into the way of peace; that, having done your will with cheerfulness during the day, we may, when night comes, rejoice to give you thanks; through Jesus Christ our Lord. Amen.*[9]

Written prayer also aids in the prevention of wandering thoughts, which are an inevitable nuisance that hampers any effort to regular prayer if offered solely extemporaneously.

The second language of prayer is extemporaneous prayer which has many advantages. We say these prayers day in and day out when we

---

[9] *The Book of Common Prayer*, 1979 (Kingsport, Kingsport Press, 1977) p. 99.

wish to bring our thoughts and needs to God. In the Garden of Gethsemane, Jesus' prayer is extemporaneous, "My Father, if it is possible, let this cup pass from Me; yet not as I will, but as You will" (Matt. 26:39). This prayer encapsulates what He wishes; therefore, this is what He prays. Paul writes to the Philippians, "Be anxious for nothing, but in everything by prayer and supplication with thanksgiving let your requests be made known to God" (Phil. 4:6). So, prayer becomes for us not just an opportunity, but is even commanded. We must be about the business of prayer, sharing with God everything.

The third language of prayer could perhaps best be called "contemplative." This prayer is our deeper thoughts for which we cannot find the words, most likely because they come from thoughts so deep within us that words simply fail to materialize. A simple yearning for God is contemplative: a deep sense of defeat and general helplessness, a deep sense of loneliness or isolation, a crying out, or a moment of exalted praise or gratitude. These things defy words and are, thus, contemplative. The "speaking in tongues" of which Paul teaches in his letters to the Corinthians would have to be a prayer of this sort, for he writes, "For one who speaks in a tongue speaks not to men but to God; for no one understands him, but he utters mysteries in the Spirit" (I Cor. 14:2). There are "mysteries" that go on inside us — deeper thoughts and feelings that we cannot understand and, therefore, cannot verbalize adequately. These are the matter of contemplative prayer. Christians who engage in contemplative prayer often find it to be very peaceful.

Another example of prayer in a contemplative language would be akin to an infant's simple sounds when he is lifting his thoughts, which he cannot understand, to someone out there, whom he likewise cannot truly comprehend. Thus, as Christians, we are taught the merits of returning to a childlike state. "Whoever then humbles himself as this child, he is the greatest in the kingdom of heaven" (Matt. 18:4).

The Seven Types of Prayer
When someone mentions to the average guy on the street that he has been praying about something, the general assumption is that he is asking God for something. The reason he is doing that is that he has exhausted every other available means of getting it. This assumption is wrong on two fronts. The first is that there is more to prayer than just "asking." The second is that, even if we are asking for something, prayer should be the first thing we do, not the last. How often have I begun a household project, like fixing the dryer in the utility room, and spun my wheels, accomplishing nothing? Then, after leaning back in frustration, I decide to ask for help! "God, I need this dryer, and I have the new part. Please help me fix it." My next attempt works out smoothly, quickly, and successfully. It takes a little bit of humility to ask Him, because it is my nature to believe I can do it myself. But I have learned something: be smart and pray first!

The different types of prayer are praise, adoration, thanksgiving, confession, oblation, intercession, and petition.

Praise — *Hallelujah! Praise the Lord from the heavens; praise Him in the heights! Praise Him, all His angels; Praise Him, all His hosts! Praise Him, sun and moon; Praise Him, all stars of light! Praise Him, highest of heavens (Ps. 148:1– 4).*

Praise is the kind of prayer we stand up and offer to God when we are moved spontaneously by joy, relief, wonder, or elation to praise Him for who He is and the wonderful things He has done. I remember early in the morning standing upon the dock of a lake, witnessing one of the most beautiful and inspiring sunrises I had ever seen. So I broke out into the ancient song, based upon the song of the angels who came to the shepherds watching their flocks by night, to announce to them the birth in Bethlehem of the Savior: "Glory be to God on high, and on earth peace, goodwill towards to His people on earth."

Praise is what we offer God, because He deserves it. His love and glory warrant it from us, His people. Therefore, though it is spontaneous in nature, there is no reason that we cannot and should not offer praise to Him whenever we gather for worship.

Adoration — *We adore thee, O Christ, and we bless thee * Because by thy holy cross thou hast redeemed the world. — Liturgy of The Stations of the Cross.*

Adoration is naturally expressed with humble kneeling. Rather than moving upward by spontaneous elation, as in praise, adoration is a humble response to God's inestimable, inexpressible, and awesome wonder. If praise is standing, adoration is kneeling. Abram falls on his face before God (Gen. 17:3). So do many others. Isaiah, seeing the Lord sitting on His throne and the seraphim about Him worshiping Him, is moved to cry out in adoration, "Woe is me ... for I have seen the King, the Lord of hosts" (Is. 6:5).

Thanksgiving — *Accept, O Lord, our thanks for all that you have done for us. We thank you for the splendor of the whole creation, for the beauty of this world, for the wonder of life, and for the mystery of love.*

We thank God for a whole host of things. We have a prayer that says, "It is right, and a good and joyful thing, always and everywhere to give thanks to You, Father Almighty, Creator of heaven and earth." Yes indeed, gratitude, duly expressed, goes a long way to keep our good thoughts about God before us. And I thank Him often that He has chosen me, to open my eyes that I might see the light of

His wonder and grace. "Why me? I do not know, but I am exceedingly grateful."

We thank Him also for those disappointments, failures, and challenges that lead us to acknowledge our dependence on Him alone. It may require gathering up an extra amount of faith from time to time, but we thank Him because He takes all the adversity in our lives, and He makes something good for us out of it (Rom. 8:28). We thank Him even though we cannot see the good that He is accomplishing on our behalf. We have to trust Him, and we express our trust by thanking Him. God has done some wonderful things for us and continues doing wonderful things. Being conscious of and expressing our gratitude, even for the smallest blessings that come our way, is beneficial to our life in Him and with Him.

Frequently expressed short prayers of thanksgiving affect our attitude in life and subsequently our thoughts toward God. Hence, Paul directs Christians to "Devote yourself to prayer, keeping alert in it with an attitude of thanksgiving" (Col. 4:2).

Confession — *Most merciful God, we confess that we have sinned against you in thought, word, and deed, by what we have done, and by what we have left undone.*

If we confess our sins, he is faithful and righteous to forgive us our sins and to cleanse us from all unrighteousness (I John 1:9).

Examining our lives, how conscious we are of our sins, and the open and honest confession of sins are critical protocols for our growth in the Lord. Through the sacrifice of Jesus Christ, God has purchased for us the most grace-filled path to a righteous life. Compared to what could have been — some arduous and painful system by which we atone for each and every one of our sins — our Lord's choice of

31

giving His Son over to death so that we would not have to die is an amazingly generous gift. Human nature, being what it is, tends to take God's grace for granted. Indeed, many Christians do just that. There is a method given to us to deal with our many sins, and we should be diligent in following it: "If we confess our sins ... He will forgive ...."

Let us look at this from our Lord's point of view: we are the object of His love, and He yearns deeply to be reunited with us. Consequently, He loathes anything that comes between us (sin). Considering His love for us and the sacrifice He made for our sake, He deserves to get what He wants. And yet, He is very patient with us. "The Lord is gracious and full of compassion, slow to anger and of great kindness" (Psalm 145:8).

For the Holy God to unite with us, we must be "righteous." Thus, He sends His Son to atone for our sins, rendering us cleansed from sin, and purchasing for us the possibility of becoming righteous. The Hebrew word for "righteous" is *tsedeq*. The word does not mean "sinless" or "good." It means "functioning exactly as it should" — precisely as it is designed and created to be. We human beings are designed and created to live in perfect union with God — we are created to be righteous. Our sin makes us unrighteous, and this causes the wonderful union to be broken. Jesus' death on the cross is the source of our restoration.

An American couple touring Israel, drove about from town to town in a rented automobile. Their engine began sputtering, and the car slowed and barely remained functioning. They limped into the next Israeli town and found a mechanic who quickly opened the hood and began working. In a short time, he got the engine purring and running again just as it ought. He closed the hood with a smile on his face and said, with a sense of victory, *"Tsedeq."* The engine was now righteous — it was running as it was designed to run.

In our sinful state, it is impossible for us to restore ourselves to righteousness. It is impossible to become *tsedeq* again. Now, with Jesus' death on the cross, righteousness *is* a possibility. We, His followers, are already treated by Him as if we are. One day, in heaven, we indeed will be.

The religion of ancient Judaism was given as a system of laws to be followed out of love for God. As a means of restoring us to God, it was doomed to fail. We were never able to close the gap no matter how arduously any of us might have tried. God created Judaism to show us the path of true righteousness and prove that we were not able to succeed. It took God choosing to rescue us — saving us from the state of separation caused by our sin to make it possible.

Therefore, any time we sin, it is a brief step back into the darkness apart from God. It is an offense to God. It is a revisiting our old haunt — the one out of which He has delivered us. Any sin we commit is going backward in a harmful way. Thus, it is painful for Him to watch us do it.

The time the Hebrew people spent under oppression as slaves in Egypt symbolically represented their life in sin. They could not escape the powerful oppression of the Egyptian Pharaoh. God did what they could not. He rescued them from Egypt, and, therefore, as a symbol, He insisted that they must never return to Egypt. They must not return, even for a brief visit, to the darkness from which they had been rescued.

> *For thus says the LORD of hosts, the God of Israel: As my anger and my wrath were poured out on the inhabitants of Jerusalem, so my wrath will be poured out on you when you go to Egypt. You shall become an execration, a horror, a curse, and a taunt. You shall see this place no more. The LORD has said to*

you, O remnant of Judah, "Do not go to Egypt" (Jer. 42:18–19).

The "remnant of Judah" represents the select group of Israelis God has saved and calls His own. The point is this: God has given an inestimable gift to us in delivering us from sinfulness. We should, out of gratitude, make every reasonable effort not to return to sin anymore and be quick to confess it when we do.

True confession requires three things: admitting we sin, being sorry, and intending to amend. For example, "I yell at my kids. I'm very sorry, and I am taking a better look into myself to assure I do not do it again." Together this makes a proper confession.

Moreover, what often lies behind a misdeed provokes the cause of it. Is it the presence of anger, fear, selfishness with my time, a driving desire to do what I want, or a need to fulfill my own self-image? The examination may reveal the cause, and the cause should be confessed as well."

What if I admit I sinned, but to be honest, I am not sorry about it? This feeling, too, becomes a sin to be confessed. What if I genuinely want to know what caused me to act so unbecomingly, but cannot figure it out? We ask God to help us see what is going on. He is much more eager to answer that kind of prayer than many others we may be inclined to ask! These, and many other associated reasons, have led the Bible to direct us to confess our sins "one to another" (James 5:16). Other Christians, especially those well-trained, can be very helpful.

Thus confessed, thus forgiven.

Oblation — *Take my life, and let it be consecrated, Lord to Thee.*[10]

*Jesus said to them, "If any man would come after me,
let him deny himself and take up his cross and follow
me" (Mark 8:34).*

Oblation is the life-changing offering of ourselves, our lives, and our labors, with the help of Christ, for the purposes of God.

Paul probably offered himself to God in a prayer of oblation when he was baptized three days after his encounter with Jesus on the road to Damascus (Acts 9). It was probably done as a matter of course at the time of his baptism, with these familiar words: "Do you turn to Jesus Christ and accept Him as your Savior? Do you put your whole trust in his grace and love? Do you promise to follow and obey him as your Lord?" These questions had to be answered positively prior to the candidate being baptized.[11] They were not just commitments of the will. They are offerings of oneself — oblations.

One's first oblation to God may be the most significant moment in one's life, a true turning point. But oblations go on through the years. For one, as we grow in maturity, we learn more about who we are. As someone once wisely pointed out, "Our commitment to God is giving all that we know of ourselves to all that we know of God." Since we learn more about ourselves as time goes by and learn more of our Lord, we have the grounds to renew our oblation to Him. He deserves all that we have. Because He purchased it on the cross, He does not cater to our holding something back. "And we all, with unveiled face, beholding the glory of the Lord, are being changed

---

[10] Hymn, Hollingside, Music, John Bacchus Dykes; words, Frances Ridley Havergal, *The Hymnal, 1982 (The Church Pension Fund, 1985) Hymn 707.*

[11] *The Book of Common Prayer* ,1979 (Kingsport, Kingsport Press, 1977) p. 302.

into his likeness from one degree of glory to another; for this comes from the Lord who is the Spirit" (II Cor. 3:18).

Our continued oblation to God can be repeated as an act of continuing love. Every Sunday in worship, beholding what He has offered on my account, makes it a joyful occasion once again to offer myself to Him.

Petition —*Have no anxiety about anything, but in everything by prayer and supplication with thanksgiving let your requests be made known to God (Phil. 4:6).*

Petition is the many things we ask for ourselves.

The truth is, the larger majority of us do not pray nearly as much as we ought. As it says, "in everything by prayer and supplication (humble requests for needs) let your requests be known ...." Along with Paul's admonition that we "pray without ceasing" (I Thess. 5:17), being awake means it is time to pray. But rather than an issue of timing, let's look at it as a matter of focus. I have needs, lots of them, and either I will try to figure them all out on my own, or I am going to figure them out in conjunction with the Lord who always wants to live His life right beside me. In other words, either I will live my life independent of God (a sin), or, through time, I will grow more dependent on Him (a virtue). "Have no anxiety about anything ...."

Moreover, my days are marked with several slight, and not so slight, instances of anxiety: what will I buy my wife for her birthday? How am I going to deal with the conflict with my next-door neighbor? It is not that I expect an answer to every such question, but His assistance of any kind always pays well, and I could easily grow to enjoy it. The directive does say, "in everything by prayer," and taking this to heart results in my praying often. I love the clever sarcasm of a Christian bumper sticker I saw (on the back of a Volkswagen Beetle) in California in 1969, "Why pray when you can worry about it?" Yes, why? Because, except when a bear is chasing me through the woods, I do not like anxiety. And when he is chasing me through the woods, I am okay with the anxiety. I just do not like the bear.

Maturing in Prayer
An element of spiritual growth is the process of maturity. As I grow up as a person, I am supposed to be making good and wise decisions. Given my way as a child, I eat the whole bowl of ice cream. Being more adult-like now, I know that is a bad idea. As I grow in the Lord, maturity includes not only asking for things that will be good in the long run but recognizing that God is smarter than I and has my best interests at heart. I should learn from Him the things for which I should be asking. Or, in other words, it is good to ask for the things I've learned He likes. He is not too keen on our obtaining lots of temporal things, so I do not ask for that much anymore. I do ask for things that I think will be good for me — like my daily bread and a house. Being older, and hopefully wiser in the matters of God, my prayers are more in line with the things He has shown me I need: transformation, the elimination of all wrong desires, the inclination to keep His law, the growth of my faith in Him, the purity of my thoughts, the perfection of love. But I am also a kid in many ways, and, as a kid, I do have some requests like, "If you are so kindly disposed, please help me get a better batting average!" Is that okay? Well, it usually is if we tack on the words borrowed from Jesus in the Garden of Gethsemane, "Yet not as I will, but as Thy will" (Matt. 26:39) and mean it!

A New Dependence
Let's talk a little more about the good and necessary growing dependence on God. I was raised, like most all-American young men, to forge my own way in life: get an education, find a good job,

develop an income stream, associate with the right kind of people, and keep myself in good physical and mental health. This protocol will bring about what my parents are very intent on, for me to become financially and psychologically independent of them. Why? So, they can live their lives without having to drag me along. They want to be free of me by my learning to be free of them. Not to say they do not love me or enjoy being with me, but they enjoy seeing that I no longer need them. Thus, the great merits of independence are well established in the basic framework of my thoughts.

And then comes the Kingdom of God. One thing that must be noted is that to learn the way of God and His kingdom, we need to re-learn some very significant ways of thinking. There are a lot of things reversed from this world to God's world. God's world is richer, more lasting (forever), more challenging, exciting, peaceful, purposeful, and rewarding. But it is different. We spoke of some of these things above: In this world, retaliation, vengeance, and retribution are expected. In God's kingdom, love, forgiveness, and sacrifice are the way of life.

Concerning my new dependence, I need to be motivated on a deeper level to depend on Him more and pray a lot more. As I said above, the Lord "wants to live His life always right beside me." To count on Him and involve Him in my life, my former independence must be put aside in lieu of a new dependence on Him. I do need Him, and I want to learn that well! Henceforth, instead of launching out with my own plans, I need to check with Him first. My plans may be great, but to accomplish what I want, I need His assistance. Therefore, I ask Him. By this change, I am certainly not returning to dependence on my parents or anyone else. The change is that I am strictly departing from dependence on myself. As one great writer teaches, "The two poles of the interior life: 'It is the true foundation of all self-distrust, and of an entire confidence in God.'"[12] I learn to distrust myself, and I gain an ever-growing dependence on God.

A good example of this took place back in my college days when I was just beginning to learn what it means to walk with and enjoy my new life with God. I was working that summer at a conference center near San Bernardino, California. My friend and I decided on our day off to drive to Disneyland in Pasadena. Great idea. Being one of the few with a car, a convertible, we had no trouble finding a couple of other guys to join us. We headed out on our own! Then it hit me: Why is it that if we are surrendering ourselves to God and praying for His will to be done every (work) day; yet we totally forget about Him on a rare day off? The question was rhetorical. It answered itself. So, I put on the brakes: "Guys, we're going to pray." All of us young, growing Christians prayed together, asking God to go with us (to Disneyland) and lead us through the day. He did. It was a perfect day. The four of us never had even a minor debate on what event, ride, performance, or activity we would do next. We ate the most incredible meals, had the best time, and we even got a chance to talk with some lonely guy about our Christian faith. We explained to him how he could turn his life to Christ, and he was very interested. We were the last car to pull out of the parking lot that night after the park closed. God went with us. He answered our prayer and showed it by scheduling and filling it as a perfect day at Disneyland. I certainly did not expect that kind of answer every time, but I knew He had something to prove to us; and He did. He wanted us to know what He can do when He was along with us!

---

[12] Jean-Pierre de Caussade, *Abandonment to Divine Providence* (Joseph Pich, 2013), p. 247

"Upward Call"

"But in everything by prayer and supplication with thanksgiving let your requests be made known to God" (Phil. 4:6).

Intercession — *We have not ceased to pray for you and to ask that you may be filled with the knowledge of His will (Col. 1:9).*

Intercessions are the prayers that we offer on behalf of others. As intercessors, we stand in between God and the people we care for, asking Him to show His mercy and goodness upon them. In Genesis 18, we find the interesting story of the Lord sharing with Abraham His plans to destroy Sodom and Gomorrah for the sins of the people there were "exceedingly grave." Abraham begins to intercede, saying, "Wilt thou indeed destroy the righteous with the wicked? Suppose there are fifty righteous within the city; wilt thou then destroy the place and not spare it for the fifty righteous who are in it?" (vv. 23–24). God relents and agrees to withhold His anger against them if there are at least a small gathering of righteous ones found in the city. It is no accident that Abraham found himself in the role of intercessor for the people. God wanted him to do this. Moses, too, interceded for the obstinate people of Israel in the wilderness so that God would not destroy them (Ex. 32:9–14).

Praying for the world, the well-being of its people, and the fulfillment of God's will is the work of Christians. By this, we are the salt and the light of the world. Prayer is powerful, and I dare say that if we (the Christians throughout the world) were aware of how much effect it had, we would be doing a lot more of it.

The end of communism in Eastern Europe and the Berlin wall's razing on November 11, 1989, were attributed to the fervent prayers of various Christian groups, especially in Poland. The world did not see the collapse coming. The startling and unexpected collapse occurred through a slate of incredible miscommunications among

40

the political leadership of East Berlin in a wave of "a stunning series of events."[13] When God answers prayers, inexplicable things just happen!

The Battle in the Heavenly Places
Whenever we pray, it helps to know the true source of the conflict against which we are battling. Paul seeks to clarify the true nature of our battle as warriors of prayer, interpreting it as a war in the heavenly places.

> *For we are not contending against flesh and blood, but against the principalities, against the powers, against the world rulers of this present darkness, against the spiritual hosts of wickedness in the heavenly places (Eph. 6:12).*

How does this affect our prayers? It broadens the scope of our thinking and adds fervency to our praying. Why? Because if indeed the battle is more spiritual than we have believed, we now have greater confidence because we know, beyond doubt, that we have no power in and of ourselves against the forces of harm. But our God does, and He is the One we are calling upon to act.

The Right Kind of Intercession
Intercessory prayer is not carrying others' burdens to God. It is a matter of lovingly presenting them before Him. Our prayer for them must be from God's point of view. "Identification with God is the key to intercession," writes Oswald Chambers.[14] Sympathizing with people is not. Fix yourself on what God wants for that person, then

---

[13] www.dictionary.com.

[14] Oswald Chambers, *My Utmost for His Highest* (Grand Rapids: Discovery House Publishers, 1992), May 3.

let your prayers ascend. Suffering and adversity are part of this life. If our only prayer for family members and friends is to get them out of this suffering, we may be praying against the greater will of God. Pray instead that they may remain strong and quickly and effectively come to the fulfillment of God's will.

To me, intercessory prayers are much like the act of holding my family and friends up before God, much like one might hold up to the sunlight a wet garment so it can dry. I am not drying the garment; I am making it possible for the sun to dry it. Holding a friend up to the Lord with a lot of sympathetic words is not an effective prayer; holding him up before the Lord so that God will move in his life is!

In the Bible, some prayers are given to us that are very helpful in our prayers for others. Paul wrote this prayer to the Ephesians:

For this reason I bow my knees before the Father, from whom every family in heaven and on earth is named, that according to the riches of his glory he may grant you to be strengthened with might through his Spirit in the inner man, and that Christ may dwell in your hearts through faith; that you, being rooted and grounded in love, may have power to comprehend with all the saints what is the breadth and length and height and depth, and to know the love of Christ which surpasses knowledge, that you may be filled with all the fulness of God (Eph. 3:14–19)

To the Colossians, he wrote this prayer:

And so, from the day we heard of it, we have not ceased to pray for you, asking that you may be filled with the knowledge of his will in all spiritual wisdom and understanding, to lead a life worthy of the Lord, fully pleasing to him, bearing fruit in every good work and increasing in the knowledge of God. May you be strengthened with all power, according to his glorious might, for all endurance and patience with joy, giving thanks to the Father, who has qualified us to share in the inheritance of the saints in light (Col. 1:9–12).

My preferred prayer is the one that Jesus prayed over the disciples the night before He dies:

I do not ask Thee to them out of the world, but to keep them from the evil one. They are not of the world, even as I am not of the world. Sanctify them in the truth; Your word is truth. As You sent Me into the world, so I have sent them into the world. And for their sakes I sanctify Myself, that they themselves also may be sanctified in truth (John 17:15–19).

I pray this prayer over family and friends daily. Jesus asks His Father to keep the disciples from the evil one (Satan). He prayed that the Father sanctify them in the truth. *Sanctify* here means to separate from them completely the influences of the world, the flesh, and the devil and leave them wholly, completely, and purely transformed into the image of God.

"Truth" is all the wonderful and sanctifying reality of Who God is, who we are, and a clear vision of His purposes for us. Lastly, He offers to sanctify Himself — to give Himself wholly to the fulfillment of God's will, making Himself a sacrifice — so that they are able to be sanctified. In our intercession with Jesus, we offer ourselves to be consecrated to God — to live righteous lives — so that those for whom we intercede will best benefit from our prayers. "The prayer of a righteous man has great power in its effects" (James 5:16).

Prayer Transforms Us
We pray to God because we want Him to do something. And sometimes we are blessedly pleased with a good and quick result. Other times, the answer comes slowly. And yet other times, God

says no. It is important to understand that perhaps the main reason God delays in answering our prayers is that the whole process of prayer becomes, for us, in our souls, an occasion for transformation. "Do not be conformed to this world but be transformed by the renewal of your mind, that you may prove what is the will of God, what is good and acceptable and perfect" (Rom. 12:2).

Upon entering Gethsemane, Jesus asked that the cup (of suffering) could pass from Him. He ended up conceding instead to the Father's will. The work of prayer was an occasion of transformation from His earthly will to surrendering to His Father's will.

Prayer for us is often the same. We begin asking for what we think we want; yet, over time, we come to realize that God has a higher cause. We come to terms with His higher will, surrendering ourselves to it. In other words, though we begin with a request, ultimately, we relent to "Thy will be done."

We learn a lot about God by being parents. I remember a few years ago, I saw a McDonald's advertisement on TV of a quite clever scene of a young boy hanging around the garage with his father — supposedly on a Saturday morning. The young boy asks his father several questions, such as "Can I run the lawnmower? Can I play with the axe? Can I paint the house?" The father has to say no to each request, but the viewer also sees how it pains the father repeatedly to deny his son, whom he loves. Finally, the son asks, "Dad, can we go to McDonald's for lunch?" Dad lights up. Finally, there is a question to which he can say, "Well, yes, son, we can!" And off they go. God loves us and truly wishes to answer our prayers, "Yes." If we, as imperfect beings, know to say, "yes" only to good things carefully and wisely chosen, how much more will our perfect Parent in heaven give only good gifts to us — His children? God "richly supplies us with all things to enjoy" (I Tim. 6:17). He loves to give us good gifts to enjoy (like Disneyland!) and continues to do so as long as they do not interfere with the higher good.

The highest good that God can give us is Himself. Think about Psalm 27:

> *One thing have I asked of the Lord; one thing I seek;*
> *that I may dwell in the house of the Lord all the days*
> *off my life; to behold the fair beauty of the Lord, and*
> *to seek Him in His temple (Ps. 27:4).*

The psalmist wishes above all to dwell in the house of the Lord and behold His fair beauty. While our earth-bound souls may think we mostly want a few more of the good things this world has to offer, our deepest soul, the highest level of our being, wishes for one thing only: union with God. The life of prayer is a journey from self to God. Knowing that this is the higher will of God and knowing that we are always better off praying in accordance with His higher will, it is most understandable that our time spent with God in prayer — as we are laying our will and requests before Him — will naturally lead us to be transformed as well.

Prayer with Persistence
I can think through my lifetime of only a few prayers of any seriousness that God has not answered, but I can think of even fewer that He answered right away. Jesus taught the disciples to pray with persistence. In Luke, it says, "Now Jesus was telling them a parable to show that at all times they ought to pray and not to lose heart" (Luke 18:1). The odd thing here is that He is speaking to His disciples — the twelve men who followed Him most closely. We naturally think that if there is anyone on earth closest to the Lord who should have faith in Him and who should receive quick answers to their prayers, it would be these Twelve. But even these faithful followers are being reminded that their prayers may not be answered

45

quickly, and, indeed, the answers may come so slowly that they will be tempted to "lose heart" — give up. Don't give up!

The parable is about a widow — seen as someone with absolutely no clout — who comes to a judge, repeatedly urging that the judge should give her legal satisfaction against her opponent. The scenario is unfavorable for her; there is no reason to hope the judge, who cares neither for God nor people, will consent to her wish. Yet, he does. Why? Because if he does not, he reasons, "by continually coming," she will "wear me out!" While he has no concern for her, he is concerned enough about himself that, motivated by nothing other than his own peace of mind, he consents. The disciples do have "clout" with their loving God. Therefore, if the widow can get her requests ultimately answered by pestering the evil judge, assuredly, the disciples can get their requests ultimately answered by pestering their wonderful God! "Pestering" strikes us as a derogatory word. Yet, this is what Jesus taught them. What may feel like pestering, by relentlessly repeated prayer requests, is not considered wrong by our Father in heaven; instead, Jesus is teaching that this approach is a manifestation of good faith and may indeed be the way to get their prayers answered.

Another parable says essentially the same thing:

> *And he said to them, "Which of you who has a friend will go to him at midnight and say to him, `Friend, lend me three loaves; for a friend of mine has arrived on a journey, and I have nothing to set before him'; and he will answer from within, `Do not bother me; the door is now shut, and my children are with me in bed; I cannot get up and give you anything'? I tell you, though he will not get up and give him anything because he is his friend, yet because of his*

persistence he will rise and give him whatever he needs (Luke 11:5-8).

One must understand that in Jesus' day, the process of getting the house and family closed up for the night with the door barred is a bit of an undertaking. When the friend asks for bread late at night, his neighbor calls out from the upstairs bedroom, saying no. But Jesus explains that after the friend has pestered his neighbor relentlessly, he will get up and "give him whatever he needs." This parable is part of Jesus' answer to His disciple's request, "Lord, teach us to pray."

This principle, therefore, is teaching about prayer. The keyword is "persistence." The word, in the original Greek, is actually "shamelessness." The meaning is, if you pray with "shameless persistence," God gives you what you want. There are other stories similar in meaning. Blind Bartimaeus cries when he hears that Jesus was coming down the road with His entourage. Those nearby try to hush the blind beggar, for indeed, it is socially inappropriate for a beggar to holler out to a noted rabbi in such a fashion. Social conventions aside, Bartimaeus begins hollering out all the more. At this shameless persistence, Jesus calls him to come. "What do you want Me to do for you?" "I want to regain my sight!" he exclaims. Jesus responds, "Go your way. Your faith has made you well." Immediately, he receives his sight.

Strange as it seems, Jesus is teaching us that we must continue praying and not "lose heart" — not give up. Jesus honors those who do not give up and explains that shameless persistence is characteristic of strong faith — a faith that believes intensely enough that, if undeterred, the fervent begging presses through to completion.

This passage begs the question: how do we pray fervently with the abandonment of this "shameless persistence" while at the same time respecting the Father's greater will and judgment? There is no simple answer to this. However, both Moses and Paul, followers very close to God, pray for something they desperately want. After repeated requests, God speaks to each of them, telling them no.[15] In both cases, there is a higher reason. They pray fervently and repeatedly until God tells them to quit. It is logical to assume that had He not, they would have continued. I do believe that we are to pray, freely and fervently, in accordance with whatever is on our hearts, in childlike trust in our Lord, until He tells or shows us otherwise. If we have faith to pray, we should trust Him to guide us in those prayers.

Forming Habits
We are human beings and must acknowledge we best operate with established patterns in our lives. Our good morning, getting out of bed, and onward-for-the-day practices are pretty much the same every day. As well, our preparations for going to bed at night are typically established practices. It is our nature to operate this way. Setting a foundation of prayer at the beginning of the day is most helpful for the entire day. Of course, if this is a new thing, we will have to work to make it happen.

The main benefit to an established time of prayer in the early morning is that it sets a kind of beginning to the day with God at the heart of our thoughts. It is easier to have prayer going in our minds throughout the day when it gets started that way. It is also a good time to cover many matters related to your thoughts, concerns, and labors of the day. We ask God to help us with any or all of our anticipated undertakings, not to mention perhaps a few sins to confess, to put them behind us. The morning prayers can become a

---

[15] Moses, in Deuteronomy 3:23–27; Paul, in II Corinthians 12:7–9.

kind of framework upon which everything else through the day will be hung, letting God's light shine on them. (There is a simple pattern of prayer in the appendix that can easily be adopted and adapted.)

There is another good reason to begin regular morning prayers. The One you are talking to loves it! In Robert B. Munger's book, *Christ's Heart, My Home*, a wonderful story drives this point home.[16] Paraphrased:

According to the story, Jesus has come for the first time into the life and heart of a young man. The booklet is an allegory about how Christ moves from room to room in the young man's life, each room representing a different aspect of his life. The dining room represents the young man's appetites and desires. The workroom represents his skills and talents. The rec room was for fun and fellowship — his social life. The library represented the things the young man let his mind dwell on. As he enters each room, Jesus begins making changes, adding things the young man needs, removing harmful things.

At one point, they entered the drawing room. This cozy room Jesus found to be very nice. It had a fireplace and two overstuffed chairs. Jesus said he liked this room and said that he would meet there every morning with the young man to spend time together. This place would be for their morning prayers together.

They met every morning, and their discussions usually began with whatever was on the young man's mind. After some months went by, the young man became quite busy with work and school. He began arriving late for their appointed time in the drawing-room,

---

[16] Robert B. Munger, *Christ's Heart, My Home* (InterVarsity Press, 1986).

leaving early sometimes and even sometimes missing the appointed time altogether.

One morning as he was hurrying out the door, through the door cracked open to the drawing-room, he saw Jesus sitting there in His usual chair. Sticking his head in the door, he asked, "Have you been here waiting for me?" Jesus replied, "I have been here every day, just as I said." The young man apologized and confessed that he had let the activities of his life take over and had forgotten about this time with the Lord. Jesus forgave him patiently and then explained, "The problem is that you have been seeing this time here together in light of what it does for you, how it helps your day. What you haven't realized is that this time here together means a great deal to me, too!"

We spoke earlier of loving and pleasing our Lord. Our established prayer times with Him are events that He loves!

In a Quiet Place
Talking with God is what we do in prayer, but, as we said earlier, there do not always have to be words. Sitting with God in quiet is a good form of prayer — contemplative prayer. I repeat here what one of the great teachers in prayer, St Teresa of Avila, said, "See, He is only waiting for us to look at Him." When I visit an art museum, I wander about, like most everyone else, taking in the many great works of art, trying to imagine how anyone can be so gifted to create this amazing piece of work. Wandering is what I do, but I notice in many of these museums, benches. The benches are here for the patrons simply to sit for a while and admire, contemplate, study, and think. Why not? It is time well spent. The same is true with God. Learning to be quiet with God and looking at Him is a great gift.

There is a power in silence.
Psalm 46 provides us with a simple and remarkably beneficent piece of advice, "Be still and know that I am God" (v. 10). "Be still" can

be translated from the original Hebrew also as "relax" or "let go," but "being still" clearly provides the notion that the strife of this world is in God's hands. If we accept this on faith, we are free simply to be still and let God do what God does. Thus, stillness in the face of God is a compliment to Him and a way of showing Him great faith. It is also great for our soul — our deep inner self. There, resting in silence, we are giving God what He likes best — love and trust — and are getting something our inner souls desire deeply — peace.

Brigid E. Herman, the author of *Creative Prayer*, wrote,

> *He, too, was a wise man who first discovered that in order to live we must stand aloof from what the crowd calls living .... and so was that other unknown scribe who told us that "silent men are kings, for they rule over a great country where none can follow them."*[17]

"Silent kings" do rule over the great, silent wonder of our inner soul; where indeed, only God and ourselves can think, ponder, and talk together. No other human being can force himself into this holy space; he may enter only if we invite him. And only rarely would we choose to do so.

If we do succeed in establishing for ourselves a habitual time of prayer, we can look forward to that time as a place of rest, peace, and certainty where we will, at least for a short time each day, know that we are in the right and suitable place — alone with God. There can be nothing wrong with being there and everything right. We are created for this relationship and this kind of moment. Our life in this world does not permit us to stay in this silence with God, but He

---

[17] Brigid E. Herman, *Creative Prayer* (Brewster, MA, Paraclete Press, 1998) p. 24.

encourages us to make frequent visits, and indeed, with time, we can learn to sort of keep one foot in the door!

Dry Times Are Okay

Be aware that there are dry times in a life of prayer — times when it may feel like God is nowhere near. The truth is, He is not far at all. St Teresa di Lisieux, another wonderful teacher on prayer, writes in her journal, "I was in complete aridity — Jesus was asleep in my little boat as usual. How rarely souls let Him sleep peacefully within them."[18] She is reflecting on the miracle story of the storm at sea when Jesus sleeps in the stern of the boat — until the disciples panic and wake Him! If we experience dry times in prayer, this notion suggests correctly that we need not be anxious or think we are doing something wrong, but simply let Him sleep! It is okay.

If God allows dryness — or aridity — let it be, for some wise teachers say that these are the times that lead to purer love and greater union with God. He is there always. Whether we sense feelings of peace and joy or by faith alone, take it that He is with us. Indeed, we remain His good and faithful servants in the right place and doing the right thing.

We Study God's Word

"If you love Me, you will keep My commandments." The commandments are revealed in the Bible. It naturally follows that loving God and drawing near Him require spending time reading, studying, and applying to our lives the things we learn in the Bible. What we find in the Bible are, in fact, the things He wants us to know. One could look at it this way: If someone becomes acquainted

---

[18] Saint Therese of Lisieux, trans. Michael Day, *The Story of a Soul* (Rockford, Il, Tan Books and Publishers, 1997) p. 119

with a new friend and, in the process of growing close to him, discovers that the new friend has written an autobiography, naturally he will want to read it — what a great way to get to know someone better than to read his autobiography. The Bible is God's autobiography, at least in the sense that His will, perspectives, commandments, and priorities are herein revealed. The Bible is a revelation, not so much of His history, as of His nature and, thus, how He wants us to live our lives.

Scripture is life-giving. It truly speaks to us, not only to our minds, but even in the depth of our hearts. Its life-guiding and life-giving power comes through the Holy Spirit.

I know this, because I experienced it. My eyes were opened to our Lord when I was 19. Living at the fraternity house at SMU, I began going to church with the young lady I was dating, a young lady who had much more interest in God than I. Before this time, I had no interest in God or anything to do with Him. To me, God and Jesus were historical figures like Abraham Lincoln and George Washington who came, did their great things, and then left; they were gone. I happened to have been at this time assigned a paper on Socrates versus Jesus, so I found a Bible and had been reading some of the things Jesus said and did. I was unmoved by anything I read and was rather bored by it. One Wednesday evening, I attended a class with her at her church and, while there, I had a life-changing experience with God deep inside my heart that first terrified me and then left me with a profound peace. My worldview was now changed. God was alive, and He knew and cared for me. First thing upon waking the next morning, I grabbed the Bible and began reading the same passages. Not only were they deeply impressive, but they also were so impactful. It felt as though they were written expressly for me!

"Upward Call"

No two persons' experiences with God are the same, but the facts are the facts: God's word in the scripture has life-changing power. The whole of Judaism is based upon the premise that reading and meditating upon God's word is essential to walking with Him and living in His favor. Every young Jew is thus taught the signature passage in the Bible, the foundation for life with God, called the "Shema" — a name taken from the first Hebrew word of the passage:

> *Hear (Shema), O Israel! The Lord is our God, the Lord is one! And you shall love the Lord your God with all your heart and with all your soul and with all your might. And these words, which I am commanding you today shall be on your heart and you shall teach them diligently to your children, and shall talk of them when you sit in your house, and when you walk by the way, and when you lie down, and when you rise. And you shall bind them as a sign upon your hand, and they shall be as frontlets between your eyes. And you shall write them on the doorposts of your house and on your gates" (Deut. 6:4–9).*

One can easily sense the value of earnestly reading, learning, and applying God's word in accordance with ancient Judaism. The words of the Bible shall be on our hearts because, by such, they guide us. Therefore, we read the Bible, listening carefully for the meaning, striving to understand the implications, and applying them to our lives. We seek to embrace what God is telling us.

> *Oh, how I love Your law! It is my meditation all the day. Your commandments make me wiser than my enemies, for they are ever mine. I have more insight than all my teachers, for Your testimonies are my*

meditation. I understand more than the aged, because I have observed Your precepts (Ps. 119:97– 100).

We Read the Bible Slowly
I recall taking a class on speed-reading my senior year in seminary, which really was not very productive. In some professional disciplines, fast reading and significant quantities of ingested literature are beneficial, but not here. Scripture is to be read slowly; we mull over the meaning of everything we read.

A parishioner once came to me wanting to begin reading the Bible. She requested a good starter-list of books in the Bible. I gave her about ten books to be read in order: Luke, Acts, Romans, Genesis, Exodus, I Corinthians, Ephesians, Deuteronomy, or something similar. I was pleased that she was motivated to do this. Two weeks later, she was back. "Do you have questions?" "Yes," she said, "What do I read now?" I suppressed a smile. Yes, she had read all of that. I explained we don't read the Bible this way, not if you want to understand what it is telling you. "Now start over and read slowly," I explained, "carefully, asking yourself, what do these things mean, and what implications do they have for me?

Inspiration and Authority
The Bible, with its 39 Old Testament books and its 27 New Testament books (66 in all), is "inspired" and "authoritative." Inspired means God is its author.

He wrote it by inspiring the Old Testament prophets and teachers to write down the things God revealed to them. And He inspired the early Christians to write down what they saw, heard, and knew about Jesus Christ and life in the Kingdom of God. How He inspired them is not certain. It is doubtful that He dictated anything to anyone word for word. More likely, He inspired them through interior motivation and circumstances to write and utilized the thoughts and perceptions that were on their minds at the time. However, God did it. He got what He wanted: the inspired word of God.

The Bible is considered inspired not only because of how it came about but also because of the words' power, as I describe above. "Trust in the Lord with all your heart, and lean not on your own understanding" (Prov. 3:5). "Seek first the Kingdom of God and His righteousness, and all these things shall be added to you" (Matt. 6:33). How many times have God's faithful people leaned on words such as these to get them through difficult times?

God has a plan, and He knows what He is doing; trust Him, and He has us covered. This truth is what we believe, but fixating on the quoted words goes a long way to bring the understanding and willing faith of the mind down the long journey to the core and peace of the heart. The inspired words have the power to do this.

Lastly, we consider it inspired because its capacity to reveal and teach us truth seems endless. No matter how many years a Christian has repeatedly and diligently studied Bible passages, no one will ever embrace everything there. Most every time I prepare a lesson on some passage of the Bible for a class I may be teaching, or a seminar I may be leading, I discover (be shown) something I did not previously know — a new perspective, a deeper understanding. And I am in wonder at it and find myself excited to share it with others, enjoying the impact these discoveries can have upon us all. Only the Bible, described as the living word, can have this power. The words are alive and relevant for all ages, revealing truths about God accurately and somehow mysteriously managing to penetrate the heart. When the words feel as though they are written solely for us, they are.

The word of God is living and active and sharper
than any two-edged sword, and piercing as far as the

*division of soul and spirit ... able to judge the
thoughts and intentions of the heart (Heb. 4:12).*

Consequently, we must understand scripture's authority in our lives.
As the passage says, it can judge us — "the thoughts and intentions
of our hearts." The thoughts and intentions of our heart are where
we go wrong, but when Jesus comes into our lives, so much begins
to turn around, and the very scriptures that once judged us now
become words that give us life. We do not judge the value of the
Bible's teaching, as some seeking to relegate it to obsolescence
might do. We uphold its strength and recognize its authority over us
as a gift from God. Inevitably, we might squirm a bit when we read
specific passages. But rather than dismiss them, humbly we
prayerfully consider how we should transform our lives into
compliance. We smile at the story of one church's "matriarch" who
commends her new pastor several weeks in a row for the fine
sermons he preaches, until the Sunday he preaches on the sinfulness
of gossip! At this she criticizes him, because now he has "gone to
meddling." Yes, the Bible has a way of "meddling" with our lives,
and this is a good thing. Rather than dismiss the scriptures, humbly
we prayerfully consider how we should transform our lives into
compliance.

It Is Authoritative
The Bible is authoritative. Having been canonized many centuries
ago with its sixty-six books, the Bible has remained the authoritative
resource ever since for the things Jesus said and did. We believe it
is trustworthy to settle any of the many theological debates
throughout Christian history.

The Bible is authoritative also because, as we say, "it contains all
things necessary to salvation." We grow in maturity and holiness
with God through our years here on earth. We never have to find
any other source to complete the journey. No one has to climb a

mountain in Tibet and sit under a Bo tree meditating with a famed Buddhist monk to gain the last pearls of godly wisdom. Everything we will need to know while on this earthly journey and everything God wants us to understand and follow is right here in the sixty-six books. Let it be understood that God has other forms of revelation: beginning with creation itself, then the historic councils of the church, the Holy Spirit, and Jesus Christ Himself who contribute significantly to the breadth of divine revelation. Scripture operates in conjunction with all of God's revelation.

Studying the Bible
How do we study the Bible? How do we extract the good things that are there? Every growing Christian needs a Bible, and, for study, each of us needs a good study Bible in which we can underline, highlight, and make notes.

We study it by reading slowly, thinking about (meditating on) any passage we may choose to consider. One scribe comes to Jesus, offering to follow Him wherever He goes. Jesus does not say yes, nor does He say no, but He wants the scribe to understand the level of hardship that would be faced on the journey: "The foxes have holes and the birds of the air have nests, but the Son of Man has nowhere to lay His head" (Matt. 8:20). So, do you still wish to follow me? Questions we might consider as we meditate on this are, "What if He asked me to follow Him? Am I ready to say yes? How does Jesus know that His Father will provide for Him? Do I have this kind of faith? What about the scribe? Do I think he began following Jesus right away just as the earlier disciples did ... without question? How about something really positive: If I begin living a life of faith, following Jesus today with all that I am, how wonderful it will feel to know that God will provide for me, and I need not have any more fears!

"Upward Call"

For a more in-depth study, such as the kind clergy do when preparing a sermon or class of instruction, there are eleven questions we ask to analyze the content of a biblical passage carefully. The scholastic word for this process is "exegesis."

We begin by selecting a passage:

And when he (Jesus) returned to Capernaum after some days, it was reported that he was at home. And many were gathered together, so that there was no longer room for them, not even about the door; and he was preaching the word to them. And they came, bringing to him a paralytic carried by four men. And when they could not get near him because of the crowd, they removed the roof above him; and when they had made an opening, they let down the pallet on which the paralytic lay. And when Jesus saw their faith, he said to the paralytic, "My son, your sins are forgiven." Now some of the scribes were sitting there, questioning in their hearts, "Why does this man speak thus? It is blasphemy! Who can forgive sins but God alone?" And immediately Jesus, perceiving in his spirit that they thus questioned within themselves, said to them, "Why do you question thus in your hearts? Which is easier, to say to the paralytic, `Your sins are forgiven,' or to say, `Rise, take up your pallet and walk'? But that you may know that the Son of man has authority on earth to forgive sins" — *he said to the paralytic* — *"I say to you, rise, take up your pallet and go home." And he rose, and immediately took up the pallet and went out before them all; so that they were all amazed and glorified God, saying, "We never saw anything like this!" (Mark 2:1–12).*

1. What is the context of the passage? (What comes before and after the passage that helps us understand what this is about?)

In the previous chapter, we learn that Jesus has gathered four disciples who have begun following Him. First are Simon (Peter) and his brother Andrew, and next are James and John, brothers as well. All are fishermen and live by the Sea of Galilee. Jesus and these disciples then come into the seaside village of Capernaum, participate in the synagogue service on the Sabbath, and later arrive at Simon's home where He heals Simon's mother-in-law from a fever. She begins to wait on them and presumably prepares them dinner. Jesus later that evening heals several ill and demon-possessed people who have come looking for Him. The next morning Jesus and His new disciples leave to preach in other nearby towns where He heals another ill person, and by the time He returns to Capernaum, His popularity has skyrocketed.

The reason all this is helpful for studying the passage is that we now see clearly the origin of His extraordinary popularity and what is motivating the large crowds to seek Him out. It explains why there was no longer room anywhere in the house and how the gathering had made it difficult to reach even the door.

2. What is the geographical and physical setting?

At the beginning of the passage in question, Jesus has returned to Capernaum and "was at home." We do not know whether this is the same home of Simon or the home of Jesus Himself, who had moved to Capernaum from Nazareth (Matt. 4:13). Nor do we know the time of day.

3. Who are the people involved?

The people involved include Jesus and (presumably) His four disciples. Also, there could be, as well, Simon's wife, children, and mother-in-law. Then, the great crowd of people gather from

Capernaum and other towns eager to see and hear Jesus. There are scribes (educated teachers of the law who are friendly with the community's religious leaders) who likely use their elevated status to position themselves in the front of the inside crowd. Lastly, there are five other men, four of whom are carrying the fifth — a paralyzed man — on his pallet.

4. What happens? Or what is being taught and to whom?

We will answer this question in order:

- Jesus, in the home, is "speaking the word" to the large gathering of people.

- Four men approach the home carrying a paralyzed man on a pallet (probably a loose blanket roll-up stretcher).

- The four men, unable to get through the door, climb up on the roof of the house and, positioning themselves above where Jesus is sitting, open up a sizable enough hole in the roof. They then lower the man on his pallet (with ropes?) near Jesus.

- Jesus sees in this dramatic undertaking a sure sign of faith, but the faith He sees is attributed to the four friends.

- Seeing "their faith," Jesus says to the paralytic, "My son, your sins are forgiven." This statement strikes the reader as rather odd; the paralytic's problem is paralysis, not sinfulness.

- The scribes reason silently that Jesus is committing blasphemy by forgiving a man's sins; God alone can forgive sins.

- Jesus, who knows by the spirit what is in the scribe's hearts, answers their criticism with a challenge, "Which is easier …?" The forgiveness or the healing? Without waiting for an answer, he heals the paralyzed man and tells him to get up. The man takes up his pallet, leaves the house, and goes home.

- The healed man does this in front of everyone gathered.
- The people are amazed and glorify God.
5. What verse(s) seem to be key to the passage?
- v. 5, Jesus forgives the paralytic's sins based on the faith Jesus sees in the four that brought him!
- v. 9, Jesus challenges the scribes' denunciation that He cannot forgive a man's sins.
- v. 11, Jesus heals the man of his paralysis.
- v. 12, the paralyzed man reveals the complete and total reversal of his fortunes by carrying out with his own strength before all present the very instrument that has been carrying him through all the time of his illness!

Four verses are seen as key, because there is more than one issue at hand.

6. What words seem to stand out (keywords)?

"Authority" (v. 10) seems to be a keyword. The miracle story is intent on showing that Jesus truly has the authority to forgive sins. The scribes are right. God alone can forgive sins. They are wrong because they are unwilling to consider the primary issue here: the divinity of God in Jesus!

7. What important biblical issues are in this passage?

Jesus chose to forgive the man his sins first before healing him of his paralysis. This order suggests that forgiveness is more important than bodily healing. So, why would forgiveness of sin be more important than healing? Because salvation in the afterlife is eternal. The suffering of this present life is no comparison with the joy of life with God in heaven. The first is maybe 80 years in duration; the rest is forever. Jesus, knowing this, sees the much greater need for forgiveness over and above the healing and well-being of a body that is only temporary.

Secondly, the power of faith is astounding. It is because of the friends' faith that Jesus heals the man. Faith unlocks numerous doors to the miraculous power of God; and, thus, Jesus spends a great deal of time teaching on the importance of faith. The friends don't just "have" faith. They put their faith to work ostensibly.

8. If there are parallel passages to this one, how do they compare or contrast?

If the same, or any very similar stories, exist in other places in the Bible, they should be perused for the presence of significant similarities and differences. The same event appears in Matthew (9:2–8) and Luke (5:18–26). In Matthew, no hole is dug in the roof even though the same large crowd ("multitudes") is present. Also, Jesus chastises the scribes for "thinking evil" in their hearts. Since the line, "But so that you may know that the Son of Man has authority on earth to forgive sins ..." (v. 6) is repeated word for word the same as verse 10 in Mark, we should take note that this may be to the gospel writer the most important part of the story. After all, this is only the second chapter in the Gospel, and the people are in the beginning stages of learning the identity of Jesus and the extent of His power.

In Luke, there is more written to set the scene of the miracle, including the interesting detail that to open the roof, the friends must remove "tiles," which makes this a different kind of house. But the story culminates in the same fashion as the others, with Jesus again saying, "But in order that you may know that the Son of Man has authority on earth to forgive sins ..." (v. 24).

9. What other passages relate to these issues?

"Upward Call"

At this point in the study, we are encouraged to search whatever other passages shed light on these issues. For instance, concerning the primacy of forgiveness of sins and salvation, one might remember that rather heavy teaching where Jesus declares,

> *And if your hand or your foot causes you to sin, cut it off and throw it away; it is better for you to enter life maimed or lame than with two hands or two feet to be thrown into the eternal fire. And if your eye causes you to sin, pluck it out and throw it away; it is better for you to enter life with one eye than with two eyes to be thrown into the hell of fire (Matt. 18:8–9).*

I know of no sane person who would opt to remove his hands, feet, or eyes, but Jesus is clear: no kind of life in this age warrants sacrificing salvation in heaven. It is better to live a completely impoverished, ill, disabled, agonizing, or otherwise harsh life on earth than to sacrifice a chance to be with Him in joy for eternity in the hereafter. And, yes, if it is necessary to separate oneself from any cause of sin and temptation physically, then, by all means, it should be done. Indeed, while everyone else present in the home in Capernaum sees the primary concern to be the man's paralysis, Jesus, who sees all things in light of eternity, knows the man's greatest need: salvation.

Concerning the matter of faith in this passage, one could choose to compare it with the healing of the woman with the hemorrhage:

> *And a great crowd followed him and thronged about him. And there was a woman who had had a flow of blood for twelve years, and who had suffered much under many physicians, and had spent all that she had, and was no better but rather grew worse. She had heard the reports about Jesus, and came up*

*behind him in the crowd and touched his garment.
For she said, "If I touch even his garments, I shall be
made well." And immediately the hemorrhage
ceased; and she felt in her body that she was healed
of her disease. And Jesus, perceiving in himself that
power had gone forth from him, immediately turned
about in the crowd, and said, "Who touched my
garments?" And his disciples said to him, "You see
the crowd pressing around you, and yet you say,
'Who touched me?'" And he looked around to see
who had done it. But the woman, knowing what had
been done to her, came in fear and trembling and fell
down before him, and told him the whole truth. And
he said to her, "Daughter, your faith has made you
well; go in peace, and be healed of your disease"
(Mark 5:24–34).*

Out of fear of punishment from those around her and because it is
unlawful for anyone with her ailment to touch the garment of
another, she says nothing. But she has faith. In that faith, she is able
to believe that simply if she could muster her fortitude enough to
press through the crowd and manage at least to touch His garment,
she would receive a miraculous healing. And she does. What is
peculiar about this event is that it is the only recorded miracle where
Jesus heals a person without knowing beforehand. Her faith is great,
and it echoes the faith-turned-into-action we see in the passage with
the paralyzed man. In both miracles, faith is what causes it to
happen, and that faith is pointed to a belief in the divinity of Jesus.

10.   What are the original readers of this passage expected to
learn from this?

The readers are expected to see that Jesus must indeed be God (is
One with the Father), that He is willing and able to forgive sins, and

that faith is a most important element to opening the door for His work in their lives. They are expected to understand that forgiveness of sins has primary importance over the healing of illnesses, because the body is a temporary vessel, and forgiveness of sins is necessary to eternal life in the Kingdom of God. They are to understand that Jesus' life and teachings stand in opposition to the teachings of religious authorities.

11. What are we to gain today from the study of this passage?

Likewise, we are to ponder with awe and wonder the presence of God that exists in the physical person of Jesus Christ. Furthermore, the faith of the four friends is impressive to see; and, while envy is typically regarded as a sin, the exception is when we are uplifted and encouraged as we envy the virtue we see in other godly Christians. We can envy their faith and strive to find in ourselves the faith to rely on God to work His miracles in our lives and through our prayers for others. We can be moved by the love for their ill friend as demonstrated in their efforts on his behalf and challenge ourselves to consider how far "loving our neighbors" should likewise motivate us. Lastly, we want to embrace the need for forgiveness ourselves and begin with the greater endeavor to see our life now as vastly inferior and subordinate to the life yet to come on the other side of death's door.

In Summary

In review, these are the eleven steps of sound exegesis:

1. What is the context of the passage? (What comes before and after the passage that helps us understand what this is about?)

2. What is the geographical and physical setting?

3. Who are the people involved?

4. What happens? Or what is being taught and to whom?

5. What verse(s) seem to be key to the passage?

6. What words seem to stand out (keywords)?

7. What important biblical issues are in this passage?

8. If there are parallel passages to this one, how do they compare or contrast?

9. What other passages relate to these issues?

10. What are the original readers of this passage expected to learn from this?

11. What are we to gain today from the study of this passage?

Performing a proper exegesis on a scholastic level requires studying keywords in their original language (Greek or Hebrew) and researching various commentaries on the passage. As for the rest of us, these eleven steps should lead us into a very effective study of scripture.

We Seek Fellowship with Other Christians

I cannot count the number of times I have encountered people who profess belief in God and Jesus Christ but do not associate with a church. Fellowship with other Christians is considered one of the initial building blocks necessary to the earliest Christian communities. (See Acts 2:42.) It is a good and valuable axiom shared many years ago: Christians are like coals in a campfire. Keep them together, and they burn well with a good, warm glow; spread them apart, and they die out.

The Greek word for fellowship is *koinonia,* and it represents the kind of sharing that engages our spiritual lives and the journey we are on with other like-minded Christians. The word itself comes from a Greek word for "sharing." In short, when Christian people gather and talk about nothing more than sports teams, the weather, and politics, it is not the kind of fellowship intended. When Christians gather for prayer, study, and sharing their victories and struggles in the Christian life, it is. We all need to do this in order to grow. Thus, when discussing these things with the churchless believers I mention above, I always tell them that whenever I find a Christian with no church or fellowship, they are willing to admit they are not growing in faith. None of them has yet denied it.

Christians in fellowship with other Christians — the proper *koinonia* — was Jesus' plan during His mission on earth. His true presence and fullness of divine activity were promised in the context of Christian *koinonia*.

> *Again I say to you, if two of you agree on earth about anything they ask, it will be done for them by my Father in heaven. For where two or three are gathered in my name, there am I in the midst of them (Matt. 18:19–20).*

It is clearly understood that when Christians come together to share their lives and journeys, Jesus profoundly places Himself in this community.

When Christians are engaged in this kind of fellowship, they relate to each other's struggles and victories. They build into their own lives a deeper understanding of how the word of God benefits their brother and sister Christians. They are encouraged, knowing how others manage to face challenges through the eyes of God and find victory. There is an encouragement to pray, study, and serve the needs of others. Above all, it is here that the commandment to "love one another" as Christ has loved us is in full play. No matter what challenges and battles remain before them, they know others are caring for them and shouldering with them the struggles they face.

"Upward Call"

Paul encouraged the *koinonia* of Christians in Rome to "rejoice with those who rejoice, and weep with those who weep" (Rom. 12:15). By following this good word, no Christian would ever feel alone.

Two of our Lord's greatest gifts are to be practiced in the context of this *koinonia:* baptism and communion. We practice baptism and communion, because Jesus expressly directed us to do so. And, as such, we do so even when we cannot be sure that we fully understand what is involved in these two great gifts. We may understand a great deal of what they are about, but certainly, things are going on in these rites that benefit our soul, things that extend beyond our understanding. Hence, they are often referred to as "mysteries," borrowing the ancient Greek understanding that there are here realities that go beyond human comprehension.

Unfortunately, the different perceptions of baptism and communion serve to sustain the division among Christendom. The disagreement is over how far do these things go. Simply speaking, one party to the matter considers each of these "sacraments" to be an "outward and visible sign of an inward and spiritual grace." In contrast, the other party considers them to be an "outward and visible sign" only of their commitment to Christ.

Baptism
Concerning baptism, those who believe there to be an "inward and spiritual grace" associated with it — that some gift of the Holy Spirit is being given at baptism, a gift that any of us would benefit from having — believe even infant children of Christian families should receive it. The intent is that the child will be raised in the faith and, along with the grace imbued in the child at baptism, will most likely arrive at an adult profession of faith in Jesus Christ. Those that believe otherwise want the candidate to hold out until he is ready to make a fully considered commitment and profession before receiving the baptism — "believer's baptism."

It is not the intent of this book to debate the issue. Instead, we shall discuss some of what we do know. Aside from the idea that the early event of Noah and the ark was somewhat a type of baptism, with the earth being submerged in water and creation getting a new start, baptism finds its origin in Judaism's most notable event: the crossing at the Red Sea. The race of Hebrew people, God's chosen people, has multiplied over the years and become "exceedingly numerous" in the land of Egypt. For fear of them and to control the race, Egypt enslaves them and forces them to build facilities in the storage cities of Pithom and Raamses in Egypt. They are enslaved by a powerful taskmaster forcing them into hard labor, and live in symbolic darkness. And this is important to the issue: they are powerless over their oppressors.

They cry out to God, and He, agreeing to rescue them, sends Moses to "bring My people, the sons of Israel, out of Egypt" (Ex. 3:10). The process of deliverance involves a lengthy showing of God's power against all the gods of Egypt. In the end, God prevails, and the rescued people begin enjoying their new freedom. Pharaoh then changes his mind and decides instead to reclaim his slaves, bringing about the crisis at the Red Sea. God separates the waters of the Red Sea, allows His Hebrew people to cross over, and then destroys the cause of their darkness and oppression by closing the waters of the Red Sea over Pharaoh's mighty army.

This event at the Red Sea is all very significant. First of all, God's people are now free. In baptism, we are freed from the power of sin and darkness. Sin keeps humanity in darkness — darkness being the metaphor to describe our inability to see God, be with God, and even find a way to God. St Augustine gave us the phrase "original sin" to describe our state at the time of our birth: we are sinful from conception.[19] Sin, the cause of our separation from God, disables us

---

[19] St. Augustine (Bishop of Hippo) *Confessions*, 8:12.

70

from seeing God and His light. Now, the Hebrew people can look back across the Red Sea and see on the far, distant shore their past in Pharaoh and his people, and all the of Egypt's evil power, with a great gulf between them and protecting them from any further oppression. Secondly, it was water that enacted the escape. Water has forever been the ultimate tool for cleansing. Now it has "cleansed" the people from oppression and slavery and, just like baptism, makes a new beginning for them possible. And, most importantly, the Hebrew people are now God's people. They belong to Him. He rescues them, purchases them, and are now His people. He does not set them free to wander off and do whatever they want. He sets them free to become something exceedingly special, His chosen race. And being His chosen race, He has a plan for them: a plan to use them to bring His law, His will, and His ways to the whole human race.

Likewise, when we are baptized into Christ and set free from sin, it is not so that we can be free and wander off to do whatever we want (which would lead us inevitably back into sin and darkness); but we are set free to become God's chosen people, His chosen race, to live through Him, by Him, and for Him. We are His, and He purchased us with His blood which He shed on the cross. Now, being His, He wishes to use us to bring His Light and Truth to the whole world.

The ancient story continues for quite a time. The Hebrew people spend many years in the wilderness learning to be faithful to God, with many successes and failures, before entering the "land flowing with milk and honey" — symbolic of heaven. We, His faithful followers, likewise see this passage of time on earth as our preparation, as well, before we enter our own version of the land flowing with milk and honey, the true heaven.

What Is Baptism into His Death?

"Upward Call"

Jesus associated Christian baptism with death, and Paul elaborated on this important issue. Jesus said, "I have a baptism to undergo, and how distressed I am until it is accomplished" (Luke 12:50). When the disciples, James and John asked for places of honor at His table in the Kingdom of Heaven, Jesus asked them, "Are you able ... to be baptized with the baptism with which I am baptized?" (Mark 10:38), meaning His death. Yes, when we share in Jesus' baptism, we too share in a kind of death. While for us, it is unlikely this will lead to our being put to death on a cross, it must lead to another distressful death, the death of our old self. For us, it is giving up living for ourselves. It is the same as answering yes to Jesus' exacting of discipleship: "If anyone wishes to come after Me, let him deny himself (a death), and take up his cross, and follow Me" (Mark 8:34).

Paul elaborates on death in baptism in his epistle to the Romans in his effort to explain that once a person is baptized into Jesus Christ, his old life, with all its sinful practices, has come to an end; a new life must begin.

Do you not know that all of us who have been baptized into Christ Jesus were baptized into his death? We were buried therefore with him by baptism into death, so that as Christ was raised from the dead by the glory of the Father, we too might walk in newness of life. For if we have been united with him in a death like his, we shall certainly be united with him in a resurrection like his. We know that our old self was crucified with him so that the sinful body might be destroyed, and we might no longer be enslaved to sin. For he who has died is freed from sin (Rom. 6:37).

72

"Upward Call"

Much can be seen here. Let us be reminded of the seminal scene at the Red Sea. Sin, oppression, and darkness are to be left behind on the distant shore. They are no longer a part of our new life in Christ; they are left behind in our "old self." Now that we have been cleansed by water, we emerge victorious in the newness of life — a resurrected life. And, thus, it behooves us to honor the Savior who has rescued us — honor and please Him by living a new kind of life where faith, love, and obedience to our living Lord has replaced the old and lifted us in expectation of our new joyful life in heaven.

All of you who were baptized into Christ have clothed yourselves with Christ (Gal. 3:27).

Some Christians believe a candidate should be baptized only after being ready to make a fully considered commitment and profession of his faith in Jesus Christ. Then and only then is it appropriate to administer baptism. Others believe that baptism is appropriate even for infants brought to baptism by believing friends and family members who commit to raising this child in the full knowledge of the faith. This conflict leaves us with a question: who is right? I believe this and many other such questions are best resolved when seen from the perspective of God Himself. For God sees us and knows us not primarily as we are now, but even more so as we shall be:

Blessed be the God and Father of our Lord Jesus Christ, who has blessed us in Christ with every spiritual blessing in the heavenly places, even as he chose us in him before the foundation of the world, that we should be holy and blameless before him (Eph. 1:3,4).

God chooses us before the foundation of the world to become holy and blameless servants of the Lord. He sees our past, present, and future together. His vision is not limited by the categories of time which He created. What matters is that we are baptized, believing Christians. Whether we are baptized and then believing or believing and then baptized, I cannot imagine matters a whit to God who sees us as we shall be.

Holy Communion

The other gift Jesus gave His people, to be practiced in the community of the faithful, is Holy Communion. Just like baptism, we do not claim to understand it thoroughly. Hence, for it, the previous description "mystery" is entirely appropriate. This gift, too, unfortunately, sustains the divisions among Christendom, for we do not agree over the same matter. Is this an "outward and visible sign of an inner and spiritual grace," or is it an "outward and visible sign" only? The question revolves around how we interpret what Jesus said, "Take, eat; this My Body," ... and with a cup of wine in His hands, said, "Drink from it, all of you; for this is My blood of the covenant" (Matt. 26:26–28). Simply speaking, many do not believe that the blessed bread and cup of wine we have in our Sunday worship is His body and blood in a tangible way because, logically, it is too farfetched to be taken literally. It is instead meant as a symbol of something relative to His presence among our fellowship. However, many believe that the blessed bread and wine indeed are His body and blood, again simply speaking, because He said so. The latter group believes that regular wine and bread can be placed on a table or altar and there, with a proper prayer, are turned into the body and blood of Jesus Christ. All the physical and chemical properties of bread and wine remain unchanged, but, in a miraculous act of God tantamount to the virgin birth, the nature of these elements is changed into Jesus' body and blood.

We can find numerous books written about these sacred elements God gave for our fellowship together. It is not the purpose of this book to debate the issues revolving around them. But, again, here are some of the things we do know: Communion is a way of our uniting with Jesus in love, perhaps *the* way. As a loving, married couple spends their lives doing many things together and much time being in close proximity with one another, there are precious occasions they physically join together in love.

Similarly, Christ Jesus is with His people, whom He loves, in many ways and times, but Communion should be considered a precious moment when His people unite with Him. Remember, from His perspective, Jesus longs to be in perfect oneness with us, that we all might be one together. Since He and His Father in heaven are one together, Jesus has spent His life on earth restoring all His people into oneness with God.

> *I do not pray for these only, but also for those who believe in Me through their word, that they may all be one; even as Thou, Father, art in Me, and I in Thee, that they also may be in Us (John 17:20–21).*

This desire for union, or oneness, together is our Lord's goal as the chief end of the great love He has for us. God is at work now, and the chief purpose of His labors is to bring us to perfect readiness to be united as one with Him. He accomplishes this by transforming us into His likeness and perfecting us in love.

In addition to union with Jesus, Holy Communion does something to imprint us with His perfect nature. We are seeking to be more like Him and less like our old selves. Receiving Holy Communion, I suggest, is like the method in ages past when documents and letters were sealed with the author's seal. Hot sealing wax was poured on the document, and then a sealing stamp was pressed into the wax, leaving the image of the author's seal, thus assuring its authenticity. I think it is fair to say every time we receive Communion, we are further *stamped* with our Lord's perfect image and brought closer to His perfect love.

Another matter associated with receiving Holy Communion includes death. Paul wrote,

> *For as often as you eat this bread and drink the cup, you proclaim the Lord's death until he comes (I Cor. 11:26).*

In discussing this, we should return to the prototype (or foreshadowing) of Holy Communion as found in the Book of Exodus. Just a matter of days before the crisis at the Red Sea, God sends forth His tenth and final plague upon the Pharaoh and the Egyptian people to force Pharaoh to let the people go. It is a plague of death wherein the first-born male of every house dies. The plague affects every family residing in the land of Egypt: Egyptians, Jews, and even livestock. It brings about "a great cry in all the land of Egypt, such as there has not been before and such as shall never be again" (Ex. 11:6). However, there is one escape from the horror of this plague, an escape that the Hebrew people utilized to void the plague from entering the walls of their homes. They are instructed in each household to take a one-year-old unblemished male lamb and put it to death. Its blood is then to be spread over the doorposts and the lintel of each house to signify that those living inside obey the decree. God said, "When I see the blood, I will pass over you, and no plague will befall you" (Ex. 12:13).

No doubt we find in this the beginning of the Hebrew worship of Passover, many symbols and representations of Holy Communion. Holy Communion requires the shedding of blood, not of one-year-old male lambs, but the One true Lamb of God. So that His blood is available for our worship, Jesus had to die. Every time it is celebrated, Communion makes a statement — a proclamation — that Jesus died and shed blood that all the world could benefit from the grace of forgiveness, everywhere and for all time. When we receive Jesus and believe in Him, we become the beneficiaries of the forgiveness of sin. Those who turn their back on Him and choose not to believe in Him are not forgiven. The death of the first-born years ago in Egypt is symbolic of our eternal death, but the blood of the Lamb saves the faithful from death. Jesus' command to us is that we continue in this fashion, eating His body and drinking His blood until He returns in the second coming.

Another foreshadowing of Holy Communion was in the manna given to the people as they wandered through the wilderness. While their "baptism" at the Red Sea set them free from sin and oppression, the next step was to learn the ways of God. So, they were led into the wilderness, received the law of God, and began the process of learning obedience and faith in God. This part of their journey allegorically represented the Christian's time on earth now, being prepared, as we said, for the entrance into the Christian version of the land flowing with milk and honey — heaven. Manna was a miraculous "bread from heaven" which sustained their lives physically throughout the years in the wilderness. Manna began soon after they left the Red Sea and entered the wilderness and continued the many years of wandering the wilderness, ending abruptly at the crossing the Jordan River into the promised land. *Manna* was the Hebrew question, "What is it?" Both its existence and content were a mystery to the people. All they knew was that manna was "the bread which the Lord has given (them) to eat" (Ex. 16:15) as food.

The comparison is clear. Communion is given as spiritual food, which God's chosen people live on spiritually while they journey through this period of earthly time until we enter His kingdom. We cannot understand it, either its origin or its spiritual content, but the faithful understand it is the "bread" — the body and blood — "which the Lord has given" us that sustains us on our journey during this period of growth and preparation for heaven.

One might question that, if he cannot see or feel any significant, personal benefit from partaking of these gifts, why should they be considered as having any great importance? There is, indeed, a great personal benefit. However, one probably does not see or feel them much because these gifts are spiritual and therapeutic for the soul, not the mind and body. Remember, when Jesus faces the paralyzed man in Capernaum, everyone wonders whether Jesus will heal the man's paralysis because, being human, this is all they see. But as Jesus sees the paralyzed man, He focuses on the man's greatest need, the defect that impairs his soul. This is what love does. The soul is the part of man that lasts forever – in heaven or elsewhere. The paralyzed man's body probably had no more than 50 years left in it, healed or not, while his eternal soul, which will last forever, is in jeopardy. Forgiving his sins heals his soul, though it is doubtful whether he felt anything at the time. Then Jesus heals his body, but says quite directly that he heals the paralyzed body "in order that you may know" that I have the authority to forgive sins (and heal the soul)!

It always benefits us to understand things better when we can view them from God's perspective. His focus is the well-being of our soul in eternity, and He repeatedly invites us to join with Him in making this our highest calling. "Seek first his kingdom and his righteousness, and all these things shall be yours as well" (Matt. 6:33). Paul writes, "Set your minds on things that are above, not on things that are on earth" (Col. 3:2). The gifts we speak of herein perform a divine ministry to the soul — the part of us that we cannot see yet lives forever. Our Lord is entirely focused and committed to its welfare. The soul is a matter of the "kingdom and its righteousness" and "the things that are above." If this is important to Him, we should know immediately it warrants the fullness of our care as well!

The Necessity of Faith

Six of us, three couples, sat together around the dinner table on the first evening of our cruise. After introductions, a wealthy, proud, crusty, old fellow asked me with a big smile on his face, "What would you say to an old atheist like me to convert me?" I took this invitation seriously and responded with, "Let's begin talking about faith." He interrupted me immediately and said he didn't want to hear anything about faith! The immediacy of his interruption caught me off guard, and I responded rather sharply. "Then our conversation on this is over." I soon realized that he didn't seriously want to learn anything about God but rather was eager to win a debate against the existence of God. Next, he told me I needed to read the scientists more. I responded, "Why? They can't teach me anything about God." Mulling this over, I came to realize that he must hold the low opinion of Christians that they believe in (this non-existent) God only to fill the gaps in their understanding of why things in the universe exist as they do. God was our science crutch. If I would just read the scientists and be smart about it, I would discover I don't need this God, either. Science itself makes sense of life and creation.

We do not believe in God because of a need to fill gaps in our understanding of science. We believe in Him because we wish to enjoy and benefit from the relationship we have with Him. We believe in Him because He is the truth. I wish I had been more patient with this atheist; perhaps a gentler response would have opened the door to further conversation. Bringing people to believe in God is our Christian mission, and it is very joyful when it succeeds.

Faith is a good place to begin; it is the key to having a relationship with God.

*And without faith it is impossible to please him. For
whoever would draw near to God must believe that
he exists and that he rewards those who seek him
(Heb. 11:6).*

Let us begin by understanding the word "faith." It is *pistis* in Greek.
Pistis is a noun, and the verb form of the word, *pisteuo*, is translated
as "I believe." In other words, while "faith" and "believing" are very
different in English, they are essentially two forms of the same word
in the original Greek. There is, however, in the Bible, a significant
difference between "believing" and "believing in." While believing
means being convinced something is true, "believing in" means
putting one's trust in it. Hence, the verse,

*For God so loved the world that he gave his only Son,
that whoever believes in him should not perish but
have eternal life (John 3:16),*

tells us that we must put our trust in Jesus Christ as the true Son of
God in order not to perish. Faith is necessary because *faith is the
God-given ability to believe in things we cannot see.* Those who
require proof before they will believe in God are sadly out of luck.

It was my son, at the age of five, who asked me one night as I was
getting him into bed, "Dad, how do we know there really is a God?"
I gave him answers about our developing awareness of God through
answered prayer and other positive experiences. He had to ask the
question twice more before I got it. "But how do we *know* there is a
God?" I then said, "We don't." He was relieved, and, now
understanding God is what we "believe in," he went on to sleep.

Faith is somewhere out there, but to engage in a life with God, each
of us will have to find it. We may have to reach deep in our inner
being and grasp what little we might find there of faith and then
employ it in our pursuit of God. If we don't, the gap between God

and ourselves will remain wide. We can employ faith by offering our first sincere prayer to God. "God, if you are out there, please help me find You," and then begin seeking Him.

The presence of faith in a believer's heart is what distinguishes the followers of Christ from those who are not, "that whoever believes in him shall not perish." It is like a wall that separates us, yet it is a wall human beings can cross over in faith if they choose. The grace necessary to believe is there for all. The ones who choose to believe are those who find in themselves faith to accept Him without seeing Him, as we learn in the following event with Thomas.

You may remember Thomas, one of the Twelve disciples of the Lord. He has the derogatory moniker of the "doubting Thomas." But this is rather unfair for a couple of reasons. First, the other disciples doubt, too; secondly, to fulfill his mission — to tell the world he had seen the risen Jesus — he has to see Him! The story goes that Thomas just happens not to be present when Jesus startles the gathered disciples late on resurrection Sunday by appearing to them in a closed and locked room. He tells them, "Peace be with you," and shows them His wounds as physical proof He is bodily alive. When Thomas returns, they exclaim they have seen Jesus and He is alive! "Unless I shall see in His hands the imprint of the nails, and put my finger into the place of the nails, and put my hand into His side, I will not believe" (John 20:25), he retorts. The following Sunday, when the disciples, with Thomas present, are together again, Jesus appears. Addressing Thomas directly, Jesus tells him to reach out and touch Him and "be not unbelieving, but believing." Thomas must have been almost overwhelmed because he responds immediately, "My Lord and my God!" What is said next has a significant impact on us:

*Jesus said to him, "Have you believed because you
have seen me? Blessed are those who have not seen
and yet believe" (John 20:29).*

Thomas now believes because he sees Jesus alive. But Jesus makes
the pointed statement that persons are blessed for believing (having
faith) without seeing. In other words, arriving at faith in Jesus Christ,
the risen Son of God, without proof is of much greater value to a
person. The blessing comes from faith. So again, faith becomes the
wall that separates the saved from the unsaved.

While many may lament that they do not have strong faith, they must
be reminded that it takes only a little. God loves even a little faith,
and from that little faith, He causes great things to happen.

> *The apostles said to the Lord, "Increase our faith!"
> And the Lord said, "If you had faith as a grain of
> mustard seed, you could say to this sycamine tree,
> 'Be rooted up, and be planted in the sea,' and it
> would obey you'" (Luke 17:56).*

It is with just a little faith that we begin seeking, knocking, and
asking until our little faith is rewarded with the discovery of our
living and loving Lord Jesus.

Will There Be Doubts?
Indeed, even the most faithful Christian is subject to doubts. As we
live our lives according to His word, there are many situations and
challenges in life where doubts will trouble us. We have Paul's
instruction that encourages the Corinthian Christians to "walk by
faith, not by sight" (II Cor. 5:7) because he knows so well this to be
true. Every day we are expected to trust what the Bible tells us about
our future, to trust the promises God makes for our provision, and
to trust in the presence of God Himself. None of these things do we
see with our eyes, nor do we have any proof of their fulfillment.

Thus, there remains a lot in the journey of life the committed Christian must tread through in faith. Naturally, there are going to be times of doubting. But the only alternative is to live without Him. Truthfully though, God rewards more and more those that follow Him, and concerns over doubts fade over the years; consequently, the richness of God's love and presence grow larger and larger. Jesus compares this kind of experience in a parable:

> *It is like a grain of mustard seed, which, when sown upon the ground, is the smallest of all the seeds on earth; yet when it is sown it grows up and becomes the greatest of all shrubs, and puts forth large branches, so that the birds of the air can make nests in its shade (Mark 4:31–32).*

What a beautiful picture this paints, not only how faith in Jesus Christ begins small and then grows across the world, but even more how it begins and grows within our hearts. It starts when a tiny seed of faith plants itself and continues to grow, filling the heart with its presence and even pouring over to the benefit of others around us ("the birds of the air"). It is the beautiful story of faith growing to its fullness in a believer's heart.

So, we press on our way, holding onto faith and banishing the doubts that maraud us daily. Faith put to use is going to grow. I recall a couple in a financial crisis coming to me looking for godly guidance. They apologize, admitting, "Here we are again," stressing over what to do when we don't have enough to pay our bills.

We talked for a while and prayed to God over the situation. She commented woefully, "I guess we will never get better about this." "On the contrary," I replied, "you are much better; the previous times you came to me, you were in a total frenzy about to spin out of the universe. This time, you are spilling out your anxiety much more calmly!" We laughed and prayed, and they went their way. They remained faithful, God provided, and I am pleased to tell you they are now well off!

Seven Applications of Faith
There are multiple ways faith should affect a Christian's life.

1. The Faith to Believe in Jesus

The first application of faith is the one we mentioned above. We put our faith in Jesus Christ. "Do you put your whole trust in His grace and love?"[20] "Yes, I do." Herein begins a Christian's relationship with God. By such words, honestly confessed, we are putting into the arms of a God we cannot see the complete guidance, sustenance, and salvation of our lives. We are also committing to a life of service to Him in whatever form this may take. It is the best possible use of faith there is.

John Westerhoff, the religious educator and theorist, writes that faith comes in stages for many children reared in the church.[21] The "affiliative faith," one of the stages in the process, is a rudimentary kind of faith, but the only kind many Christians know how to embrace. It is the faith professed by the church member's faith community. If, for example, he is asked, "What do you believe?" he answers that he is a Methodist. He professes to believe what his supporting community believes and has no pressing reason to think, question, or believe otherwise. An affiliative faith is an academic acceptance — the mental acquiescence — of a selective body of Christian doctrine.

---

[20] *The Book of Common Prayer*,1979 (Kingsport, Kingsport Press, 1977) p. 302.

[21] John H. Westerhoff, *Will Our Children have Faith?* (Morehouse Publishing, 1976).

An "owned faith," on the other hand, is the mature faith a Christian "owns" when he or she discovers there is indeed a living, active God Who knows us intimately and invites us to repent and commit our lives to Him. An owned faith either emerges over time or is the result of a life-changing spiritual experience. Either way, the Christian with an owned faith now knows confidently he has put his faith in the living Jesus.

At the senior high session of the summer camp many years ago, we began early in the week explaining the difference between the affiliative faith and the owned faith. These kids were now senior teenagers, and it was time for them to be sincere in their commitment to God. Some of the counselors came to me the second evening greatly concerned. Some of their kids were now saying they did not think they were Christians. It was easy to see what was happening, and I told them not to worry about it. These kids are coming to the realization there is something more to this. Do not worry; we have all week! Sure enough, by the end of the week, many of those great kids left the camp delighted with their new "owned faith" in Jesus Christ the Lord.

2. *The Faith to Remain Loyal to God*

In the Book of Esther, we are introduced to a faithful servant of God named Mordecai. His willingness to sacrifice his own life for the honor of God is the cause of the story. It begins as the king of the Persian Empire names a new prime minister.

> *After these things King Ahasuerus promoted Haman the Agagite, the son of Hammedatha, and advanced him and set his seat above all the princes who were with him. And all the king's servants who were at the king's gate bowed down and did obeisance to Haman; for the king had so commanded concerning him. But Mordecai did not bow down or do*

85

obeisance. Then the king's servants who were at the king's gate said to Mordecai, "Why do you transgress the king's command?" And when they spoke to him day after day and he would not listen to them, they told Haman, in order to see whether Mordecai's words would avail; for he had told them that he was a Jew. And when Haman saw that Mordecai did not bow down or do obeisance to him, Haman was filled with fury. But he disdained to lay hands on Mordecai alone. So, as they had made known to him the people of Mordecai, Haman sought to destroy all the Jews, the people of Mordecai, throughout the whole kingdom of Ahasuerus.

Haman is a classic example of an arrogant, self-consumed, egotistical tyrant. In his egoism, he wants all the people of the Persian Empire to bow down to him whenever he is present. Mordecai, a faithful Jew, will bow down and show obeisance to God alone. So, he refuses. To retaliate, Haman threatens to execute Mordecai, and not only Mordecai, but all the Jews living in the Persian empire, including his lovely niece, Esther! Though Mordecai's refusal jeopardizes the entire Jewish race, he remains unbending; God deserves nothing less. One will need to read the book to learn how it ends, but in short, the story could not have turned out better.

The take-away from the story is to be faithful to God under all circumstances and never, ever turn our back on Him, and God will reward us greatly.

Blessed are you when men revile you and persecute you and utter all kinds of evil against you falsely on my account. Rejoice and be glad, for your reward is

great in heaven, for so men persecuted the prophets
who were before you (Matt. 5:11–12).

Faithfulness to God is both an Old Testament and a New Testament virtue. When we stand strong for honor and obedience to God, it pleases Him greatly. Translating from the original Greek, the words of the verse above actually say, "Rejoice and be exceedingly glad ...." Truly, the promise is that when we are persecuted and harassed for upholding the honor and will of God before the adversity of opponents, we are promised a very great reward in heaven. It is a reward so great that the teaching says we should rejoice and be exceedingly glad now! The history of Christianity is paved with the blood of its martyrs. Throughout history, multitudes of people have become believers through the testimony of bloodshed by the many Christians who have died for their faith. When non-believers see how far Christians are willing to go, even to death, to stand up for Jesus, many have become convinced that their joyful relationship with Jesus must be real, and they become converts themselves.

Jesus goes on to say,

> *Everyone therefore who shall confess Me before*
> *men, I also will confess him before My Father who is*
> *in heaven; but whoever shall deny Me before men, I*
> *also will deny him before my Father who is in heaven*
> *(Matt. 10:32–33).*

It sometimes takes strong faith to confess Jesus as our Lord before other people, especially in the face of adversity, but what a great reward awaits those who do!

3. The Faith to Obey God

When we accept Jesus Christ as who Christianity claims Him to be, we elevate Him to an unprecedented level. He is God. Therefore, whatever He says to us is no longer just good advice that we should consider following. He is God; what He says to do is the word of God. We must do it immediately. The New Testament likes to use the word "immediately" to describe the faithful way Jesus' followers responded to Him.

> *And passing along by the Sea of Galilee, he saw Simon and Andrew the brother of Simon casting a net in the sea; for they were fishermen. And Jesus said to them, "Follow me and I will make you become fishers of men." And immediately they left their nets and followed him (Mark 1:16–18).*

> *After this he went out, and saw a tax collector, named Levi, sitting at the tax office; and he said to him, "Follow me." And he left everything, and rose and followed him (Luke 5:27–28).*

Jesus commands the disciples to come and follow Him. They respond immediately; they leave their homes, families, occupations, and lives behind. This action takes faith. We do not know what interchanges between Jesus and these three disciples preceded this moment, but we know their immediate, unhesitating response was what He expected. Jesus was accustomed to His followers obeying anything promptly He told them to do. "Then he commanded them all to sit down by companies upon the green grass. So they sat down in groups, by hundreds and by fifties" (Mark 6:39).

We can understand these things and can well imagine the kind of charisma that emanated from Jesus. Today, however, we do not get to see the warmth in His eyes or hear the commanding presence of His voice. But whenever we have good reason to believe He — through the Holy Spirit — is telling us to do something, we are nevertheless expected to respond accordingly and promptly. And, like the early disciples, we are seldom told why! Our obedience is the sign of our faith.

Bishop Fanuel Magangani of Northern Malawi told the following story with even the joy of laughter. He was visiting a priest whose parish was far north, remote from the rest of the diocese. Few clergy in this region of Africa had transportation; many get around simply on foot. While staying with this priest, God told the bishop to give this priest his car. This action seemed preposterous because he needed the car more than the priest. So, he questioned what he thought he heard. He heard it again; it was not a loud, audible voice, but he heard it as a message sent straight to his heart. His perplexity grew greater. Just as he was about to preach the sermon at the church the following morning, the message was sent a third time, and he knew then what he had to do. He gave his car to the young priest. The following week, while receiving some Americans who had come to visit, he was astounded — almost to tears — when they announced they had come to give him a car!

I think we could all agree. God would make "following" Him and obeying His commands a lot easier if He just explained to us in detail why He wants us to do what He wants. But that is not going to happen. As I said above, faith is the filter that separates the righteous from the unrighteous, and our faith must grow and mature as we use our faith to obey His every command. Yes, God commands His people to act in faith. No, He does not tell us why. We are supposed to obey Him not because His command is rational but because He is God.

4. *The Faith to Pray for a Miracle*

There are many things written in the Gospels that are perplexing. Many of them promise God's intervention if we will just pray in faith. My favorite, mainly because it is so bold and almost brazen, is this promise from Jesus,

"Upward Call"

Therefore I say to you, all things for which you pray and ask, believe that you have received them, and they shall be granted you (Mark 11:24).

I say it is my favorite because it strongly challenges me; it indeed raises the bar. How do I ask for something and cause myself to believe that I have, in fact, received it? I might ask my dear wife or a friend to do something for me and believe they will. But my request is reasonable. Now, I am talking about God, who might do some things I ask, but not others. So, how am I going to apply this promise as presented? What about the many things I want but do not know whether He wants?

Spiritual maturity is part of this. Hopefully, I have learned more about what God wants. If I were to ask Him to give me the money to take a series of luxury world cruises so I can completely forget about the needs and wants of the poor, I am mature enough to know He will probably not do it! Nor if I ask that He make me the greatest ballplayer in the state so I can lap up lots of praise and become egotistical, I remain convinced He will not comply. But if, on the other hand, I realize that I lack the kind of love He expects of me and ask Him to make me more loving, I believe He will do it. While this distinction is clear, there remain many things in between for which I may pray though I am not sure He wants.

It is a matter of maturity. I am faced with many issues in my life and the lives of friends and family, country, and the world, over which I dutifully pray — and pray a lot. Sometimes, I pray with great urgency. It depends on how I feel about it. Love dictates all of this. Love dictates that we pray with sincerity, and Jesus dictates that we pray in faith. So, when my heart begins feeling the heavy weight of something that calls for prayer, I pray heartily and repeatedly. I let my heart guide me.

"Upward Call"

As a result, I have seen many prayers answered and miracles of healing take place. I recall one such event which took place in Pittsburgh, Pennsylvania. It is Friday evening of a weekend conference that we are holding for teenagers. The teens are told where to come, but since we do not start until everyone is present, we stress the need to call if there is a delay. Or if anyone has trouble finding the church, please call! The phone number that is given (long before cell phones) is the church's phone number. Everything is in order, but there remains one teenager yet to arrive. The phone begins to ring. Our one oversight is that the phone we need to answer is in the office behind a locked door. Repeatedly, we hear the phone but could not answer it. On another phone, we begin calling everyone connected to this church who might help us open the locked office, but to no avail. Finally, I get my house key out of my pocket in desperation and ask God to please make this key work! He does. The office door opens, we get to the phone, and everything works out for a great weekend. When I try the key the next day in that same lock, it did not work.

Associated with this application of prayer is the teaching of our Lord mentioned in an earlier chapter. We are to pray with persistence. When a miracle is needed, we do not pray once and then give up. The parable mentioned above is the one with the widow and the unjust judge. At first, the unkind judge chooses to ignore her, but her tenacity gets her requests answered. It is her persistent, unrelenting pestering that causes him to change his mind. It is how the parable ends that clarifies this point. Jesus said, "When the Son of Man comes, will He find faith on earth?" (Luke 18:8). Yes, persistent, unrelenting prayer that does not cease until it is answered is the kind of prayer being honored by God and driven by deep faith.

As for the specific promises Christ gives us in these verses, they do indeed set the bar high. They serve to call us forward, an upward call, to become the kind of Christians whose faith is so strong that it drives us to pray and to believe with growing certainty over all the matters God puts before us.

5. *The Faith to Trust in God's Preservation*

> *Therefore I tell you, do not be anxious about your life, what you shall eat or what you shall drink, nor about your body, what you shall put on. Is not life more than food, and the body more than clothing? Look at the birds of the air: they neither sow nor reap nor gather into barns, and yet your heavenly Father feeds them. Are you not of more value than they? And which of you by being anxious can add one cubit to his span of life? And why are you anxious about clothing? Consider the lilies of the field, how they grow; they neither toil nor spin; yet I tell you, even Solomon in all his glory was not arrayed like one of these. But if God so clothes the grass of the field, which today is alive and tomorrow is thrown into the oven, will he not much more clothe you, O men of little faith? Therefore do not be anxious, saying, "What shall we eat?" or "What shall we drink?" or "What shall we wear?" For the Gentiles seek all these things; and your heavenly Father knows that you need them all. But seek first his kingdom and his righteousness, and all these things shall be yours as well (Matt. 6:25–33).*

Jesus is preparing the disciples for their ministries on earth. In short, as they journey through the towns and cities along their mission, He tells them to focus on their message and ministry and not be distracted by the needs of their livelihood. Jesus promises that His Father will personally see that their temporal needs are all met. It is a type of trade-off: You seek first My kingdom, and I will take care of your livelihood. It is a general principle for all Christian ministries.

It is faith that enables us to obey God by trusting in His provision. Faith, in this sense, is letting go. It is saying, "I will not be anxious about tomorrow's need because my Father in heaven has this matter covered."

Bill Hickinbotham was blind, but that never stopped him from his ministry. He traveled from church to church throughout the country, praying, preaching, teaching, and transforming people's lives in Christ. He rarely stopped smiling and laughing. He often talked about his friend, an Anglican priest in Alaska, who would annually organize a preaching mission for Bill in the Yukon Valley in northern Alaska in the winter! As the plane was revving up one afternoon for a flight to one of the mission stations, Bill, donned in his heaviest coat, asked the priest where they would be staying that night. "I don't know," he said as he busied himself with the flight plan and cockpit instruments. A few minutes later, Bill asked, "Where are we eating dinner?" "I don't know," he repeated with a bit of irritation. Bill laughed as he remembered his friend, who never concerned himself with such incidental matters in all his preparations. The priest organized the meetings and the gatherings of the people but always left it to God to "worry" over temporal issues such as food and housing. There was never a problem, and Bill would return saying the missions were so successful you would think the Day of Pentecost had happened again!

Faith in God's promise to make provision for our necessities is, for one, a way of living a simpler, more peaceful life. If God says He has this, why should we concern ourselves with it? Our faith sets us free to be unconcerned, and this pleases God. God does provide. We love being able to trust Him, but He does have a way of challenging us. It has to do with His timing. If, for example, we need $500 by

Thursday, why would God provide it for us on Tuesday? Since we are expected to trust Him, there is no need for the provision to arrive early. Do we have the faith to trust Him fully? Typically, by Tuesday, we begin getting a little anxious. Faith has to be grown, so this is a learning experience for us. Our faith needs to last to Thursday!

One Saturday morning, while in seminary in Chicago, I was driving to my weekend church job. I was complaining, "whining," I prefer to say. Since I always give ten percent of my income away (tithing), the way I figure it, I am entitled to whine to God when I have financial problems. And I did; I had bills sitting on my desk at the apartment I could not pay. As I was driving down the road, registering my complaint to God, He began speaking in the recesses of my mind: "Do you have gas in your car?" I checked the gauge. "Yes, I do." "Do you have a shirt on your back?" "Yes." "Do you have food in your belly?" "Yes." "Then what are you worried about?!" These questions humbled me profoundly and gave me great insight into how God sees these matters. A few days later, just before the bills were due, we received a check from a source I never expected.

It is good to ask God to provide for our needs whenever we have them ("give us this day our daily bread"). But we might want to remember that the ultimate act of faith in God as the provider is to forget about these "incidental" matters, as the pilot-priest did since we know "He's got it."

God's provision comes in a variety of ways, yet let it never be misunderstood, labor is a proper element of our life in God, who has commissioned us since the time of Adam, "In toil you shall eat of the ground all the days of your life ... by the sweat of your face, you shall eat bread" (Gen. 3:17,19). In the Bible every prophet, priest, king, and disciple of the Lord was working at his job when God pressed him into divine service.

6. *Faith in the Face of Fear*

Our problem is not that we have no faith; it is that we have too little faith. The faith that we have must grow; it must increase. We find in Luke 17:5, "The apostles said to the Lord, 'Increase our faith!'" Jesus answers by telling them about the power of faith. Yes, He expects them to have more faith and put their faith to work.

> *On that day, when evening had come, Jesus said to them, "Let us go across to the other side." And leaving the crowd, they took him with them in the boat, just as he was. And other boats were with him. And a great storm of wind arose, and the waves beat into the boat, so that the boat was already filling. But he was in the stern, asleep on the cushion; and they woke him and said to him, "Teacher, do you not care if we perish?" And he awoke and rebuked the wind, and said to the sea, "Peace! Be still!" And the wind ceased, and there was a great calm. He said to them, "Why are you afraid? Have you no faith?" And they were filled with awe, and said to one another, "Who then is this, that even wind and sea obey him?" (Mark 4:35–41).*

It is not clear precisely what they are afraid about, whether it is the awesome power of Jesus or that they are about to drown. They wake Him because it looks like the boat is on the verge of sinking (and who wouldn't be afraid in that situation?). The Gospels report that, overall, Jesus urges the disciples about a dozen times not to be afraid. Our lives are in God's hands. From beginning to end, if we remain faithful to Him, nothing can truly hurt us. If we should die, we die; we know we will sooner or later, anyway. Our faith speaks powerfully to the assurance that we will be with Him in eternity. Nothing can truly hurt us.

It is an attitude against fear. Jesus has no fear. He knows that His Father has all things in His hand; and we, when we develop the faith to cast all our cares on Him, are able to banish all fears, as well. "Perfect love casts out fear" (I John 4:18).

7. The Faith to Accept All Circumstances with Joy

Nothing is more empowering to us live a transformed, victorious life than to fully believe in and embrace this powerful promise given to Christians:

> *And we know that God causes all things to work together for good to those who love God, to those who are called according to His purpose (Rom. 8:28).*

The "good" spoken of here is the progress God is making in re-shaping His followers, "those who love Him," into His image. It is the goodness of making us more like Him, more holy, more loving, and more available to Him; freer to serve Him, more effective in our prayers, more in peace, and more of a witness for Him in this world. The Holy Spirit does this work in each Christian's life. In His infinite wisdom and omnipotence, God can and does take all the misfortunes that a Christian encounters in life, and like a master-sculptor, God utilizes them to shape him into His image and accomplish His greatest good.

The classic biblical example of suffering is Job. No one can imagine experiencing the loss of all things more than he. He loses his health, property, and family all at once. Yet, despite his grief, he refuses to be angry with God. Instead, in faith, he surrenders every outcome to the glory of God. "The Lord gave and the Lord has taken away. Blessed be the Name of the Lord" (Job 1:21). If we insist that we must understand and make sense of everything God does through all the trials He allows in our lives, I suppose our lives would be very different. But the truth is, God intends that we learn our greatest lessons trusting Him in things that make absolutely no sense at all, including the untimely death of loved ones. "Trust in the Lord with all your heart, and do not lean on your own understanding" (Prov. 3:5). Like a shepherd leaning for support on his staff as he watches over his sheep in the meadow, by nature, we try to lean on our understanding when things are going amiss. "Why would God allow this?" But the proverb says for us to lean on nothing, absolutely nothing, but our trust in Him.

Faith in distressful situations has the power to draw us more closely into God's heart and mind. Faith enables us to say, "Thy will be done." Faith enables us, like Mary, the mother of Jesus, to say, "Be it onto me according to your word" (Luke 1:38). Faith, therefore, enables us to hold before God an open hand — the open palm of our hand. God wants our open hand so that He can put in — "the Lord gives" — and take out — "the Lord takes away" — whatever He wants. When God grants to us a blessing that we enjoy, it is natural for humans to grab and hold on. Our loving Lord wants instead that we keep the palm open because after He puts something in; later, He likely takes it out. And then there is room for another good thing He puts in and wants to be free to take it out, too.

So, we leave our hand out to God, palm open. Seeing this, He says, "Well done, my good and faithful servant, you have been faithful over a little, I will set you over much; enter into the joy of your master" (Matt. 25:21).

Our faith tells us God knows what He is doing; it tells us all things that happen God works out for the best. Our faith says that He is accomplishing wonderful things in our lives that we cannot understand now, but we will later. Our faith says that we are His chosen followers, belonging to Him, and indeed, He may do with us what He wants. His good, which we will see later, is much greater than anything we can imagine!

How Can a Believer Increase His Faith?

After hearing about and seeing so much divine activity associated with faith and the new kind of miracle-filled life that opens to a believer who has faith, it is no surprise that the disciples urged Jesus, "Increase our faith!" Jesus answers by explaining once again the power of faith:

> *If you had faith like a mustard seed, you would say to this mulberry tree, "Be uprooted and be planted in the sea"; and it would obey you" (Luke 17:56).*

His point was for them to learn just how powerful faith was: "If you had faith ... you would say." The nuance of the Greek verb is even more so: "You would say ... and ... it would have already obeyed you," suggesting that heaven's power is so effective that it would respond immediately — even before you finished asking!

Their faith grew tremendously. What happened first was listening to and taking to heart what Jesus just said ... faith is extremely powerful. The second was the coming of Pentecost. Jesus had commissioned His disciples after His resurrection to go into all the world, and this they did, each going to different places. But they were instructed first to wait in Jerusalem "until you are clothed with power from on high" (Luke 24:47–49). The power came just a few days later. On the day of Pentecost, the Holy Spirit — the power of which He spoke — came down upon them all; filled them with a kind of internal, spiritual presence and power; and demonstrated to them that it was the Holy Spirit that was speaking the message of the Gospel through them.

The third thing was that they would learn about faith as they began using it. A classic case took place soon after Pentecost when Peter and John were entering the temple at 3 o'clock one afternoon. Peter turned to a man lame since birth, sitting by the temple gate, and healed him miraculously through faith, just as Jesus had promised. The man followed them into the temple, walking and leaping and praising God!

For us to increase our faith, some similar things need to happen. We begin likewise by hearing and taking to heart the several teachings from Jesus about faith and its effectiveness. Secondly, we submit to God the Holy Spirit by offering to be of complete service to Him in whatever way He chooses for us, promising to obey Him in whatever He commands us. (See Acts 5:32.) And thirdly, we begin praying in faith. Our faith can grow in much the same way we build up a muscle in our body; we use it. The more we use a muscle, the more we work it, the greater the load we require it to move, the stronger it grows.

It is not a matter of simply praying over more things. It is beginning to live a life of service to our God. It is about being a dedicated servant of the Lord in whatever place and role we find ourselves. God intentionally spreads His servants out into every corner of society and, wherever we are, we begin a life of service to Him, walking in faith and prayer and being His voice, love, and light. Life everywhere requires prayer and faith, and so we begin with this in the place He gives us, and we do it all for Him. Prayer and faith will cause us to pray, believe, and see our faith increase more and more.

To Be Transformed by Love

To understand God is to understand His love. We know He loves us, but it is not easy to understand why.

We love God, too, as we said in an earlier chapter. The love we have for Him is not the feeling kind, or at least it does not begin that way; it is expressed in obedience to Him. "If you love Me, you will keep My commandments," says Jesus (John 14:15). Love is a decision of the will.

Our struggle with understanding love is, in part, the consequence of sloppiness in our language. "Love" is used in many ways, too many, and this leads to confusion. We say we love pepperoni pizza or a beautiful sunset, or we can say this man and woman fell in love or fell out of love or talk about making love secretly in the back seat of the car. Then, it is out of love for us that Jesus dies on the cross. There is a lot of diversity here, and, yes, it does confuse.

The Greeks are much wiser about this and have several words for "love." We need to talk about two of them, *eros* and *agape*.[22]

Eros is the word from which we get such unflattering English words, such as "erotic" and "eroticism." Eros, though, is not altogether that bad. It is the human love or desire with which we are born. The object of *eros's* love is itself, so it is often referred to as "self-love." It drives the engine that struggles for our self-preservation. This *eros* is also called "pride" because it is a principal sin from which all human beings suffer, and it is also referred to as the "original sin" into which all human beings are born.

---

[22] Much credit for the discussion on this subject should be directed toward the valued classic by Bp. Anders Nygren, *Eros and Agape*, (London: Society for Promoting Christian Knowledge, 1932).

Self-love always wants its own way; this is its nature. It has powerful desires that are never fulfilled. Therefore, it is constantly driven forward and is never satisfied or secure. It seeks to be liked and admired by people all around. It seeks its own, strives to be in control, and is quick to justify its choices of behavior and fervent endeavors at self-promotion. It loves possessions, popularity, power, prestige, and its own pleasure. It bristles at injustice, wants revenge when it has suffered wrong and is very prone to jealously. It is compatible with the society of human beings within which it lives and generally evaluates itself based on how well it has achieved favor, communion, and status. Self-love has gained an empire over human hearts and is "loathe to relinquish" that control to anything, including God's love.[23]

The nature of human beings is like this *eros*. When they justify themselves by saying, "everyone else does it, too," this is quite true. But clearly, when we step back and have a good look with unveiled eyes at this self-love within us and all its power and aspirations, we know we are not happy with it, do not wish to live with all its driving pressure, and certainly do not want to die this way. But the truth is that this is the only nature in human beings and, therefore, it is impossible for us to step out of it, because we have nothing else to step into.

We had nothing else to step into, that is, until Jesus Christ came, died, and gave us His life. Jesus provided for us a new life and a very new kind of life. "I am the way, the truth and the life," says Jesus, "no one comes to the Father, but through Me" (John 14:6). The life He gave us, which was His nature, is *agape*. The reason it was even possible for us to step out of self-love as our principal operating system and step into Christ was that His grace was given

---

[23] Jean-Pierre de Caussade, *Abandonment to Divine Providence* (Joseph Pich, 2013), Ch 11, Letters Book 4, letter XII.

to us first. Many believe that, in baptism, grace is given to the recipient. It is His grace that opens our eyes well enough to see that something more is needed, certainly that something better is wanted, and then grants us the gift of faith necessary to accept it.

Jesus Christ says, "If anyone wishes to come after Me, let him deny himself, and take up his cross, and follow Me" (Mark 8:34). Denying oneself is the seminal requirement in becoming a disciple of Jesus Christ. To "deny oneself" is renouncing the *eros*/self-love within us. We know it is not gone away, but our renouncing it is a declaration it is no longer our choice of operation; whatever influence it continues to have on us is not with our permission. With God's help, we will be working to give it no further place in our words, thoughts, and deeds. "Taking up one's cross" is adopting the new nature that Christ gives us, *agape*. Agape is the sacrificial love that Jesus taught us on the cross, and the power of Jesus' death on the cross enables us to renounce the former and adopt as our own the new *agape*. The cross is the symbol of *agape* because *agape* is sacrificial love, and the cross is the instrument of Christian sacrifice. *Agape* is not yet perfected within us, but by this declaration, we are saying this is now the kind of love by which henceforth we are living our lives. It is good when we wear a cross to remind us.

The "follow Me" means to be with Him, watch Him, and imitate Him so that we can learn from Him how to make *agape* our own. This last part — "follow Me" — is a long process for which we must be patient. But we aggressively apply ourselves to its adoption by practicing it with every opportunity provided.

The Bible does a wonderful job of describing *agape*. One should note the ways it contrasts with *eros*. Paul wrote to the Corinthians,

> *Love is patient, love is kind, and it is not jealous; love does not brag and is not arrogant, does not act unbecomingly; it does not seek its own, is not*

provoked, does not take into account a wrong suffered, does not rejoice in unrighteousness, but rejoices with the truth; bears all things, believes all things hopes all things, endures all things. Love never fails (I Cor. 13:48).

Paul precedes this passage by saying regardless of any manifestations of Christian faith and practice, a believer has nothing and is nothing unless *agape* is at his heart.

Where the object of *eros* love is the self, the object of *agape* is others. God and our neighbors are the others whom we are to love. When Jesus repeated the Old Testament commandment, "You shall love your neighbor as yourself" (Matt. 22:39), He means that with the same level of sincerity, and devotion that you are accustomed to loving yourself, you shall now begin loving your neighbor. This action changes the work of *eros* to *agape*. In the way you once loved yourself, now practice this love on others. This change cannot be any more dramatic.

"Love is patient, love is kind, and it is not jealous." Agape always approaches other people with their best interests at heart. It is difficult for us who have been trained all our lives in *eros* to imagine that love wants the best in all others and that we shall never be jealous of them. *Agape* has no desire to brag about anything because bragging does not benefit our neighbors. Bragging is done to elevate oneself, and *agape* has no desire to do that. *Agape* never elevates itself, and it never "seeks its own," which makes it the opposite of *eros* by definition. It rejoices when others' eyes are opened, and they discover the truth in Jesus Christ. It rejoices when others come to know Jesus Christ as their Lord and discover the great love He has for them. Love "bears all things." Paul, who is imprisoned, stoned, lashed, shipwrecked, left to drown, cold, hot, and starving all for the sake of the Gospel writes this — for the sake of seeing others come to Jesus, for the sake of the privilege of honoring God by acts of extreme sacrifice.

Agape is "uncaused" love. This curios description means that for us to love someone, there is nothing they need to do or not do, be or not be, befriend us or not, before we sincerely take their best interests to heart and regard them as valued by God. The Good Samaritan had no reason to care so deeply for, and spend so much time and money on the badly wounded Jew, except he was motivated by God's "uncaused" *agape* love. After hearing Paul's testimony, King Agrippa replied to Paul, "In a short time you will persuade me to become a Christian." Paul then said to him, "I would wish to God that whether in a short or long time, not only you, but also all who hear me this day, might become such as I am, except for these chains" (Acts 26:28-29). These are the things agape love says and does.

The concept of *agape* opens the door to many people for Jesus. Because of Jesus' great *agape*, he could effortlessly love even the sinners, outcasts, and criminals just as easily as He could the closest friend. The *agape* of which we speak is in Jesus Christ thoroughly, and this energy and intensity burst forth upon people long before they could do anything to earn it. Jesus could socialize with and reach out to anyone of any state in life, because *agape* love is never dependent upon people's behaviors.

The Pharisees reached out only to the righteous people among them, hanging their behavior on biblical verses, such as, "The eyes of the Lord are toward the righteous ... the face of the Lord is against evildoers" (Ps. 34). It was no surprise that they denounced Jesus for spending His time with outcasts. Jesus explained that He "did not come to call the righteous, but sinners" (Matt. 9:13), and they denounced Him for that. He said to His followers, "But I say to you, love your enemies, and pray for those who persecute you" (Matt.

5:44). These actions were what *agape* does, and it was diametrically opposite from what the religious leadership in Jerusalem would ever consider doing.

The new life in Christ has *agape* as its complete mode of operation. By the power of His Spirit, Jesus infuses this love into those who follow Him. He modeled *agape* always, but most strikingly on the cross: "God demonstrates His own love — *agape* — toward us, in that while we were yet sinners, Christ died for us" (Rom. 5:8). He obligates us to *agape*: "A new commandment I give to you, that you *agape* one another, even as I have loved you" (John 13:34). We are obligated because we are not able to pay Him back for what he did for us in taking our sins upon Himself. He wants us to feel indebted to Him, but His commandment is that we pay the debt forward in love to others.

Standing at the cashier of a grocery market, a poor man realized he did not have enough to pay for the milk and cereal he was trying to buy. A Christian man who had been standing behind him, stepped forward and paid for it all. When the deeply appreciative poor man asked him why he would do that, the man replied simply, "God has been good to me; should I not be good to others?" In actions such as this, a believer is paying back our love to Jesus Christ.

The True Role of Marriage
Should you ask a hundred people what the true purpose in marriage is, they would likely all get it wrong. Possible suggestions will include companionship, to feel loved, for the bearing of children, for rearing children, for sex, to avoid loneliness, etc. Truthfully, all of

these things can occur without marriage. The answer is to grow holy. Growing holy is the true purpose of marriage.[24]

Marriage began actually as a commandment before the commandments. Notably, marriage began even before the Fall in Genesis 3, when Adam and Eve, in contravention to God's commandment, ate from the fruit of the tree of good and evil and were cast out of the Garden of Eden. Marriage began in Genesis 2, in what we call the primordial law, a kind of governing law that God gave Adam and Eve before sin came into the world: "For this cause a man shall leave his father and his mother and shall cleave to his wife; and they shall become one flesh" (Gen. 2:24). By this, marriage came into being.

From the modern perspective, marriage happens now because a man and woman meet and become attracted to each other. He sees her and begins to think how good it might be to marry her, and she sees him and thinks the same. After several dates, they probably have found many things they have in common, so this is looking even better. He likes to go to movies, and so does she; she likes Italian food, and so does he. They drive the same kind of car or read the same books. They have the same college, church, or field of work and, so, now it is getting exciting.

What he sees in her is that she will be great as a wife, and what she imagines about him is that he is going to make a great husband. To clarify this, men, statistically, have an order of most important things to them in marriage; they are considered his needs, and they are ranked in order. Likewise, women also have an order of needs, statistically, and the interesting thing is that they are all different

---

[24] Appreciation is extended to Fr Homer Rogers, St Francis Church, Dallas. It is believed it was through his writings that this purpose for marriage was first brought to my attention.

than the man's list.[25] These aren't necessarily what each man or woman would list as a conscious need, but they are, in order, what leads to marriage difficulties if they are not met. Sex ranks number one on the man's list. Many times in marital counseling or pre-marital training, I have asked the woman what she thinks is number one on the woman's list. She always guesses it correctly: affection. She wants hugs, flowers, phone calls during the day, special attention, loving notes, and hugs. If he is cold and indifferent to her and provides none of these, the marriage begins to suffer, and she, hurt, begins to wonder why she should go out of her way to please him if he is doing nothing to please her. If she does not provide him what he wants, he soon becomes resentful and wonders why he should even try to make her happy. At this point, the marriage deteriorates and begins to fall apart.

Man's second need in this survey is "recreational companionship." Recreational companionship means that when he marries her, he expects that she will be beside him while he does all the activities he likes to do but does not like doing them alone. These activities can include hiking, attending football games, going to parties with friends, etc. Her second need is conversation. We mentioned conversation in an earlier chapter. Here the woman gains a sense of intimacy through heart-to-heart conversation with her husband. She looks forward to this almost daily.

The point of all this is that it is *eros*, plain and simple, that gets couples together in marriage. He marries her because *eros* tells him he wants her, and the reason he wants her is because when he is married to her, she will please him in many wonderful ways. She marries him, dreaming the same *eros*-driven fantasy: he is going to

---

[25] Willard F. Harley Jr., *His Needs, Her Needs* (Ada, MI, Revell, 2001).

make her happy. All of this is God's plan; He uses *eros* to bring couples together. But then something happens. While in the courtship stage, all they could see was that they were very similar, compatible people. Soon after marriage, the blinders start coming off, and they find themselves covenant-bound to a person who has many more differences than they could realize. I cannot help but think of this as one of God's most clever tricks.

One of three possible outcomes stands before this couple when they find themselves in great conflict. One, they split up. Two, they go on surviving together in a frustrating form of unhappy co-habitation. Three, they begin learning *agape*. The *agape* turn-around says this: "I admit I was disillusioned about how this marriage was going to go, but I made a commitment to God to stay in it; and so, to make this work, I must get to work to provide her with what she wants in this marriage whether she does the same for me or not!" And, of course, if she says the same thing, this will develop into a very positive, happy marriage, with two people working hard to build and practice *agape* love between them. This description is the way marriage is supposed to work.

God-instituted holy matrimony is all about making two people holy. Marriage is a laboratory for holiness. Another way to express holiness is to say they have become perfect in God's love, *agape*. As the couple replaces the original underlying motivation for their marriage (*eros*) with *agape*, they are conducting a holy event. We can and should learn from Jesus what *agape* looks like and practice it with every person we encounter. The other seven billion persons in this world represent to a Christian seven billion opportunities to practice *agape*. But in no place is this more effective than in Holy Matrimony because in no other place are we bound to another person in a covenant. If we do not like how some other person treats us, it is easy enough to walk away, but not in marriage. The covenant commits us to work through the most challenging times. And let us remind ourselves that in the deeper levels of the human psyche, it is, in the first place, the titillating, strange differences in our spouse that arouses our infatuation, not the similarities. I would never have become attracted to someone who was just like me — what a bore!

Consequently, we have many opportunities in married life when we must choose how we are going to act. What happens when the husband and wife crawl into bed, exhausted at the end of the day, finally fall asleep, and the baby begins to cry? Do we pretend still to be asleep and accidentally nudge the spouse, hoping he or she will get up and tend the child? Or do we quickly and quietly get up so the spouse can stay asleep? These are actions that choose between *eros* and *agape*, and there are dozens every day. While I live in a loving relationship with my wife, she, for her good, needs to live in a loving relationship with me. Consequently, I need to let her and help her find ways to love and make sacrifices for me. It is the loving thing to do.

Agape *is a Commandment*
Agape was not just an improved attitude; it is a commandment. A lawyer — an expert in the Jewish Law — once asked Jesus what he should do to inherit eternal life. Jesus answered him, "What is written in the law? How do you read?" And he answered, "You shall love the Lord your God with all your heart, and with all your soul, and with all your strength, and with all your mind; and your neighbor as yourself." And Jesus said to him, "You have answered right; do this, and you will live" (Luke 10:26–28). When the lawyer proceeded to ask Jesus, who is this "neighbor" that he must love and what category of persons was this commandment restricted to, Jesus answered with the parable of the good Samaritan. The good Samaritan found a badly beaten Jew, treated and bandaged up his wounds, brought him to an inn, and out of his own pocket fully paid for the completion of all needed medical care until he was well. Thus, in answering the question, Jesus was explaining that the

neighbor referenced in the commandment applies to any and every person we encounter who had a need for which we can offer any help. It was an unrestricted group of people.

The action of loving one's neighbor as ourselves, as explained earlier, means that with the same level of focus, sincerity, and devotion that one is accustomed to loving himself, with this same intensity, he shall now love his neighbor. The good Samaritan does for the wounded stranger precisely as he would have done for himself. It is not hard to figure out how to do this. All one has to do is ask the simple question, "What is needed here?" Or, rather, "What would I want someone to do for me if I were in his place?"

This commandment is loving one's neighbor as himself. As powerful as this dictate is, Jesus gives them a new commandment which is even more powerful — a new commandment that raises the bar even higher. The day celebrated every year in church calendars, the Thursday before Easter, is called Maundy Thursday. Maundy is related to the word "mandate," and the name is given because on this night, the night before He dies, Jesus gives the disciples this new commandment.

> *A new commandment I give to you, that you love one another; even as I have loved you, that you also love one another (John 13:34).*

It does not sound very new; it is very much like the old one. But there is something new about it. Instead of asking ourselves, "What would I want someone to do for me if I were in his place?" now we are to ask ourselves, "What would Jesus do for me?" And then we let this answer dictate the course of action we take in loving our neighbor. Of course, Jesus has already done it. He says just a little later,

*This is my commandment, that you love one another
as I have loved you. Greater love has no man than
this, that a man lay down his life for his friends (John
15:12–13).*

After saying this, Jesus goes out to the cross and dies. The height of
our sacrifice is now greater: what is commanded of us to do for our
neighbor is make the ultimate sacrifice — to lay down our lives for
our friends. *Agape* has now been given its fullest definition.

St Alban was one of the first Christians to be martyred in Britain. In
the third century, Alban, a soldier in the Roman army, gave shelter
to a Christian priest who was fleeing from persecution and was
converted by him. When officers came to Alban's house, he dressed
in the priest's garments and gave himself up. Alban was tortured and
martyred in place of the priest. There stands now the Cathedral of
St. Alban on the spot of the martyrdom, the place where, in the name
of *agape* love, Alban laid down his life for his friend.[26]

Paul's Battle for Agape

Paul taught a lot about *agape* and *eros*; he most often referred to
them as the Spirit versus the flesh. He writes to the Galatians,

*For you were called to freedom, brethren; only do
not use your freedom as an opportunity for the flesh,
but through love be servants of one another. For the
whole law is fulfilled in one word, "You shall love
your neighbor as yourself." But if you bite and
devour one another take heed that you are not
consumed by one another.*

---

[26] *Lesser Feasts and Fasts, 1997 (New York, Church Publishing, Inc.,1998), "Alban". P. 276.*

But I say, walk by the Spirit, and do not gratify the desires of the flesh. For the desires of the flesh are against the Spirit, and the desires of the Spirit are against the flesh; for these are opposed to each other, to prevent you from doing what you would (Gal. 5:13–17).

It is like a battle that Paul urges the Christians in Galatia to fight. He urges them to choose the side of the Spirit (*agape*) and resist the desires of the flesh (*eros*). "Through love be servants of one another." Make this their practice. Jesus Christ delivers us from the power of the flesh. The temptation to resort once again to the flesh is always present, but Christ has empowered us to live different lives. With His help, we do it. Paul is very open about this struggle, even within himself. He writes to the church in Rome,

I do not understand my own actions. For I do not do what I want, but I do the very thing I hate. Now if I do what I do not want, I agree that the law is good. So then it is no longer I that do it, but sin which dwells within me. For I know that nothing good dwells within me, that is, in my flesh. I can will what is right, but I cannot do it. For I do not do the good I want, but the evil I do not want is what I do. Now if I do what I do not want, it is no longer I that do it, but sin which dwells within me (Rom. 7:15–20).

The good thing about this is that Paul knows he is not the sin. He has chosen to live by the Spirit. He wills at every turn to do what the Spirit tells him to do. He chooses to follow *agape*. He has been redeemed by Jesus Christ. It is the "sin which dwells within" him that is the cause of the things he hates, not him. Paul ends the passage with the promise that brings him great comfort,

Wretched man that I am! Who will deliver me from this body of death? Thanks be to God through Jesus Christ our Lord! (Rom. 7:24–25).

In the end, when his life on earth is finished, he knows the battle will be won and he is no longer harassed by the nagging desires of *eros* "thanks be to God."

The Final Judgment Is Based on Agape
Whether we realize it or not, God is busy perfecting *agape* within us. John the Apostle wrote,

So we know and believe the love God has for us. God is love, and he who abides in love abides in God, and God abides in him. In this is love perfected with us (I John 4:16–17).

"Abiding in love," that is, practicing love (*agape*), is the way we are perfected in *agape*. Making a habit of practicing the *agape* Jesus gives us enables God to shape it into our very nature. And indeed, this is the question by which we will be assessed on the day of judgment.

When the Son of man comes in his glory, and all the angels with him, then he will sit on his glorious throne. Before him will be gathered all the nations, and he will separate them one from another as a shepherd separates the sheep from the goats, and he will place the sheep at his right hand, but the goats at the left. Then the King will say to those at his right hand, "Come, O blessed of my Father, inherit the kingdom prepared for you from the foundation of the world; for I was hungry and you gave me food, I was thirsty and you gave me drink, I was a stranger and you welcomed me, I was naked and you clothed me,

I was sick and you visited me, I was in prison and you came to me." Then the righteous will answer him, "Lord, when did we see thee hungry and feed thee, or thirsty and give thee drink? And when did we see thee a stranger and welcome thee, or naked and clothe thee? And when did we see thee sick or in prison and visit thee?" And the King will answer them, "Truly, I say to you, as you did it to one of the least of these my brethren, you did it to me." Then he will say to those at his left hand, "Depart from me, you cursed, into the eternal fire prepared for the devil and his angels; for I was hungry and you gave me no food, I was thirsty and you gave me no drink, I was a stranger and you did not welcome me, naked and you did not clothe me, sick and in prison and you did not visit me." Then they also will answer, "Lord, when did we see thee hungry or thirsty or a stranger or naked or sick or in prison, and did not minister to thee?" Then he will answer them, "Truly, I say to you, as you did it not to one of the least of these, you did it not to me." And they will go away into eternal punishment, but the righteous into eternal life (Matt. 25:31–46).

After an initial reading of this passage, one might naturally conclude that the Christian teaching on salvation is that a person gets saved and goes to heaven if he feeds the hungry, gives water to the thirsty, visits prisoners, cares for the ill, receives strangers, and gives clothing to those that did not have any. So, everyone better go out and do these things! But this is not what Christianity teaches, nor is this what the passage is saying. Look more carefully at the curios part: none of them, neither the sheep nor the goats, knows what they are doing. "You like that we fed You, Lord, when You were hungry?" say the sheep, "When did we do that?!" In some secret way, the Son of Man has been living His life through the indigent and suffering people, but still, neither the sheep nor the goats knew this. Therefore, the difference between the sheep and the goats is that while not knowing there was anything special about the needy, the sheep cared for them anyway! And answering the question of why they made this choice, it is because the sheep are the ones that have *agape* alive and active within them! Truthfully, they may still not have known it; in serving the needy, they were just doing what had become natural to them.

It happens in this fashion. Jesus Christ, our Lord and Savior, has been presented before them. The sheep have accepted Christ as their Lord and Savior. In moving into their lives in the person of the Holy Spirit, God, who is love (*agape*) — Jesus — has begun infusing His presence and nature into them. Said differently, Christ Himself has begun living His life within them. Now *agape* is manifested as it emerges from them in their humble actions. Therefore, the point of the parable is not about what the sheep do. It is about the kind of servants that they have become! *Agape*, by its very nature, loves all others as Christ has loved all of us. Therefore, without thinking about it, questioning it, or even wondering why, the sheep have begun responding to every person they encounter in accordance with their need, just as Jesus would. The sheep are blessed to have Jesus, He has transformed them from *eros* love to *agape* love, and their reward is to "inherit the kingdom prepared for them from the foundation of the world."

The Spontaneity of Agape

Agape is not natural to this world nor anyone born in it. It is a gift from God. Christians who have God's Spirit operating within them are no longer "of the world." They do not belong to this world; they belong to God. However, filled with His Spirit, these Christians Jesus has sent into the world. They live their lives for Him. His light and *agape* shines through them. They are no longer compatible with this world. Jesus has prayed, and continues to pray, for them to the Father that they may be kept from the world and from the "evil one" (John 17:15–18). Those who have begun to operate by *agape* are different, and, indeed, we are. This Spirit, this *agape*, is our new nature. When Christians are operating out of their new nature, they do what is natural — they practice *agape*.

In the third century Roman empire, a great plague swept through the land. Many who could afford to escape the big cities found refuge in the fields and towns. They left afflicted friends and even family members behind in their effort to avoid dying themselves. But Christians, who were still in the minority, did just the opposite.

They found these friends and family members ill from the plague and abandoned in the streets — complete strangers — and brought them to their own homes and nursed them back to health. The Christians put themselves at significant risk for doing so; they are exposing themselves to the illness. They did it because *agape* was in them, and Jesus said, "Greater love has no man than this, that he lay down his life for his friends" (John 15:13). The consequence was, though some Christians died in the process, many of those they ministered to lived. And the pagan Romans, especially those that survived because of the care shown them, began asking the natural question, "Why did you do this?" The answer was that they did it, "Because Jesus Christ, who lives within us, did it for us and taught us to love others." The further consequence of this charity is that thousands of pagans became Christians, bringing about tremendous growth in the church.

We do what is natural. Call it a new natural, but natural just the same. Oswald Chambers puts it this way:

> *We don't deliberately set the statements of Jesus before us as our standard, but when His Spirit is*

116

*having His way with us, we live according to His
standard without even realizing it ... The nature of
everything involved in the life of God in us is only
discerned when we have been through it and it is in
our past.*

*The evidence of our love for Him is the absolute
spontaneity of our love, which flows naturally from
His nature within us. And when we look back, we will
not be able to determine why we did certain things,
but we can know that we did them according to the
spontaneous nature of His love in us.*[27]

Thus, it is not really up to us to imitate the marvelous description of
agape quoted above from I Corinthians 13, or in Matthew 25 with
the sheep and the goats. Instead, it is up to us to abide in Jesus, seek
to draw closer to Him, follow Him, live in His blessed *agape*
ourselves, and be amazed at the spontaneous actions of *agape* that
naturally emanate from us.

---

[27] Oswald Chambers, *My Utmost for His Highest* (Grand Rapids: Discovery House Publishers, 1992) April 30.

117

The Value of Humility

Humility is somewhat of an elusive virtue. If one ever thinks he has acquired it, this itself is evidence that he probably has not. I like to think of humility as the second greatest virtue — second to love — because it is necessary to the growth of all other virtue. Humility puts us in the proper disposition before God — it makes us teachable. Humility in our soul has the spiritual effect of putting humus around a tree to make it grow, and, yes, even the words "humility" and "humus" have the same root. God allows the dumping of unappealing debris around our feet because it helps us see what is lacking in us and helps us grow into His likeness.

What is humility? Humility is not false humility. That would be concert pianist, Van Cliburn, saying, "Aw, shucks, I'm not a good piano player." That is not humility. It is a lie. True humility would say, "Thank you very much. I am good, but only because God has granted me the gift to be so." Humility is truth, the clear, unobstructed assessment of reality. It is a fair and honest acknowledgment of our limitations. It sees God in all His greatness and sees the self for all its weakness. Being humble means God can have His way with us, with no resistance, because being humble means we claim no rights for ourselves. Mary, the mother of Jesus, said to the angel, "Behold the handmaid of the Lord; be it done to me according to your word" (Luke 2:38). We are instructed to humble ourselves before the Lord because humility is the greatest antidote against the birth defect of self-love.

Humility brings us peace. If *eros* drives us to significant accomplishments and manmade success, humility puts a halt to that. Instead, we can claim, "I am God's cherished child even now. I do not need to accomplish anything now. I do not need to struggle to understand anything right now. I do not need to stay on my toes, ready to protect myself from any possible conflict I might encounter."

King David wrote a psalm about humility. Sense how much peace one finds in these words:

> *O Lord, I am not proud; I have no haughty looks.*
>
> *I do not occupy myself with great matters, or with things that are too hard for me.*
>
> *But I still my soul and make it quiet, like a child upon its mother's breast; my soul is quieted within me.*
>
> *O Israel, wait upon the Lord, from this time forth forever more (Ps. 131).*

Humility makes us strong. We only have to look to the rock hard saints. We see them as kind, attentive, sensitive, hospitable, and compliant; yet inflexible when it comes to issues of faith and obedience. Even the threat of death does not deter them. The main reason outsiders could not deter them from faith and obedience to God is that being humble persons, they do not care what anyone thinks of them. Humility gives them clarity, and what they know is that pleasing anyone else was not at all important compared to pleasing and loving God. Jesus explained,

> *If any one comes to me and does not hate his own father and mother and wife and children and brothers and sisters, yes, and even his own life, he cannot be my disciple (Luke 14:26).*

Jesus does not intend for us to harbor ill feelings towards any of these persons. On the contrary, he expects us to love our neighbor, but He also expects our love for Him and willingness to serve and obey Him to exceed our love for any neighbor.

"Upward Call"

Whom have I in heaven but Thee, O Lord? and having Thee I desire nothing upon earth (Ps. 73:26).

Some of us may have greatly tender souls. One unkind word, one hint at criticism, one expression of disinterest from a neighbor, and we feel devastating rejection. We tend to cower from or patronize others in a valiant effort to prevent a devastating confrontation. We may think our weakness is an expression of humility, but it is not; our problem is, at least in part, a lack of humility. We strive for others to like and accept us when we should strive alone for a place in the heart of God. St Paul writes, "I press on to make Christ my own; because Christ Jesus has made me his own" (Phil. 3:12). It is as simple as that. We let go of the great need to win approval from others. Humility makes us strong.

Humility then brings us peace; humility makes us strong; and third, humility can bring us great joy. It brings great joy, because the humble person is free of concerns of this world and, most significantly, of his place in it. His place in the world is established and protected by Jesus Christ. We have this written about St Francis of Assisi who when asked by his companion, Brother Leo, what is perfect joy?

> *I return from Perugia and arrive here in the dead of night; and it is winter time, muddy and so cold that icicles have formed on the edges of my habit and keep striking my legs. And all covered with mud and cold, I come to the gate and after I have knocked and called for some time, a brother comes and asks, "Who are you?" I answer, "Brother Francis." And he says, "Go away; this is not a proper hour for going about, and you may not come in." And when I insist, he answers, "Go away, you are a simple and a stupid person; we are so many and we have no need*

of you." And I say, "For the love of God, take me in tonight." And he answers, "I will not, go somewhere else."

"I tell you this," St Francis said to Brother Leo, "If I had patience and did not become upset, there would be true joy in this and true virtue."[28]

It took me a while to understand how that might be joy. St Francis meant that humility frees us from the concern of how we are thought of and treated by others, even in a situation so extreme as this. St Francis was a humble man and knows who he was in God; in this freedom, he was not trapped by the rudeness of another person's weak character. He did not let it affect him; he did not choose to counter on equal terms, either in word or emotion. His response was in liberty and joy.

Humility Is Necessary to our Ministries

While God accomplishes great things in this world, it is curious that He chooses individuals through whom He does His work — flawed, sinful human beings. There is a humorous story about this. Jesus returns to heaven after he had risen from the dead and ascended. The angels gather around Him and ask Him how it went, "Did You accomplish everything You went there to do?" "Yes," He answers. "Did you bring salvation to the whole world?" "Yes," He answers again. "And what did you do to see that the message of salvation is shared throughout the world?" "I left it in the hands of twelve men." "Twelve men?!" the angels asked Him, stunned. "What if they fail? What is Your Plan B?" "There is no Plan B," Jesus answers.

Yes, it does seem strange that He leaves the message of His Kingdom in the hands of fallible people. Yet, this is precisely what He does. *Agape* love, now planted and thriving in the hearts of His

---

[28] Unidentified writing on St Francis of Assisi

followers, energizes them into sharing the message of salvation through Jesus into the whole world. This sharing of the gospel will continue until He returns at the end of the age.

The problem, of course, is that each of us who hears His calling is still a sinner. We have *eros* still demanding attention, and it continues its demands on those who now seek to do great things for God. It is no wonder that even the disciples were caught more than once discussing who was the greater disciple.

> *And they came to Capernaum; and when he was in the house he asked them, "What were you discussing on the way?" But they were silent; for on the way they had discussed with one another who was the greatest. And he sat down and called the twelve; and he said to them, "If any one would be first, he must be last of all and servant of all" (Mark 9:33–35).*

After Jesus' departure, they are each destined to move out into society and accomplish great things for God in spreading the good news of His Kingdom throughout the world. It is imperative that they not lose sight that all the good they can accomplish will occur not by their might but by the Holy Spirit operating through them. Therefore, Jesus stresses over and over the necessity to maintain humility within themselves. In the passage above, He even appeals to their *eros* — their natural desire to be great, "If any one would be first ..." He explains that in the Kingdom of God, many things are just the opposite. Why? Because in the Kingdom of God, the only form of love is *agape,* the desire to serve others. And whoever chooses to be, not first, but last will be the greatest of all. A*gape* works in this way: it never yearns to be above or greater than others. It yearns and hungers to build up joy and show great love to all others, and the greatest in the Kingdom of God will do just that.

122

Jesus knows His followers are still defective in the sense that *eros* is still part of who they are and that sin still dwells within them. On the other hand, he knows *agape* has been planted within their hearts also, and so the mixture of the two will exist together within them, like Paul's Spirit waging war with his flesh.

Jesus knows that as they go out into the world, guided by His Spirit, they will be very effective. He knows they are about to accomplish great things for the Kingdom of God, but He knows they will be faced with opposition and obstacles. One of the greatest obstacles they will have to confront is their pride. Therefore, humility continues as a topic of discussion even the night before He dies when He washed their feet.

> *Jesus, knowing that the Father had given all things into his hands, and that he had come from God and was going to God, rose from supper, laid aside his garments, and girded himself with a towel. Then he poured water into a basin, and began to wash the disciples' feet, and to wipe them with the towel with which he was girded. He came to Simon Peter; and Peter said to him, "Lord, do you wash my feet?" Jesus answered him, "What I am doing you do not know now, but afterward you will understand." Peter said to him, "You shall never wash my feet." Jesus answered him, "If I do not wash you, you have no part in me ...."*
>
> *When he had washed their feet, and taken his garments, and resumed his place, he said to them, "Do you know what I have done to you? You call me Teacher and Lord; and you are right, for so I am. If I then, your Lord and Teacher, have washed your feet, you also ought to wash one another's feet. For I*

have given you an example, that you also should do
as I have done to you" (John 13:3–15).

Peter's objection represented the thoughts of all the disciples: Jesus should not be washing their feet. If anyone should be washing feet, they should be the ones washing His. Such was the protocol of that day. If you were to accept the invitation to visit a friend's home, when you arrived, it was a typical custom of the host to have one of his servants wash your feet, much like nowadays when the host offers to take your hat and coat. But protocol dictated that it was the youngest, lowest servant whose humble job was to get on his knees and wash the feet of the newly arrived guests. So, in keeping with all the other reversals that shall be discovered in the Kingdom of Heaven, Jesus got on His knees and, stripped to His waist, washed their feet.

This event will serve as a show-and-tell kind of thing. The disciples will not forget seeing their Lord and Master on His knees washing their feet. And they will remember what He said, for He was not going to let them pay the favor back to Him: "If I then, your Lord and Teacher, have washed your feet, you also ought to wash one another's feet. For I have given you an example, that you also should do as I have done to you." He will make them not pay it back to Him but forward it to each other; He is telling them to be each other's lowest servant.

The word "should" in Greek is our word for "ought" in the sense of "debt" such that since He washed their feet, they now have a debt they owe Jesus, and they need to pay it by being the lowest servant to each other. Though the commandment is to wash each other's feet, the whole point is not washing dirty feet. It is to humble themselves before their fellow disciples to act as each other's lowest servant! That is how their debt to Jesus must be paid.

"Upward Call"

Peter's Wound

Pride is an enemy to the work of God. It thrusts itself upon every throne that the Lord may build as He elevates us to accomplish the work of Jesus Himself in this world. Therefore, pride must be deeply wounded. Pride is what happened to Peter.

By Jesus' direction, Peter was heir apparent of leadership in the fledgling church. He was the most outspoken and had naturally become the speaker for the whole group. When they were caught discussing which of them was the greatest, surely many "votes" were leaning toward him and quite probably even his own. Again, on the last night Jesus was with them, Jesus, calling Peter by his original name, said,

> *"Simon, Simon, behold, Satan demanded to have you, that he might sift you like wheat, but I have prayed for you that your faith may not fail; and when you have turned again, strengthen your brethren."* *And he said to him, "Lord, I am ready to go with you to prison and to death." He said, "I tell you, Peter, the cock will not crow this day, until you three times deny that you know me" (Luke 22:31–34).*

I am sure Peter did not believe this. He knew his determination; he knew he loved the Lord. He knew the importance of loyalty, and he knew that Jesus said, "Whoever shall deny Me before men, I will also deny him before My Father Who is in heaven." So, no, even if all the others denied Jesus during the impending crisis, he would not.

But Peter did deny Jesus. The power of Satan caused Peter to deny knowing Jesus even to a servant girl, one of the lowest persons in the strata of society. Standing around the campfire, he denied Jesus three times. And when he heard the cock crow, he went out and wept bitterly. He wept out of shame. He grieved the deep wound to his

"Upward Call"

pride. For now, he had to face the fact that he was not the strong, faithful follower he claimed to be.

Jesus knew that this was going to happen. Satan had obtained permission to "sift you like wheat." Why is wheat sifted? To get the impurities out before it can be used to make good bread. So Satan had received permission not to destroy Peter but to sift him in order to draw out his impurities. And what was the impurity? That Peter, in the natural state of *eros,* believed "he" could do it. His impurity was his pride.

The resurrected Jesus came to Peter several days later and asked him if he loved him. They were again standing around a fire, the only such instances of a campfire in the gospels. The scene is recreated, and Jesus asked Peter three times if he loved Him. Each time Peter said yes, Jesus affirmed to him the great commission that He was putting on him: tend My lambs and shepherd My sheep (John 21:15–17). Three denials around the fire, three times re-commissioned around the fire, and three times Peter had the opportunity to tell Jesus that he loves Him. Was Peter demoted for his acts of apostasy? No, now more than ever, he was ready. With his pride wounded, the newly humbled soul of Peter was ready to begin his work.

Paul's Thorn

Paul was no exception. God knew the plans He had for Paul — to bring the gospel of salvation through Jesus to "the Gentiles and kings and the sons of Israel" (Acts 9:15). Paul was blessed with a great revelation from God to show him paradise and hear "inexpressible words, which a man is not permitted to speak" (II Corinthians 12:4). Because of all of this, it was determined that Paul, too, needed to be humbled. So, in this case, God sent,

A thorn in the flesh — a messenger of Satan to harass me — to keep me from exalting myself. Three times I besought the Lord about this, that it should leave me;

126

"Upward Call"

but he said to me, "My grace is sufficient for you, for my power is made perfect in weakness" (II Cor. 12:7–9).

Paul was told the reason for this "thorn in the flesh" was to keep him from exalting himself. As with all the Lord's ministers, the war being waged between *eros* and *agape* — the flesh and the Spirit — must be fought constantly for the soul to remain an effective agent of Jesus Christ.

Just like Paul our job is to humble ourselves. But since we are humble enough to admit we are not capable on our own of satisfactorily humbling ourselves, God must help us, and, therefore, He does.

The added benefit we gain from studying this episode with Paul is that he explains that the weakness caused by the "thorn" is itself a great grace. The Lord's power is perfected in weakness. God chooses to use us. It is not because of any particular capability we have that makes us valuable to God. It is because we are empty vessels fraught in weakness that gives us usefulness to God. It is because of our humility that we can be useful to God. Paul said it succinctly, "When I am weak, then I am strong" (II Cor. 12:10).

In Pennsylvania in the early 1980s, we did a series of weekend retreats for high school teens that proved remarkably successful. Many teens came to know Jesus Christ through this program, and many grew stronger in their walk with the Lord. One of the program's key elements was that though adults were present and active, the primary leadership of the weekend was run by Christian teenagers who had been through the program, trained, and came back as "staff." They steered the weekend for the participants, lead the groups, and gave almost all the talks. Blessedly, we had many great teens to choose from when selecting staff, but we were still cautious to choose the one young person to chair the whole weekend. One time, we had a difficult decision to make. We liked the young man we were considering, but he had a very quiet personality. We had always trusted his faithfulness, but could he guide a group of teens for a whole weekend, keep them from getting out of hand, and keep them on schedule? One of the adults drew him aside long before the scheduled weekend and was honest with him, discussing his strengths and the part that caused us concern. His answer, "I understand your concern, but I know I can do anything that God calls me to do." His faith and humility won us over. We chose him to lead, and we never saw a more effective leader over the years of doing this. Paul understood the importance of humility, "When I am weak, then I am strong." I am strong because, in my weakness, my pride is not an obstacle to God. He is free to work through me, and there is no one stronger than my God!

Therefore, we should not be surprised to find the frequent exhortations toward a life of humility in the Bible. "Every one who exalts himself will be humbled, but he who humbles himself will be exalted" (Luke 18:14). "Humble yourselves before the Lord and he will exalt you" (James 4:10). "Whoever humbles himself like this child, he is the greatest in the kingdom of heaven" (Matt. 18:4).

It was a beautiful Easter morning, and I was still in bed, ruminating over the events of last night. There was no early service this Sunday because we had conducted the Easter Vigil the night before. So, I enjoyed my free time reflecting on what a good job we had done last night. It was splendid. I loved the music, I thought my sermon was great, and the whole liturgy came off without a stumble. We had pulled off a good one, a great memory to think about. And then a yellow jacket stung me on top of my head!

I jumped out of bed, dispatched the evil creature, and went into the bathroom to treat the wound with bee-sting medicine. What was a yellow jacket doing in my house? Why was he in my upstairs bedroom? Why did he sting me on the top of my head?

I soon began to laugh. God made certain I didn't take credit for anything good He did for me or through me. But why so quickly? I blamed God for that yellow jacket or gave Him credit for it, whatever the truth may be. He had made His point, and the distraction was effective. The ungodly train of thought was ended — no more self-exaltation about a good service of worship.

Humility is of great importance. One of my favorite authors writes,

> *Therefore, if He is prodigal of His gifts, He expects to receive all the glory of them, and would be compelled to withdraw them if He found that we appropriated any part of them through self-satisfaction.*[29]

Yes, He will withdraw them or send stinging insects to remind us who gets all the credit.

Humiliations are part of the Christian journey. While we do not like them because they are wounds to our pride, we must be accepting of them and grateful for their benefit. Jesus says this very thing the night before He dies. He instructed the disciples that He is the vine, through whom the life-giving sap runs, and they are the branches upon which the fruit would be grown. "I am the vine; you are the branches. He who abides in me, and I in him, he it is that bears much fruit, for apart from me you can do nothing" (John 15:5). Apart from the vine, the branch can do nothing. But, attached to the vine, it bears much fruit. The God-sent humiliations that come in our lives all

---

[29] Jean-Pierre de Caussade, *Abandonment to Divine Providence* (Joseph Pich, 2013) Ch. 11, Letters, Book 4, letter III.

serve to keep the branches well attached to the vine. There is in this same parable a vine-keeper; He is God the Father. And His role is described as two things: "Every branch of mine that bears no fruit, He takes away, and every branch that does bear fruit He prunes, that it may bear more fruit" (John 15:2). Every servant of Christ is subject to this revelation: either he will be lopped off if he is proving to be of no value to the kingdom, or if he is showing himself useful to God, he will be pruned. The prunings are events that humble us, but the promises are clear. Everyone humbled will later be exalted. Those branches that are pruned will bear even more fruit.

St Catherine's Two Crowns
Catherine of Siena, a devoted Christian of the church who lived in the fourteenth century, was well known for her devotion and service to God. At an early age, she became a tertiary of the Dominican order. At one point in Catherine's life, she brought a complaint to God. She had to bear up with other women in her order who were painfully harassing her. She asked and pleaded with God that He would remove them from her. His response to her was riveting: I have two crowns for you to wear, Catherine, a crown of thorns and a crown of gold. I intend that you wear the one of thorns now and the one of gold later. But if you had rather, I will give you the gold one now and save the one of thorns for the hereafter. She withdrew her request.

Our life as Christian servants in this world is marked with taking up the cross of Christ. So bearing it is what servants of Jesus agree to do when they commit to discipleship: "take up the cross." Thus, this image helps us understand that in this lifetime, true servants of our Lord wear a crown of thorns as He did, so that in the next lifetime, we may, with Him, wear a crown of gold.

"Upward Call"

How Can We Grow in Humility?
As we remain in His service, God prunes us so that we will bear more fruit for Him. He humbles us from time to time, as needed. I say "as needed" because if we take the lead and humble ourselves, God does not need to. In the scriptures, we find, "Humble yourselves in the presence of the Lord, and He will exalt you" (James 4:10). In other words, humble yourselves in the presence of the Lord, and He does not need to! I do not like the bee stings He sends my way; I would rather beat Him to it. Though our efforts are undoubtedly imperfect, there are things we can do. Humility, first of all, is a mindset. Therefore, it is most helpful to keep the right mindset well in place.

Raymond of Capua, a spiritual director and confessor for St. Catherine of Siena, reported this most valuable event in Catherine's life:

> *The Lord Jesus appeared to her and said, "Do you know, daughter, who you are and Who I am? If you know these two things, you will be blessed. You are she who is not; whereas I am He Who is. Have this knowledge in your soul and the Enemy will never deceive you and you will escape all his wiles; you will never disobey my commandments and will acquire all grace, truth and light."[30]*

The author goes on to explain: "Small words, yet of great value." This truth is profound. Regarding the words, "You are she who is not," he writes,

---

[30] Blessed Raymond of Capua, *The Life of St Catherine of Siena* (Rockford, Il, Tan Books and Publishers, Inc., 2003) pp. 79–80.

All creatures are made from nothing, for "to create" means to make something from nothing. When creatures are left to themselves, they tend to return to nothing, and if the Creator ceased for one moment to preserve them in existence, they would rapidly be reduced to nothing again ... Who can glory in anything he does, when he knows that he himself has not done it, or imagine himself to be superior to others if in his heart of hearts he knows himself not to be? ... Further, how will he dare to call things of the world his own when he knows that he himself is not his own property but belongs to Him who made him?

We do not regard the words of other Christians, no matter how holy they may be, as "the word of God." The Bible alone holds that distinction. But when another Christian has great insight, this revelation can be for the benefit of us all. Paul wrote, "Set your mind on the things above, not on the things that are on earth" (Col. 3:2). These are the "words of God," and they mean the same thing. The words from Catherine tell us that nothing that comes solely from us has any value whatsoever, and everything that comes from God has great value. Therefore, we strive to let God live His life through us, for then everything we do comes from Him and has great value to us and the world about us. Continue seeing all things from God's point of view, and we will have kept ourselves safely in the right mindset about humility.

Another thing we can do is that as soon as something exalts us in even the slightest way — any compliment, accomplishment, or award — then immediately thank the good Lord, who loves to give good gifts to His children, giving Him full credit.

Conquering Sin

As I walked up during lunch, the table discussion was on sin. She seemed to make a quick assessment, and then I heard her say, "I have sinned six times in the last week, and my last sin was on Tuesday." I smiled to myself and asked, "When was the last time I sinned?" When was the last time I worried about something I needed instead of trusting God? Or when was the last time I was hoping to be the one noticed or complimented? Or when was the last time I was not loving God with all my heart, soul and mind; and when was the last time I was not loving my neighbor as myself? In other words, my thoughts gravitated quickly to the question not when was the last time I sinned, but when was the last time I was not sinning! There is special kind of internal peace one finds in realizing that no matter how much we sin, God has got it. There is a blessed spiritual benefit in knowing Christians remain in the constant glow of His grace and mercy.

We need to realize that there is a source of sin in us that is fundamentally impossible to get away from. It is a birth defect. It is what Paul calls the "flesh," and it is that part of him that he laments, "Wretched man that I am! Who will set me free from the body of this death? Thanks be to God through Jesus Christ our Lord!" (Rom. 7:24–25). Yes, Jesus Christ has done and continues to do that which is impossible for us. The better side of this is that Paul explains that it was no longer he who is causing his faults and failures, but the "sin which dwells within" him (Rom. 7:20). Paul has chosen to be a servant of our Lord, and anything that could offend that Lord, he does not want to do. The cross of our Lord Jesus Christ delivers Paul from darkness and enables him to be a follower of Jesus. The power of the cross conquers the darkness of sin within us that keeps us from life and salvation in God and set us free to live our lives for Him.

"Upward Call"

Whereas, before, we could not ever leave the life of sin and darkness, now we can. Paul writes in II Corinthians a beautiful verse, "But we all ... beholding as in a mirror the glory of the Lord, are being transformed into this same image from glory to glory" (3:18). So, while this verse promises us that God is in the process of transforming us into His likeness, another verse tells us that the responsibility of transformation also belongs to us, "Do not be conformed to this world, but be transformed by the renewing of your mind, that you may prove what is the will of God ..." (Rom. 12:2). While God the Holy Spirit is working on us to transform us from inside out, we work on ourselves from the outside in. To say this more clearly, God has given us the power to stop sinning through the cross of Jesus Christ.

I was invited to be on the staff for a week-long youth conference during the summer in western Massachusetts. On the first day of the conference, I began visiting with an attractive 21-year-old woman. She had been coming to this conference for several years in a row, and being 21, this would be her last time to attend as a participant. She had a sadness in her eyes, and she told me she would make her confession during the week as she always had, enjoy the conference, and then she would go back to her boyfriend and regrettably resume their sexual activity. "That is the way it always happens," she lamented. I cannot explain why I said what I said. It just sprung out this way, "Then, when you make your confession, you need to confess that you are spitting on the cross." She blinked back hard and asked, "What do you mean?" "That's right," I told her. "You are telling Jesus that His death on the cross was not good enough for you; it wasn't good enough to deliver you from your sins. Your sins are too big for Him. He may need to die on the cross again; the first one did not work." She still looked stunned, so we talked further. "Jesus' death on the cross enabled you to stop sinning. You confessed it, He forgave you, and He gave you the power to live a new life. You can change this." This assurance gave her great hope. She was not entrapped after all in a sinful behavior she did not want. We did not speak again that week, but she found me at the end of the conference to tell me that when she made her confession, she confessed to "spitting on the cross." Her smile showed me there was peace inside her, and I knew she was going home this time to raise the bar and begin living a truly transformed life, not the one she had before. She knew now she could do it.

Something very similar happened to a woman in the Bible. She had been caught in the act of adultery. She was about to be executed at the hands of the angry crowd as the Jewish law dictated that she should. Jesus interrupted the execution and invited that whoever among the angry crowd was without sin to throw the first stone. No one did, and they all left. Jesus told her that no one, including Himself, was going to condemn her, and then He said, "Go your way; from now on sin no more" (John 8:11). It wasn't just an act of mercy, but in His words, "sin no more," He empowered her to do just that. God never tells someone to do something without giving them the power to do it.

Jesus breaks the power of Sin within us — Sin with a capital "S." It is the nature of sin, or self-love, or pride — all the same thing. We sometimes spell the nature of Sin with a capital "S" to distinguish it from the individual actions of sin (spelled with a lowercase "s.") Jesus' death on the cross rescued us from the overwhelming power of Sin. Our responsibility then is to benefit from that freedom and, with the help of God's Holy Spirit, work to eradicate every act of sin (spelled with a lowercase "s") we commit.

We do this with the help of confession, which we discussed in an earlier chapter.

Most merciful God,

*we confess that we have sinned against You in
thought, word, and deed,
by what we have done, and by what we have left
undone.
We have not loved You with our whole heart;
we have not loved our neighbors as ourselves.
We are truly sorry and we humbly repent.
For the sake of Your Son Jesus Christ, have mercy
on us and forgive us;
that we may delight in Your will, and walk in Your
ways,
to the glory of Your Name. Amen.*[31]

Acts of sin include sins committed through our actions, words, and thoughts, sins against God and sins against other people, and sins of commission and omission. Sins of omission occur when we fail to do the things our Lord has told us to do. Since He told us to love our neighbor as ourselves, failure to love our neighbor is a sin of omission. Sins of commission are the things we do but should not have done. As anyone can imagine, if one were to write out a composite list of all the possible individual sins, it would be quite lengthy. Nevertheless, these kinds of lists do exist and can help prepare for a confession. They help us remember sins we have done (and not done) that warrant confessing.[32]

I borrowed one such list, compiled by my friend and mentor, Fr Homer Rogers, for his parish.[33] I gave a copy of this list to teenagers participating in a weekend conference in Texas and Pennsylvania.

---

[31] *The Book of Common Prayer*,1979 (Kingsport, Kingsport Press, 1977) p. 320.

[32] *St Augustine's Prayer Book*, Ed. Loren Gavitt (New York: Holy Cross Publications, 1967), p. 112.

[33] Fr Homer Roger, St Francis Parish, Dallas, Texas.

"Upward Call"

Making a confession was voluntary, of course, but it was surprising how many teens wanted to do it. One may have been surprised how thoroughly engaged in preparation many of these kids were. Though some people might protest that the preparation would only enhance guilt, it did just the opposite. It was normal that these teenagers were at a stage in life when they discovered good things about themselves and, as well, many actions, thoughts, and words of which they were not at all proud. They believed they are good persons but were puzzled that they think and do bad things. The confession puts all the ugliness behind them. And beyond this, seeing these sins listed, they came to realize that so many ugly thoughts, words, and deeds are things that do not have to be part of their lives. It was a riveting realization that God truly wanted to set them free from sins. They could see the potential for living the kind of life they wanted, not one they were quietly ashamed of. The weekends not only introduced hundreds of young people to Christ but gave them great hope for a new kind of life of which they will be proud.

In the absence of such lists, one is well served by taking the time simply to review the Ten Commandments and look not just at the explicit nature of each Commandment but the collateral sins implicit in each. There are also the "seven deadly sins": pride, envy, anger, greed, gluttony, sloth, and lust. One could use this list effectively in the same way.

I was asked to participate in a weekly series of sermons at a church in downtown Fort Worth. The senior pastor asked seven priests to select one of the seven deadly sins and preach about it. When he called me, he admitted I was the seventh one called, and, by now, there was only one sin left to choose from. I knew automatically which one I was getting: "Lust. No one wanted to talk about that." He said I was right. I did the best I could.

"Upward Call"

I find it odd that one sin many Christians make a big thing about is accidentally saying a bad word. I have even been asked, "Don't you think the young Jesus probably said a bad word when He hit His finger with the hammer in the carpenter shop?" I do not know. But I find it odd, because of all the sins one could feel guilty about, these unpremeditated outbursts are probably the least horrific if indeed they are sins at all.

Late in the evening, well into darkness, I headed to my room at the lodge on Likoma Island in central Malawi. I was dressed in my suit and at the end of a long, hard day. It was dark, but I could make out the flagstone pathway in front of me and was eager to get to my room. All of a sudden, my toe hit on the edge of a step I did not see and, within one second, slammed my face to the pathway. I barely saved myself from a significant injury. As soon as I hit my face, a four-letter word flew out of my mouth, a word I do not use and hardly knew it existed within me. But there it was. And yes, there were persons I knew well within hearing. They came running to see if I was alright. Fortunately, with only one minor scrape on my cheek, my body was okay. Out of kindness, no one mentioned my embarrassing outburst. Was that a sin? No, I must say it was not. A significant part of the gravity of sin has to do with intent, and there was none.

There is another sin I wish to comment on. It involves a Dallas atheist group that purchased the right to display ads on the sides of Dallas city buses. The ads were large posters that advertised, "Good without God!" Unlike accidental outbursts, these are premeditated and make a pitiable statement that they are very comfortable living without God. According to the Bible, not believing in God is considered by some as the worst of all sins. I pity atheists, for I am convinced they will wake up on the other side of death's door and discover the awful reality they are still awake and far separated from the God who created them. Secondly, it is one thing to arrive

138

honestly at the conclusion that God does not exist, but rather than keep the door open on the subject, honestly willing to hear otherwise, a statement such as this goes a long way to shut the door to their soul and make their resistance to Him firm. Lastly, it is sad to note that people honestly think that Christians believe in God to bolster their endeavors to be good people in this world. That is hardly the reason devoted Christians choose to believe in God. And, by the way, "good?" Jesus said, "No one is good but God alone!" (Mark 10:18).

One last topic for this discussion is "habitual sin." Habitual sins are simply sins that are hard to stop committing because we have let them become a habit. Most of the sins under the heading of gluttony are probably habitual, like chocolate. But a lot of things can become habitual. For example, I do not want to eat too much chocolate, but I do. I have a refrigerator magnet that says, "Save the earth! It is the only planet with chocolate." So, I have to do my best to curb my appetite for chocolate and other sweets, but it is not easy to do since the pattern is so well established. I think God allows habitual sins because they keep us a little on edge, striving to do right, and they certainly keep us humble.

The point of this whole discussion on Sin and sins is that if we wish to answer the "upward call of God," we need to take the matter of our sins seriously. While the bulk of the modern Christian world takes the matter of sins lightly, God does not. Sins hurt Him, because they draw us further from Him. Because He has an intense desire to be in oneness with us, He has an intense distaste for anything that keeps us from it. Sin does this. We often say that it helps a lot to see things from God's point of view. Sin is no exception. From His perspective, the sins that we make no effort to stop are like leaving a dead squirrel in the closet. It may be something we can get used to, but there is a stink there that only continues to get worse to Him. So often, people try to cover it up or make excuses, like burning incense or using aromatic sprays to cover the stench. But until we deal with the dead squirrel directly, it will not go away, and He knows it. By the way, if we bring the matter before God directly and honestly, He is very good at eradicating dead squirrels. I apologize for the imagery, but I hope it paints an accurate picture. If we love God in *agape* love, with all our heart, soul, and mind, we are going to take His cares directly into consideration, show our love for Him by striving to please Him and do His will, confess and ask forgiveness for our sins, and work toward an amended life.

"Upward Call"

Understanding Salvation

No one has ever asked a more important question than what the Philippian jailor in Acts 16 asked his prisoners, Paul and Silas. Paul and Silas sang hymns of praise to God after being severely beaten and locked in the inner prison in stocks. When an earthquake disrupted the prison and the two made no effort to escape, undoubtedly, they had something the jailor himself wanted. Falling on his knees before them and bringing them out of prison, he asked, "What must I do to be saved?" Translated, this means, "I want what you have! How can I get it?"

As human beings, we are not born saved. Our default status is to continue on into eternity separated from God in a place referred to as the eternal fire. Being saved means that we are delivered from that fate and have gained, as our destiny, eternity with God in the Kingdom of Heaven. Paul and Silas answer the jailor, saying, "Believe in the Lord Jesus and you shall be saved, you and your household" (Acts 16:30–31). He believes, and he and his household are baptized that night, and all rejoice together. It is a perfect end.

Paul writes to the Ephesians,

> *For by grace you have been saved through faith; and this is not your own doing, it is the gift of God — not because of works, lest any man should boast (2:8–9).*

We are saved by grace through faith. This defining statement is not hard to understand. God gives us the grace that makes our salvation possible — the grace to believe. We respond by faith by believing in the Lord Jesus, who died to save us. God has no faith. Faith is the God-given ability to believe in things we cannot see; there is nothing He cannot see. We have no grace. For man, it is impossible. Our salvation is by His grace, responded to by our faith. Paul emphasizes that it is not by our works, meaning there is no way it can be earned. This revelation is rather thunderous!

Judaism has long been the religion of salvation through keeping the law — the law given by God to Moses. "It will be righteousness for us, if we are careful to do all this commandment before the LORD our God, as he has commanded us" (Deut. 6:25). Thus, the Jewish community has embraced the fervent keeping of the law as the means of salvation for over 1400 years. Those who keep the laws zealously from their youth forward are blessed by God, prosper as a reward in the present, and be further rewarded for their piety in the Paradise to come.[34]

This shared understanding existed for centuries, so it is no wonder that the disciples were perplexed when Jesus taught them a very different perspective on salvation. The "rich young ruler" came to Jesus asking what he needed to do to obtain eternal life. Jesus first spoke to him about keeping the commandments. He responded by saying he had kept them since his youth. Jesus loved him and said to him, "'One thing you lack: go and sell all you possess, and give it to the poor, and you shall have treasure in heaven; and come, follow Me.' But at these words, his face fell, and he went away grieved; for he was one who owned much property" (Mark 10:21–22). It was a sad moment for everyone. Jesus then explained to the disciples how hard it is for a rich man to enter into heaven. The disciples were "amazed" at His words. Indeed, anyone keeping the commandments and blessed by God with a prosperous life was bound to be saved. They had been taught this understanding all their lives. Apparently, in Jesus' day, this young man was a model for a

---

[34] *The Interpreter's Dictionary of the Bible* (Nashville, Abingdon Press, 1962) Volume 4, "Pharisees."

saved person in the disciples' perception, as well as the perception of many Jews. Any Jewish mother would have given her eye teeth to see her daughter married to a righteous, successful man such as this. Yet, Jesus revealed that he is not saved, and it would be hard for him to be so. The disciples were "even more astonished" and said to Jesus, "Then who can be saved?" He responds, "With men it is impossible, but not with God; for all things are possible with God" (Mark 10:27).

This truth is a significant reversal. It sets the whole of Jewish salvation theology upside down. Jesus teaches us that salvation is not the result of human effort; it is an act of God. Throughout time, all the world's major religions have taught what a person must do to reach up to God — all of them, except for Christianity. Christianity teaches that no person can reach up to gain favor with God. It is impossible. Christianity is the story, instead, of how God reaches down to man. The proclamation that "with men salvation is impossible" is possibly the most significant theological declaration in the New Testament. It makes a statement that contrasts everything the world has ever believed about a moral code, an ethical God, or a religious purpose. "With men," Jesus said, "it is impossible." It also stands in stark contrast with *eros*, the self-love part of us, which strives to control our life and destiny. Thus, to the most important question a person can ever ask, "What must I do to be saved?" this statement answers, "It is impossible." And then He follows it with, "but not with God; for all things are possible with God." If God does make it possible, if He does prompt a person to have faith as He did the Philippian jailor, this man is saved.

A saved person is not a renovated version of the old person. Instead, he is a newly created person, a person with a new foundation, being built with a new operating system (*agape*), and with a completely new purpose and view of life.

"Upward Call"

If any one is in Christ, he is a new creation; the old has passed away, behold, the new has come. All this is from God, who through Christ reconciled us to himself and gave us the ministry of reconciliation" (II Cor. 5:17).

This work of God is part of the reason that with man, it is impossible. Perhaps we can improve ourselves, but we can't recreate ourselves. God's new creation has a new foundation, which is Jesus Christ, upon which he builds his house (I Cor. 3:11–15). He has a new moral code, *agape*. He has a new purpose in this world, to be the light of the world (Matt. 5:14). He has a new joy, the joy of Jesus (John 15:11).

Sitting by the community pool in our new neighborhood, I was pleased to meet a new acquaintance. I soon learned we had a lot in common, especially since we were Christians, and he had a very lively faith. He was an emergency room physician, recently retired. We talked about our experiences as Christians and shared our stories about how we came to know Christ as the living Lord. I then asked Tom what he would say to describe the first significant difference he realized about himself after his conversion. In other words, in what way had life become different? He thought for a while, for he was intent on giving a good answer to the question. Then he answered, "I realized I had a different worldview."

What an insightful answer! And so true. We are new creations, and from the point of view of our new foundation, we see the world and our place in it very differently. Perhaps one of the most convincing proofs of the existence of the living Lord is the change He causes in the minds and hearts of His followers.

We Are Saved by Election
Returning to the idea of being saved by grace, we come face-to-face with an even more humbling truth. It is more proper to say we are

saved by election. Election means I am a believer and follower of Jesus Christ, because God chooses to save me. He causes me to hunger for Him, that is, to recognize in some sense the God-shaped vacuum in my heart. He opens my eyes to understand the need for Him. He touches my heart in such a way I want to be close to Him. He gives me faith. Jesus said,

> *No one can come to Me, unless the Father who sent Me draws him; and I will raise him up on the last day (John 6:44).*

He said also,

> *For this reason I have said to you, that no one can come to Me, unless it has been granted him from the Father (John 6:65).*

In summary, Jesus says it is impossible to come to Him unless God the Father grants it to happen. It is impossible to come to Jesus unless God the Father draws him to Jesus. Each person who believes in Jesus and hopes to be saved does so because God the Father has made the specific decision that this person is chosen to be drawn to Jesus in faith.

For one, this evokes the mystery, "Why me?" We have no answer. We have to admit we have done nothing to be granted this remarkable gift. He chooses me before I choose Him. I am astonished, joyful, and grateful beyond words. But I remain baffled. Why me and not the next person?

It also helps me understand why many do not come to Jesus. I know non-believers with whom I have been talking, arranging repeated visits, trying to bring them to believe in Christ. I want them to open their eyes and see what I see about Him. I want them to know He exists, that He knows them, and deeply loves them. I want them to see what I see and feel what I feel, but they smile politely and explain they are just not interested. It is hard for me to understand. The gift of salvation is free, and the love of God brings such peace, but they are just not interested. I will not give up, because this is what I want to do and I am supposed to do. But the fact remains, no matter how hard I try, unless and until God the Father prompts them, faith is not a possibility.

It is not easy to understand this truth. We must return to the words of God from the prophet Isaiah who said,

> *For my thoughts are not your thoughts, neither are your ways my ways, says the LORD. For as the heavens are higher than the earth, so are my ways higher than your ways and my thoughts than your thoughts (55:8-9).*

We clearly never fully understand God's way of doing things, at least in this lifetime. His greater knowledge and plans are bigger than the universe itself. This truth leaves us only to trust Him, love Him, and obey Him, because He is who He is. (See Ex. 3:14.). His name, "I Am Who I Am," fills us with wonder, love, and awe.

When Is a Person Saved?
The various perceptions of what constitutes "salvation" are unfortunately something that contributes to the divisions in Christianity. Perhaps it is the main thing. Evangelicals say a person becomes saved when he accepts Jesus Christ as his Lord and Savior. I qualify.

It was a Wednesday evening in the springtime of 1969 that God opened my eyes with great trepidation, and I flung myself into God's hands as His servant. I soon began hanging around several Christians at the university. They all said, "This was the time when I got saved." It was a remarkable life-changing point in my life. I described it as "the 25 seconds that changed my life." Before this, there was no way I could say I "know God." After that evening, I felt I had a personal relationship with God, and I have had it ever since. Before, I was not saved, and now I am.

I train groups in evangelism, and bringing someone to accept Christ is the goal of all evangelistic efforts. The reason? Not only has God taught us and directed us to do this, but out of love for any person, the greatest gift we can ever give them is to introduce them to Jesus Christ. Some classic biblical examples include the eunuch who served in the court of Candace, queen of the Ethiopians.

While returning home from Jerusalem, the eunuch was met by Philip, the deacon, who asked him if he understood the passage he was reading in Isaiah. He said he did not. After Philip joined him in his chariot, he explained to the Ethiopian that it was about Jesus Christ who had recently died and returned from the dead. The Ethiopian was convinced. When he saw water alongside the road, he said with excitement, "Look! Water! What prevents me from being baptized?" Some early versions of the Bible say Philip responded, "If you believe with all your heart, you may." The Ethiopian answered, "I believe that Jesus Christ is the Son of God." Together they went down into the water, and Philip baptized him (Acts 8:26–39). The Ethiopian was then "saved." Other stories of conversion are quite similar.

This understanding of salvation made sense, at least until I started pondering that God knew me before this time and had, in all probability, planned this event to happen precisely when it did. In some sense, from His perspective, I was already saved but just did not know it until the great conversion event happened.

Oswald Chambers seems to concur when he writes,

> *I am not saved by believing — I simply realize I am saved by believing ... The danger here is putting the*

emphasis on the effect, instead of on the cause. Is it my obedience, consecration, and dedication that make me right with God? It is never that! I am made right with God because, prior to all of that Christ died. When I turn to God and by belief accept what God reveals, the miraculous atonement by the Cross of Christ instantly places me into a right relationship with God. And as a result of the supernatural miracle of God's grace I stand justified ... The Spirit of God brings justification with a shattering, radiant light, and I know that I am saved, even though I don't know how it was accomplished.[35]

Chamber's profound description gives us much to ponder. In essence, it says we cannot in any way credit our salvation to ourselves based on a decision we make, but entirely on God's grace and carefully arranged revelation.

Moreover, our thoughts are further set in awe of God by pondering what Paul said to the Ephesians, that God

chose us in Him before the foundation of the world, that we should be holy and blameless before Him in love (1:4).

Thus, we know now that our conversion, as significant as it may have been, did not just happen but was well-planned. God has had us in His focus since before we were born, and, if we are reading this right, even before the foundation of the world was set in place!

---

[35] Oswald Chambers, *My Utmost for His Highest* (Grand Rapids: Discovery House Publishers, 1992), October 28.

There is no room for taking personal credit. Moreover, it causes us to realize that God's plan of salvation for us began at our conception, if not sooner. And since the plan, as Paul describes, includes that we should become holy and blameless before Him, one might just begin to think that salvation is not a single event but the lengthier episode that follows us to perfection in heaven. Some others in Christendom think of "salvation" in this way.

None of this higher revelation distracts me from my efforts to evangelize non-believers. Just because it is hard for me to see the whole picture does not mean I am not part of it. God's plan for everyone's salvation requires that some Christian somewhere begins sharing the truth in Jesus Christ with the non-believer, and I am honored and pleased to be that person whenever the opportunity is presented. Despite God's grace and my fault-filled self, He still promises great rewards to those who engage in the service of His Kingdom. Nor does any of this higher revelation diminish the value I naturally attach to that springtime evening in 1969 when everything in my life soared to a new height, and everything about it began to change. I simply know I am deeply appreciative and dramatically humbled before my God and Savior, who gave His life for me.

For the Sake of the Kingdom

We Are God's Temple

Everything we do to draw ourselves closer to God will spiritually benefit not just us but everyone around us. The more Christ can exercise His life in us, the more His presence emanates from us. "He who abides in Me and I in him, he bears much fruit" (John 15:5). We focus on abiding in Jesus. He takes over the life we are living.

One of the most uniquely remarkable claims of Christianity is the promise to believers that God has come to dwell within us. The Holy Spirit is here. We are His vessels, sworn to be in His service, available to be used by Him in whatever way He chooses. He dwells within us.

Christians need not go anywhere to encounter their God. Whereas, the Jews of Old Testament times would want to go to the mountain or to the temple in Jerusalem, or Muslims to Mecca to be closer to God, Christians need not travel anywhere. He is here. He has chosen as His dwelling place our own heart; He dwells within our body.

A popular Christian speaker and teacher shared an interesting story. When she accepted an invitation to travel out of town for a speaking engagement, she often stayed in the host family's home. On one such occasion, she found herself staying at a home that was full of contention. So much so that as dinner time approached, she dreaded leaving the sanctity of her upstairs bedroom to be around the tension and harsh words exchanged over the dinner table. But because she did not really have a choice, she made a special request of the Lord. She told Him she did not want to go down to dinner so that she would stay in her room, and He could take her body and go downstairs in her place! She wasn't going to be the one going, He would be there in her body, and He could say and do whatever He wanted! It worked. As if she were on remote control, she simply walked down the steps, took her place at the table, and the whole time remained aloof to let Christ say and do whatever He wanted through her. It worked! Her prayer was answered. It was an amazing evening. She managed to retain her peace, and He managed to say and do things that helped the family. I have tried this experiment myself on a couple of occasions, and it proved very beneficial.

In Jesus' day, the temple in Jerusalem was God's precious dwelling place. But, in each of the four Gospels, we read the story of Jesus cleansing the temple. He went to the temple — His Father's house — and found that the temple was being used for unwanted purposes: buying, selling, and changing money.

> *The Passover of the Jews was at hand, and Jesus went up to Jerusalem. In the temple he found those who were selling oxen and sheep and pigeons, and the money-changers at their business. And making a whip of cords, he drove them all, with the sheep and oxen, out of the temple; and he poured out the coins of the money-changers and overturned their tables. And he told those who sold the pigeons, "Take these things away; you shall not make my Father's house a house of trade." His disciples remembered that it was written, "Zeal for thy house will consume me" (John 2:13–17).*

In the Gospel of Luke, we read that Jesus protested, "It is written, 'And My house shall be a house of prayer,' but you have made it a robbers' den" (Luke 19:46). Jesus' Father, the Lord God, has a temple in Jerusalem, and Jesus is drawn to it. Temples, by definition, are dwelling places of God. It is a place where Jesus teaches, hears the word of God, and prays. It is not to be used for any other purpose; it is His Father's house. To use it as a marketplace, or as Jesus said, "a robbers' den," is a "sacrilege," a word that means, etymologically, "theft of holy things."

I suppose some may conclude that Jesus, by His example, is setting before us a model of how to keep the temple in Jerusalem "cleansed" from misuse so that it may continue unimpededly, as God wanted it, a house of prayer for all nations. The problem with this conclusion is that the temple was destroyed in AD 70, sometime before the writing of at least some of the gospels, and there is no longer a temple in Jerusalem to keep clean.

But Jesus' purpose is not lost. His temple continues. Paul wrote to the Corinthians,

> *Do you not know that you are God's temple and that God's Spirit dwells in you? If any one destroys God's temple, God will destroy him. For God's temple is holy, and that is what you are (I Cor. 3:16–17).*

I heartily agree that Jesus is indeed teaching us exactly how to keep the temple of God clean and set aside for its proper use. That temple is now you and I — every person in Christ. We who have Christ within us are indeed the temple of the Lord, as Paul wrote. We are not only His temple. We are now, since AD 70, His only temple! The message now has a tremendous and powerful impact, for Christians know something more of what He expects and wants for all of us. He makes us His temple, and He wants us to keep these temples clean from things that impede their use. He wants us ceaselessly and exclusively to use them for the purpose intended: prayer.

Keeping the Temples Clean
When our temple is cluttered with stuff that does not belong there, our ability to be in union with our Lord is severely hampered. Some

of the most serious impediments result from faulty relationships with others. John, the apostle, could not have said it more bluntly,

> *If someone says, "I love God," and hates his brother, he is a liar; for the one who does not love his brother whom he has seen, cannot love God Whom he has not seen (I John 4:20).*

God does not tolerate the facade of loving God while plotting evil towards one's neighbor. God knows this kind of thing occurs, and it is to Him detestable. For this reason, Jesus, in the Sermon on the Mount, taught,

> *So if you are offering your gift at the altar, and there remember that your brother has something against you, leave your gift there before the altar and go; first be reconciled to your brother, and then come and offer your gift (Matt. 5:23–24).*

I have known several persons who make a good showing with their demeanor in church on Sundays but who remain adamant in refusing to forgive a family member: a father, a brother, or a spouse. Their hardness of heart leaves them separated from God in ways that, though they could not see it, I could. They refuse to forgive, refuse to reconcile, and stand by that decision decidedly. The Bible says, "God is compassionate and slow to anger" (Joel 2:13), and He readily draws any of these persons close to Him when they repent. But their refusal to reconcile is a grievous cluttering of their temple, and the only way to remedy it is to follow our Lord's dictate by going to the brother and reconciling to them. There is no other way around it.

If we make sincere efforts to do what it says and go to that "brother," and they refuse, then we have done what we need to do and may return to the "altar" of God with a clean conscience. But we need that "brother" to know we are sincere about our love and forgiveness. Then, whenever they are willing, we will be reconciled. There are philosophical disagreements we might have with people, and if we cannot "agree to disagree," then we go our separate ways but must do so in the peace of the Lord.

The point is easy to understand. I cannot cleanse someone else's temple, but I can be adamant about keeping mine clean. My temple is my responsibility. I am an appointed steward over the temple within me, and knowing it is His chosen place to dwell within me, out of love for Him, I must regard its upkeep as my highest calling.

Unforgiveness, hate, revenge, and irreconciliation are all intolerable before the face of God. Any claim to love God while retaining any of these misdemeanors against one's brother constitutes hypocrisy, according to the writings of I John above. Jesus tells Peter he must forgive his brother even if his brother sins against him seventy times seven. The associated parable, described in an earlier chapter, is about the king's slave who owed him the absurd amount of $170 million. He is imprisoned and tortured because he refuses to forgive his brother for even a small matter. "So shall My heavenly Father also do to you, if each of you does not forgive his brother from your heart" (Matt. 18:35). How much more can our Lord say to stress the importance of this matter? Nothing our Lord says to us in scripture is just window dressing. He means what He says.

As stewards, it is as if we are watchmen on the wall carefully watching over and guarding what we allow in our temple courts — the center of our prayer life. Human beings can perpetrate all sorts of evil to us; what comes into the temple is not based on what they do but on how we respond.

The desert fathers were the collection of men in the first centuries A.D. who found that they could best live out their Christian lives isolated in the wilderness. Monastic communities grew up out of those pilgrims who had fled the city life for a quieter, less sin-filled environment. One of the favorite stories that emerged from their shared wisdom involved two hermit brothers who shared a hovel and garden. They had developed a reputation for their humility. A man from the city came one day wanting to test it. Seeing them working in their garden, he found a hoe and began chopping up and destroying all their vegetables. He went from one end of the garden to the other. When he reached the end of the garden, one of the monks came to him with a kind smile and said, "Look, we found a cabbage that was not destroyed. Won't you stay and have lunch with us?"

What is most remarkable about the monks' magnanimity is not that they chose to act this way, but that they *could* act this way. Their temple is so clean, and Christ's *agape* love so active within them, that they, even in light of this assault on their lives, could still respond as only His love would. *Agape* is "kind ... does not seek its own, is not provoked, does not take into account a wrong suffered, does not rejoice in unrighteousness ... bears all things ... endures all things" (I Cor. 13:47). Whether the story is real or legendary, the monks make excellent examples both of Christ's love and the great caution with which they oversee the temple within themselves.

With regard to keeping our temple clean, Jesus has something to say about our wandering thoughts. In the Gospel of Mark, we learn that "He would not allow anyone to carry anything through the temple" (Mark 11:16). We learn that the temple in Jerusalem was situated such that there was a lot of city on three sides of the temple compound where a great deal of movement and business is conducted from one side to the other. It was only natural that people carrying goods would be inclined to take the shortcut through the temple courts, especially if the load was heavy. Jesus put a stop to this. His Father's house was a house of prayer, not to be used for other purposes. This dictate suggests that we should curb the inappropriate wandering thoughts and reflections that come into our minds. They come in but ought not be allowed to stay. It is credited to Martin Luther for writing, "You cannot keep birds from flying over your head, but you can keep them from building a nest in your hair."[36] Our hearts and minds constitute our temple, and as good stewards of it, this is good guidance. We cannot stop ourselves from thinking about many ungodly thoughts and reflecting on all sorts of self-inflating idealizations. But, like birds of the air, we want to shoo them on their way and allow none of them to settle in for lengthier musing in the Lord's temple. Unhealthy imaginations are out there, and we cannot help that, but we can send them out on their way to other places as we vigilantly oversee what is allowed in the temple proper. Paul writes,

> *Finally, brethren, whatever is true, whatever is honorable, whatever is just, whatever is pure, whatever is lovely, whatever is gracious, if there is any excellence, if there is anything worthy of praise, think about these things (Phil. 4:8).*

Filling the Temple with Prayer
As much as we stand like watchmen on our temple walls, preventing our precious temple of God from being abused by sinful things, we just as vigorously want to assure the temple is being used for the right purpose. We fill it with prayer. "My house shall be called a house of prayer" (Matt. 21:13). The temple is where people in Jesus' day went to pray. Our temple inside us is where we go to pray.

In 2015, a Christian-based movie hit the theaters called, *The War Room.*[37] The elderly Miss Clara had in her house a closet she had

---

[36] A saying attributed to Martin Luther (1483–1546).

[37] War *Room*, written by Alex Kendrick and Stephen Kendrick, Sony Pictures, 2005.

prepared exclusively for prayer. She called it her War Room. She went there to pray, and the greater the problem, the stronger and more enduring were her prayers. In the movie, Miss Clara says, "In order to stand up and fight the enemy, you need to get on your knees and pray."

It would hardly hurt at all for any of us to have in our homes a "war room" such as this, but indeed, this kind of intense, dedicated prayer is precisely what God's temple in our own body is intended for. In the movie, Miss Clara spends most of her time praying for the troubles people she knows are having. But the one thing that best marked Miss Clara is the faith she has in her prayers, a faith that accomplishes a lot of good.

To write at any length on the proper use of our temple of God would be simply to repeat the various lessons about prayer and faith found in the previous chapters. We are created, designed, and appointed to be God's place in this world — His temple. From this temple should go forth a life of prayer driven by faith. All we have to do is envision Jesus thrashing about with a whip of cords because zeal for His Father's house consumed Him.

This zeal now belongs to us; it is His zeal for us. When we envision His zealous cleansing of the temple, we can imagine a parent zealously protecting His children from assault and abuse. We can envision a Lord deeply desirous of His children, who shall become the places where He will live out His life and light in this world. So, we pray for our family members, our Christian friends, the non-Christians we hold before God, our nation, our leaders, our church, our world, and ourselves. None of our prayers is lost.

To broaden our understanding of how this temple — our soul — should be used, one should think about how Jesus used the temple. What did He do there? He taught there, healed there, rested, walked about, sat, observed people and their actions, even cried out to all the people there to come to Him. He was drawn to the temple. When His parents came searching for the youthful Jesus, He politely chided them for not looking there first: "Did you not know I had to be in my Father's house?" (Luke 2:49).

Perhaps, as followers of Christ, it is helpful simply to regard our soul and body as the place where Jesus lives, rests, and works. In other words, when we think of ourselves as His temple, simply let Him live His life in us!

Listening to God

On the night before He died, Jesus explained at length the gift of the Holy Spirit that was being sent to the twelve apostles. He told them,

> *And I will pray the Father, and he will give you another Counselor, to be with you for ever, even the Spirit of truth, whom the world cannot receive, because it neither sees him nor knows him; you know him, for he dwells with you, and will be in you (John 14:16–17).*

The "Counselor" is a translation of the Greek word, *Paraclete*, which describes someone who goes with the apostles wherever they go, to be an "advocate" who countermands the efforts of the "adversary" (the devil), who accompanies the apostle as a companion, and who supports and helps him in the fulfillment of his calling. We get the image of someone like a best friend except with divine power. Only baptized followers of Jesus can receive the Counselor. And those who receive Him, the Counselor dwells with them and is in them (as in God dwelling inside His temple).

The Holy Spirit (the Counselor) is also called the Spirit of Truth, for, in God, all truth dwells. When He comes, Jesus tells his followers, "He will guide you into all the truth" (John 16:3). Certainly, this Holy Spirit is at work through the church's early history when, over the years that follow, many misguided conceptions of Jesus, His true identity, and his role in the Trinity gained popularity. The Holy Spirit leads the church out of such "heresies" and guides the church "into all truth."

When the Holy Spirit came at Pentecost fifty days after the resurrection of Jesus, He made a spectacular debut with sounds, sights, and ecstatic utterances by the apostles. We learned that this same outpouring of God's *Paraclete* was intended not solely for the institution of the church, but, in fulfillment of the prophecy of the Old Testament prophet, Joel, it was an outpouring "upon all mankind" (Acts 2:17).

Therefore, all believers in Jesus can receive this same Holy Spirit who will lead them and guide them as well.

> *And in the last days it shall be, God declares, that I will pour out my Spirit upon all flesh, and your sons and your daughters shall prophesy, and your young men shall see visions, and your old men shall dream dreams; yea, and on my menservants and my maidservants in those days I will pour out my Spirit; and they shall prophesy (Acts 2:17–18).*

All baptized Christians who love God, seek to please Him, follow Him, and do His will are blessed with the indwelling and guidance of the Holy Spirit. But the practice of listening to and following the Holy Spirit is something we must learn. The beauty of doing so produces in us ready and effective servanthood that accomplishes many beautiful things for our Lord.

"Upward Call"

Learning to Listen to God
Brigid E. Herman writes in a splendid book on prayer the following beautiful description of the lives of the saints. Every segment of life that requires skill, dedication, or talent has its ultimate heroes: the ones known for being the best of the best in what they do, whether business entrepreneurship, basketball, violin, or gardening. They are the people in these fields we look up to and may even secretly aspire one day to reach their level of skill or devotion. In the realm of closeness to Jesus Christ and dedication to service in Him, we refer to these people as "saints." The saints have, through His grace, become models that Christians aspire to be like. Some of the most well-known are St Francis of Assisi, St Patrick of Ireland, and St Teresa of Calcutta. However, in truth, all they ever do is obey their Lord in the most complete and straightforward way, knowing that whatever significant things they may accomplish are wholly attributable to Him. Brigid Herman wrote,

> *When we read the lives of the saints, we are struck by a certain large leisure which went hand in hand with a remarkable effectiveness. They were never hurried; they did comparatively few things, and these not necessarily striking or important; and they troubled very little about their influence. Yet they always seemed to hit the mark; every bit of their life told; their simplest actions had a distinction, an exquisiteness which suggested the artist. The reason is not far to seek. Their sainthood lay in their habit of referring the smallest actions to God. They lived in God; they acted from a pure motive of love towards God. They were as free from self-regard as from slavery to the good opinion of others. God saw and God rewarded: what else needed they? They possessed God and possessed themselves in God.*

160

Hence the inalienable dignity of these meek, quiet figures that seem to produce such marvelous effects with such humble materials.[38]

I have long been moved by her insight in this matter and the wisdom she reveals. While there is much in this characterization of saints worthy of discussion, I wish to focus on the line, "Their sainthood lay in their habit of referring the smallest actions to God." The saints of which we speak *are* saints because of this. One way or another, they have learned to listen to and obey God. There lies in this a great secret to living one's life for God: "Do what God tells you to do; do not do what He tells you not to do." They live close to God, they listen to God, and they do what He says.

While many Christians, in their enthusiasm, seek to accomplish as much as they can for the kingdom of God and undertake many new or expanded ministries, they may succeed in little that has any lasting value. "If it sounds good, then let us do it" is their motto. I have been guilty of this. I can remember a great deal of energy being expended in gathering volunteers, hours of planning, and pages of logistics to accomplish a big event. And then, a year or so later, after the project is done, there is nothing to show for it. Why? I can almost hear the Lord saying, "I didn't tell you to do that."

We speak of God "telling" us to do things. How does God "tell" us? There are three ways the Holy Spirit communicates with us, three forms of communication: audible, mental, and spiritual.[39] The terms describe how a message from the Holy Spirit comes to us.

---

[38] Brigid E. Herman, *Creative Prayer* (Brewster, MA, Paraclete Press, 1998) p. 13.

[39] Saint Teresa of Avila, trans, E. Allison Peers, *Interior Castle* (New York: Doubleday, 1961) Sixth Mansion, Ch. 3. The footnote references P. Francisco de Santo Tomas, O.C.D., in his *Medula mystica* "has a succinct description of the three types of locution referred to by St. Teresa." He refers to the three types as "corporeal," "imaginary," and "spiritual or intellectual."

"Upward Call"

An audible message is the rarest. I have never received such a message. It is God speaking such that the person hears His voice audibly and may wonder even from what direction or whom the voice came. I have known a couple of Christian folks in the church to whom this has happened. I recall one fellow telling me about this in private lest others would think he was crazy. I know he was not, I can assure you. God spoke an audible word to him while he was driving down the road. He stopped the car to assure himself no one is hiding in the back seat. He is perplexed, but to me It makes some sense; he is a newly renewed follower of our Lord. Is God simply affirming his renewed commitment?

A biblical example of hearing God's voice involves the youthful Samuel.

> *Now the boy Samuel was ministering to the Lord under Eli. And the word of the Lord was rare in those days; there was no frequent vision.*
>
> *At that time Eli, whose eyesight had begun to grow dim, so that he could not see, was lying down in his own place; the lamp of God had not yet gone out, and Samuel was lying down within the temple of the Lord, where the ark of God was. Then the Lord called, "Samuel! Samuel!" and he said, "Here I am!" and ran to Eli, and said, "Here I am, for you called me." But he said, "I did not call; lie down again." So he went and lay down. And the Lord called again, "Samuel!" And Samuel arose and went to Eli, and said, "Here I am, for you called me." But he said, "I did not call, my son; lie down again." Now Samuel did not yet know the Lord, and the word of the Lord had not yet been revealed to him. And the Lord called Samuel again the third time. And he arose and went*

*to Eli, and said, "Here I am, for you called me."
Then Eli perceived that the Lord was calling the boy.
Therefore, Eli said to Samuel, "Go, lie down; and if
he calls you, you shall say, 'Speak, Lord, for thy
servant hears'" So Samuel went and lay down in his
place.*

*And the Lord came and stood forth, calling as at
other times, "Samuel! Samuel!" And Samuel said,
"Speak, for thy servant hears" (I Sam. 3:1–10).*

Samuel, the young boy, knowing nothing of substance about God
and His ways of communicating, heard an audible voice and had to
be instructed how to respond.

The second type of communication as it comes to us from the Holy
Spirit is called "mental." While it comes into the mind as clearly as
if audibly spoken, the person knows it was not received in the ears.[40]
If God speaks this way, His message is quite clear and may even use
words with which the person is unfamiliar. An example of this also
involves Samuel when he was much older. The Lord sends him to
anoint one of the sons of Jesse of Bethlehem as king of Israel. When
Jesse with his sons arrives at the feast, Samuel admires the oldest
son, Eliab, and says to himself, "Surely the Lord's anointed is before
me." But the Lord speaks to him saying, "Do not look on his
appearance or on the height of his stature, because I have rejected
him; for the LORD sees not as man sees; man looks on the outward
appearance, but the LORD looks on the heart" (I Sam. 16:7). The
Lord continued to reject each of Jesse's seven sons as presented, and
they have to send for the eighth and youngest son, David. When he

---

[40]Saint Teresa of Avila, trans, E. Allison Peers, *Interior Castle* (New York: Doubleday, 1961) Sixth
Mansion, Ch. 3. Described by P. Francisco de Santo Tomas, a seventeenth century author, these
messages are not heard in that way (by the power of hearing in the ear) "but the impression
apprehended and received by the 'mental' faculty is the same as though they had been."

arrives, the Lord tells Samuel to anoint him as the next king of Israel. There is no evidence of an audible word, but the message Samuel received "mentally" was clear.

Personally, I have had a mental communication only once in my lifetime. God spoke to me as I was getting out of bed one morning. It was a specific six-word sentence. The words were not mine, the idea of what the voice was telling me was nothing I would have chosen, and the sentence included words I never use. I had to look one word up in the dictionary at the library to get the full impact of its meaning. (It just so happened that I was headed to the library that morning.) The voice explained what God was accomplishing in me through the struggles I was having at the time. I was startled and elated that God the Holy Spirit spoke to me in this fashion, though, at the time, I was not particularly pleased with the content of the message.

The third form of a message from God is much more common. It is called "spiritual" because it is a message that we sense as it witnesses to our spirit. Paul wrote,

> *I am speaking the truth in Christ, I am not lying; my*
> *conscience bears me witness in the Holy Spirit, that*
> *I have great sorrow and unceasing anguish in my*
> *heart (Rom. 9:12).*

He said, "His conscience bears me witness in the Holy Spirit." In this case, it was about the sorrow he felt for his fellow Jews who were turning their back on Jesus Christ.

The Holy Spirit communicates with us in subtle ways, bearing witness to us, gently guiding us to affirm an idea, or not, to call a friend, to support a proposition, to attend a conference, or to accept a job offer. It is usually a message from God of something very unexpected, but when it is communicated and considered, it is accompanied with a significant peace felt deeply in our interior. This peace is the witness of the Holy Spirit. If, on the other hand, God wishes to lead us away from a decision we are leaning toward, the feeling we get may be anything but peace.

The most profound experience I had in this spiritual way of hearing is related to my first trip to Africa in 1982. By the strangest channel of communications, a youth leader in Johannesburg, South Africa, heard about the successful work we were having with youth in Pittsburgh, Pennsylvania. He, an Anglican priest, actually came to visit me, though he did not let me know that he made the long trip for that purpose. After arriving and getting to know me, Fr Girdwood invited me to come to Johannesburg to help him start the same program among the youth in his diocese. "Come show us how to do this." I got my bishop's approval and began making arrangements.

A few days later, while he was staying at the home of my secretary, Fr Girdwood called me and said I needed to come over to her house right away. I remember protesting because the hour was late, and we had a visiting relative from out of town. He insisted, and I came. There were five or six of us present when we settled down. I asked what was going on. "We think when you come this September, you should bring a whole team of adults and teenagers with you!" I balked immediately; the idea was preposterous. As it was, we had been struggling with figuring out how to afford getting me to South Africa. "Now you are asking me to bring a whole group of young people!" The expense was off the charts, not to mention this would require getting parents of a dozen teenagers to allow them (along with the schools themselves) to skip two weeks of school in September and go to a foreign country where there was already great political strife over the tension of apartheid. I told them there was no way. Why were you even suggesting this idea? They had barely begun talking when a wave of peace — an inner spiritual witness —

spoke in the core of my being that this was absolutely right! No rationale could have been as convincing as the "truth" I felt inside. This message was from God the Holy Spirit saying in my spirit to do this. I halted their appeal, told them what I sensed, and that I was now convinced they were right — perhaps even more than they.

I shall not unfold the long story with all its extraordinary twists and turns, but we all went, four adults and 12 teenagers. Upon arrival in Johannesburg, we met a great group of South African adult leaders and teenagers, trained them in putting on the program, led them through their first weekend, and left them the materials and equipment they would need to sustain it. It was a tremendous success, so successful that the program was adopted by all 16 dioceses in South Africa over the next ten years, covering the entire country. What was the pivotal moment? When God sent me a message saying for us to bring an entire team.

Hearing such a message deep in our spirit is not that uncommon. We are told to be constant in prayer (Rom. 12:12). There are times that the Holy Spirit speaks. There are times He is silent. If God speaks, He is offering His guidance; if He is silent, He expects us to make up our minds based on the information we have at hand. He does expect us to listen. As Brigid Herman's characterization says, He expects us to refer all things — even the smallest — to Him. This attribution to God suggests a growing dependence on the Lord for all we do, which is precisely the point. We do not grow independent as we grow closer to Him. We grow blessedly more dependent on Him every day, and this He likes.

The Keys to Hearing — Listening and Obedience
There are two keys to hearing the spiritual voice or sensing the "nudge" of the Holy Spirit as He guides us through our choices and decisions. The first is listening; the second is obeying. An interior stillness is necessary to listen. I mentioned earlier those many

Christians who in their enthusiasm seek to accomplish as many projects as they can for the kingdom of God. I question whether they ever wonder what God thinks of their ideas. To hear Him, we pretty much need to have this mindset about us: "What does God want?" To know the answer to that question, we must listen; God does not like to shout. The "still small voice" is the term most often used to characterize the voice of the Holy Spirit. It is taken from the passage in I Kings when Elijah, the faithful prophet, escapes from evil Jezebel, wife of King Ahab, who has assured him he was to be assassinated. He flees to the mountain, and there he meets God.

> *And he (God) said, "Go forth, and stand upon the mount before the Lord." And behold, the Lord passed by, and a great and strong wind rent the mountains, and broke in pieces the rocks before the Lord, but the Lord was not in the wind; and after the wind an earthquake, but the Lord was not in the earthquake; and after the earthquake a fire, but the Lord was not in the fire; and after the fire* a still small voice. *And when Elijah heard it, he wrapped his face in his mantle and went out and stood at the entrance of the cave. And behold, there came a voice to him (19:11–13).*

Historically, God has made His awesome presence known to the Hebrew people through thunder, lightning, and dark clouds, but God communicates very differently in the voice of the Holy Spirit. It is not in the strong wind, nor the earthquake, nor in the fire, but in the "still small voice" that Elijah hears the voice of God. Likewise, it is in a "still small voice" that God speaks to us, and, to hear it, we must be quiet enough to listen. It reminds us also of the great wisdom we learn from Psalm 46, "Be still and know that I am God" (v. 10). The busyness of mind and mouth do not enhance listening. Instead, we still ourselves, at least interiorly, and then we can listen.

The second key is to obey. I suppose it is a matter of simple logic: does God speak to us if we are not listening? Does He offer His guidance if we are not going to obey?

The grounds upon our listening to and hearing the words of God must be on the grounds of a willingness to obey what we are told. Therefore, as Peter says to the high priest in Jerusalem, "We are witnesses of these things; and so is the Holy Spirit, whom God has given to those who obey Him" (Acts 5:32). The Holy Spirit is God, and we should never expect His guidance on the grounds that if He communicates something to us, we give this opinion good consideration before making our decision. No, the ground upon which God guides us is that we do what He says, just as Mary, the mother of Jesus, said immediately, "Be it onto me according to Your word."

I admit that I have disobeyed a "spiritual" message from God several times and every time regretted it. It was never willful disobedience. Though I did hear something, I chose to listen to other thoughts or guidance from other people. On one such occasion, I asked God if I should take a course at a nearby seminary. The course was over a topic I was eager to study; I was glad to have the opportunity. I asked God if I should do this, and the message He sent was, "No." So, I compromised. I did not take the course for credit; I chose instead simply to audit it. This way, I could just drop out if things weren't going well without any consequence to my transcript. After several weeks, the course was not turning out to be as I hoped. I was not getting what I expected, my altered schedule impacted my good health, time was being taken from other things, and family conflicts began to emerge. Realizing how wrong I had been not to follow God's guidance, I dropped the course. Due to misunderstandings between the faculty and the administration, I received a flunking grade on my transcript, adversely affecting my grade point average. It took over a year and a half later, many headaches of conversations, and the threat of hiring a lawyer before the error was rectified. I did not have to ask the Lord why it took so long to remedy this trouble even though I had confessed my disobedience. I knew the answer: "So you will remember to obey Me the next time I speak." Unfortunately, that was the basic answer every time I did not go with the message God had given me. I must say, over time, I learned. And when a big and difficult decision had to be made, I learned to hear and obey Him, rather than the popular route many others encouraged me to take. As always, His guidance was the right choice.

Both St Teresa of Avila and St John of the Cross write about these three types of messages God the Holy Spirit sends His people.[41] In their books, almost half of what they write on this matter is along with warnings to their readers on the mistakes devoted listeners might make. Despite the guidelines stipulated above, the best rule is never to act upon a serious decision, supposedly being given by God, without conferring with other trusted Christian men and women who have the spiritual maturity to help interpret what is being heard.

Learning to Live in the Present Moment
In Romans, Paul writes,

> *God's love has been poured into our hearts through the Holy Spirit which has been given to us (Rom. 5:5).*

When is the love of God poured into our hearts? Was it when we receive the Holy Spirit? Yes. But the gifts of God are dynamic. By this, we mean the love of God is being poured out upon us in a continuous and productive stream.

---

[41]St Teresa of Avila, *Interior Castle*, "Sixth Mansion," Ch. III; St John of the Cross, *Ascent of Mount Carmel*, Book II, Chaps. XXVI – XXXI.

"Upward Call"

I've been backpacking in the mountains, and I loved it. Once I camped beside a roaring mountain stream in the late spring. I was amazed there could be this much water coming out of a single mountain day and night, weeks on end. There were hundreds, if not thousands, of gallons of water each minute rushing by. The only downside to this location was the loud, endless roar.

God's love is not loud, but it comes to us like this rushing mountain stream. It does not stop. One day, in the Kingdom of Heaven, we will experience this amazing unconditional love fully, but now just partly. When we learn to live our lives in the present moment, a practice the saints of old taught, we will begin to experience this constant, flowing love and peace in a greater fashion.

All of God's grace, love, compassion, and joy flows upon us in this present moment. Being humans who live in this chaotic world, it is no surprise that our thoughts bounce all over the place. We think about later this evening or tomorrow or wonder about a month from now, or we are thinking about something that happened yesterday, regretting something a year ago, or wishing longingly for some good ol' times in the past. This mental wandering is what we do. But God and all His wonder and grace are being poured into every one of us to its fullest at this present moment. God focuses all the energy He has directed toward us right now.

God is not very interested in your past; He has already taken care of it. "Forgetting what lies behind ..." writes Paul (Phil. 3:13). God is not interested in your future; it has not arrived yet. He is fully capable of providing for it when the time comes. Our Lord throws Himself into your life at this present moment, even while you read this.

Why is it that we, as human beings, allow ourselves to be so consumed with thoughts about our past, focus so much on the future, and even let ourselves get so enslaved to the opinions of others?

What are we doing with all this debilitating, excessive mental activity? We are subconsciously engineering our lives, trying to control and direct them. For what reasons, we do not know. Perhaps it is a bad habit born out of fear that our lives will fall apart if we do not concentrate on them. This attempt at control is what happens when we live our life without entrusting it to God. It is what *eros* insists we must do. So, we stay constantly vigilant about our lives. If we only knew! God has our past and our futures securely in His hand. In the meantime — in the present moment — He has for us a wealth of love flowing into our hearts as the waters of that flowing mountain stream.

Please allow another metaphor. I have enjoyed experimenting with a magnifying glass in the summer sun. It fascinates me that I can take a portion of sunlight and focus it into a burning spot so hot it can ignite a fire. Technically speaking, a five-inch magnifying glass focused on one small spot can produce 1200 times the intensity of light and heat. I share this image to help us appreciate that of all God's love poured into our lives, in this present moment, is an intense flood of love aimed directly at us. Is this surprising? I am around grandparents for whom the highlight of their week might be to watch their little grandchild play a board game on the floor, play the piano at a recital, or kick a soccer ball at a match at their school. If we, in all our imperfections, can love this intensely, how much more does God pour out His love watching us enjoy ourselves living out our lives in His kingdom?

Perhaps the greatest teacher for this is a seventeenth-century French spiritual director named Jean-Pierre de Caussade. His writings are published under the title, *The Sacrament of the Present Moment*.[42]

---

[42] Jean-Pierre de Caussade. Also, variously published under the titles of *Abandonment to Divine Providence,* and *The Joy of Full Surrender*.

"Upward Call"

Regarding those "souls" who learn to live in the "present moment," he writes the following,

> *All their attention was focused on the present, minute by minute; like the hand of a clock that marks the minutes of each hour covering the distance along which it has to travel ... They know only that they must allow themselves to be carried along in God's hands, to serve him in his own way. Often they will not know for what purpose, but God knows it well. The world will think them useless ... Everything in these solitary souls speaks to us of God. God gives their silence, quiet, oblivion and isolation, their speech and their actions a certain value, which unknown to themselves, affects others ... There remains one single duty. It is to keep one's gaze fixed on the master one has chosen and to be constantly listening so as to understand and hear and immediately obey his will ... So these souls are by their nature solitary, free and detached from everything, in order that they may contentedly love the God who possesses them in peace and quiet, and faithfully fulfil their duty to the present moment according to His wishes. They do not allow themselves to question, turn back or consider the consequences, the causes or the reasons ... Thus, the present moment is like a desert in which simple souls see and rejoice only in God, being solely concerned to do what He asks of them ... And so we leave God to act in everything, reserving for ourselves only love and obedience to the present moment. For this is our eternal duty. This compelling love, steeped in silence, is required of every soul ... It is necessary to*

be disengaged from all we feel and do in order to walk with God in the duty of the present moment. All other avenues are closed. We must confine ourselves to the present moment without taking thought for the one before or the one to come.[43]

Herein lies one of the greatest secrets to living one's life in the Holy Spirit. Whether we are walking, driving, sitting, waiting, or resting, we can confine ourselves to the present moment and find there the God who pours into this moment all the love, guidance, wisdom, instruction, and joy that we will ever need.

A couple of helpful practices redirect our thoughts from the chaotic habits to which we are accustomed to a pace that brings us closer to the present moment. For one, as often as possible, do all things slowly. Slowing our body helps to slow our mind; hurrying our body hurries our mind.

Avoid in your actions, whether exterior or interior, all eagerness, hurry ... accustom yourself on the contrary, to speak, to walk, to pray and to read quietly, slowly, without overexerting yourself no matter for what.[44]

Spending patient time with the Psalms is a second helpful practice. Meditating on Psalm 131, in particular, does a lot of good:

---

[43] Jean-Pierre de Caussade, trans. Kitty Muggeridge, *The Sacrament of the Present Moment* (HarperSanFrancisco, Harper Collins Publishers, 1966) pp. 1–15.

[44] Jean-Pierre de Caussade, *Abandonment to Divine Providence* (Joseph Pich, 2013) Ch 11, Letters Book 3, letter 3.

O Lord, I am not proud; I have no haughty looks.
I do not occupy myself with great matters, or with
things that are too hard for me.
But I still my soul and make it quiet; like a child upon
its mother's chest; My soul is quieted within me.
O Israel, wait upon the Lord, from this time forth
forever more.

The transition from living a lifestyle common to this chaotic world to one compatible with the kingdom of God often feels slow in coming. But as it starts happening, Christians find it blessedly rewarding.

We Share What We Have Been Given

When Jesus sent the twelve apostles out, He gave them specific instructions. Tell the people, "The Kingdom of Heaven is at hand." Then He says, "Heal the sick, raise the dead, cleanse the lepers, cast out demons; freely you received, freely give" (Matt. 10:7–8). What had they received that they could give? Jesus Christ. They had received by God's pure grace, Jesus Himself. Now it was time to "give" Him away, to share the gift of salvation that they had so freely been given.

The work or ministry of sharing the good news of Jesus Christ is what Christians have done since Jesus walked among us. Salvation in Jesus is never a secret. It is not, nor has it ever been, something to be kept to oneself. It is the good news of salvation for all humanity, and it is up to us — the followers of Jesus Christ — to spread it. We receive it as a gift; we do not earn it or merit it in any way. Thus, we give it away as freely as we got it.

One summer at the senior high session at the diocesan summer camp, I began the afternoon session with a cup of candy. By a random game of chance, one young boy won the entire cup. He took it to his seat on the floor and began munching away. I stood there and pointed out right away that there were precisely 87 skittles in the cup; I had counted them out — "one for each person here." I stood silently, saying nothing while he slowly ate one after the other. I repeated, there was one skittle for "each" person here and again waited. Everyone looked at him, he smiled back, and he ate and waited for what was next. After the third time of emphasizing the point that there was enough for everyone, some of his friends suggested, "I think you are supposed to give them away." Ah hah! With a little help, he got it and began to share them around; from that point, I resumed talking. The session was on our obligation (or privilege!) to take the free gift of knowing Jesus Christ and giving this gift to others.

Giving it away is what Christians do. I know many of us grew up under the social guideline of never talking about religion or politics with others. But this particular element of social protocol never came from the lips of Jesus Christ. "Go and tell" is the message He orders His followers. Sometimes we are met with a welcome, and sometimes we are met with resistance when we bring up with a non-believer the subject of belief in Christ. But the reasoning is simple: if we love another person, we care for their wellbeing. And as we have said before, there is nothing more valuable to anyone than their salvation into eternity. The most loving thing I can give anyone is the good news of Jesus Christ. I can share it. Whether they receive it is up to them. But I am doing what I am supposed to do: offering them the greatest gift ever.

Jesus used the following parable:

> *You are the light of the world. A city set on a hill cannot be hid. Nor do men light a lamp and put it under a bushel, but on a stand, and it gives light to*

all in the house. Let your light so shine before men,
that they may see your good works and give glory to
your Father who is in heaven (Matt. 5:14–16).

To say we are the light of the world is simply to say we have been
given Jesus Christ freely, and now His life is shining through us into
this world. God has put us into society so that wherever we live,
wherever we work, wherever we shop, or play, or go, that light of
Jesus Christ is in us and shining through us.

Then He says that no man would logically light a lamp in his house
as evening approaches and put it under a shade — a bushel basket
— to prevent the light from being seen. In the same way, we are
never to hide the light. Instead, the command is stated clearly, "Let
your light so shine before men," just as that light was meant to shine
throughout the house. Let people see who you are as a sincere
Christian and tell them about the light.

Speaking at a diocesan convention once, I referenced this parable,
and then I asked for a show of hands. How many of those present
have publicly committed themselves to share the faith of Christ with
non-believers? Only a few hands went up. I then asked how many
of them have ever attended a baptism in one of the churches in our
diocese. Every hand went up. I then said, "Did you not know that at
every baptism in our churches, you were asked directly, 'Will you
proclaim by word and example the Good News of God in Christ?'
and you said, 'I will, with God's help'"? We all laughed, and then I
repeated the previous question, "How many of you have publicly
committed yourself to sharing the faith of Christ with non-
believers?" All the hands went up.

I share my faith with almost anyone willing to talk when I am seated
by them on a plane, in a taxi, or on a bus. I have received the full
gamut of responses. I never push. If they do not want to talk about
it, the conversation is over; I conclude this is not God's time. But

people have opened up often. If there is no immediate positive response, they frequently acknowledge they are left with "something to think about." Well enough. The decision to set self aside and commit one's life to Jesus comes from the core of our being and should never be entered into lightly. I have encountered people who already knew they wanted Jesus, but just didn't know how to "find" Him. It became a time of great joy for both of us.

It is absolutely a great joy any time we have a part in bringing someone to Jesus Christ. The occasion does not have to be emotional or tearful, though it often is. Either way, we thank God for the great event that has just happened. Jesus said, "There is joy in the presence of the angels of God over one sinner who repents."

There are three ways we share our faith. One is through example. We subtly let people know we are believers in Christ (a cross we wear, perhaps). Then we live our lives consistently in the way that pleases our Lord, treating all people just as He would, and this becomes our example. It is what Jesus said, "Let your light so shine among men that they see your good works and give glory to your Father who is in heaven." There is an excellent example of this regarding a manager of an automobile assembly plant in Detroit, Michigan. Gene is long retired from that post, but he gets a phone call the night before from a previous employee. The man says that they had never talked about God or Jesus or religion at all. But he knows his boss is a Christian, and the consistent way he has conducted his life with truth, love, and integrity made a deep impression on him. He makes a promise to himself, even while he still had his job there, that if he ever gets baptized as a Christian, his former boss, Gene, is going to be the first one he calls.

Hence, the phone call. Gene is quite taken aback but is pleased and excited to share the story, and we are delighted to hear it. Gene barely remembers the man yet is deeply encouraged to hear the news.

A second way we share our faith is by a conversation with a non-believer about Jesus. What we want to tell them is what happened to us that changed our lives. In other words, we share our story of how we became believers ourselves and the effect it has had on us. Paul does this often, and the telling of his story appears twice in the Book of Acts. "I was on my way, approaching Damascus about noontime ..." (Acts 22:6). He explained what happened and how his life was changed by meeting the resurrected Jesus Christ while on the road to Damascus. On this occasion, he is speaking to a mob of angry Jews in Jerusalem. The second occasion is before King Agrippa in Caesarea, "As I was journeying to Damascus with the authority and commission of the chief priests, at midday, O King, I saw on the way a light from heaven" (Acts 26:12–13). In telling our stories, we want to explain what life for us was like before we met Christ and how life has changed since asking Christ into our hearts. This life change becomes our story; it is not now a bed of roses, but our lives are now on a much different plane. Jesus Christ has come into our lives and made us different people.

A third way we share our faith is not with the telling of our stories, but by explaining in as clear a fashion as we can what the process of salvation is. There are four steps to understanding the Christian message of salvation:

1) God created us. We explain that God first created us good. The relationship between God and man as it is described in Genesis 2-3 is a beautiful, perfect relationship.

2) We sinned. Humanity sinned (initially through Adam and Eve), resulting in the breaking of the relationship and a separation

between God and us. There is no way the efforts of any human being can bridge this gap. It is impossible.

3) Christ died for us. It took an act of God. He sent His Son Jesus Christ to die for us on the cross, and by this, a pathway or bridge by which we can cross back over to be one with God.

4) We decide. The fourth and last thing that must be done is to believe in Jesus Christ (put our faith in Him) as our Lord and Savior. We invite Him into our heart. By doing this, we cross over the bridge into the lordship of Christ. The relationship is restored.

When a non-Christian is ready to do this, we pray with them, giving them guidance on what needs to be said: a) they ask the Lord to forgive them for their many sins, b) they ask Him to be their Lord and agree to follow Him, and c) they thank Him so much for forgiving them and coming into their heart. After such a prayer, we assure them God heard them and further assure them they have made the most important decision of their lives. It now becomes our job to help them get to a church and get them baptized.

We are entrusted with sharing faith in Jesus Christ throughout this world, but we do not convert anyone. God is the One that causes conversion; we cannot enter anyone's heart and cause them to repent. Our work is to evangelize; His work is to convert. He does not evangelize. He waits for us to do the evangelizing, and when a person does convert, our Lord shares the joy with us and credits us with the reward.

The Identity of Jesus

Jesus stands apart as unique from any person who ever lived. Much has been said and written about Him, and I am sure all the books of this world could not hold all that could be said. Following are 14 points that help us describe the incomparable Jesus Christ.

Jesus Is Eternal

> *Everyone whose name is not written in the book of the life of heaven of him who was slain before the foundation of the world (Rev. 13:8).*

For us to understand eternity is simply not possible. We are too constrained by a lifetime of events that arrive in chronological order. We naturally think about all things having beginnings and ends, time past, and times yet to come. We know God is not constrained by what He creates, and He created time. Accepting the idea of eternity is to accept concepts beyond us as true and allow paradox to exist in our understanding of things of the spirit. In all the existing order, there remains a significant difference between the Creator and the things created — between God and us. While it is true that we are being re-formed into the image of God and that one day "we will be like Jesus" (I John 3:2), it always remains to be true, even in heaven, that there is a difference between the Eternal Creator and the created — between the Trinity and us. Jesus is of eternity. While the verse above is translated variously between different Bible versions, there is in there a hint of eternity: things happened before the beginning of time as we know it. Jesus was slain before the foundation of the world; our names were written in His book before the foundation of the world!

180

Jesus Is Both Man and God

Jesus was both man and God; He was 100 percent man and 100 percent God. Both natures were in Him in their most complete form. He existed as God, "But when the fulness of time came, God sent forth His Son, born of a woman ..." (Gal. 4:4), and He condescended to become the "Son of Man." Jesus was in every way a man like the rest of us, except He was without sin.

When did we see Him as a man? He was as a man when He prayed to His Father and in His hunger and thirst. He was like us in that He grew tired and sleepy at times. We saw Him as a man when He faced temptation (though never gave into it), when He had great sorrow in the Garden of Gethsemane, and when He stood accused before Pilate. He approached His beatings, crucifixion, the crown of thorns, and agony as a man. He died with suffering as a man would die. He did not know who touched Him when the woman with the hemorrhage touched the fringe of his cloak, nor does He know when He will return at the second coming.

When did we see Him as God? He was as God when He sent Peter to retrieve a stater from the mouth of a fish to pay the taxes (Matt. 17:27) when He walked on water and stilled the wind and the sea (Matt. 14:25; Mark 4:39). We saw Him as God when He knew that the temple would be torn asunder, stone from stone, and when He knew He would rise after three days from the dead. We saw Him as God when He knew Satan had received permission to take Peter and "sift you like wheat," and that Peter would deny Him three times before the cock crowed (Luke 22:31–34). We saw Him as God when He could have opted out of the agony of the crucifixion (Matt. 26:53), though he did not.

Jesus Is the Only Savior

Jesus is indeed the only "Savior" through whom anyone can come to God the Father and find salvation. There is no other path. Some of the reasoning for this will be expounded on in later chapters. Responding to the apostle Thomas,

> Jesus said to him, "I am the way, and the truth, and the life; no one comes to the Father, but by me" (John 14:6).

Three things of significance here: First of all, Jesus used for Himself the terminology, "I am." "I am" (Greek: *Ego eimi*) is the Name of God in Greek, the name which was a capital crime for anyone to use for himself in Israel. It was the name God gave Moses before the burning bush when he asked who it is that I shall say sent me. "You shall say to the sons of Israel, 'I Am' has sent me to you" (Ex. 3:14). As we saw in the Gospel of John, Jesus used it often and, for doing so, had to evade being executed. (See John 8:58–59.) By using the terminology, He equated Himself with God the Father.

Secondly, unlike other religious leaders who revealed to their followers the supposed proper way to God, which consisted of making the right moral choices, Jesus said there are no methods to get to God. He said that the only way to God was through a union with Him. Methods, morals, and religious practices did not get anyone to God. Jesus was the door, and for this to work for us, we had to enter into a relationship with Him.

Many have asked, "What about those who came before Jesus?" The answer is the same. We entrust our lives to the Savior Jesus, who walked this earth many years ago. Those before Him entrust their lives to the promised Savior yet to come.

Jesus is God's Prophetic Message to the World

God sent Jonah to proclaim the prophetic message to the Gentile city of Nineveh. He walked from one end to the other crying out, "Yet forty days and Nineveh will be overthrown" (Jonah 3:4). The people all converted, put on sackcloth, and fasted — all of them — even the animals. John the Baptist came with a message, appearing in the wilderness, saying, "Repent for the kingdom of heaven is at hand ... Prepare the way of the Lord, make His paths straight" (Matt. 3:2–3).

Jesus was a prophet. Did He come proclaiming a message? What was His message? Jesus did not have a message, because He was the message. Christ, His words, His healing power, His love, His sacrifice, His whole life was itself a message. And it was the Message that God sent to us. Jesus Christ was what God wanted to say to the world.

Jesus Is the Messiah

The Jews have long awaited the Messiah. The idea of the Messiah began in the writings of Moses. It was further developed under King David, where the description of the coming Messiah is found in the Psalms, many of which were attributed to David. The Messiah is expected to be a "Son of David," meaning that he is of David's lineage and character. By the eighth century B.C., under the prophecy of Isaiah, the nature and success of the Messiah acquire the fullest expression.

> *For to us a child is born, to us a son is given; and the government will be upon his shoulder, and his name will be called "Wonderful Counselor, Mighty God, Everlasting Father, Prince of Peace." Of the increase of his government and of peace there will be no end, upon the throne of David, and over his*

183

kingdom, to establish it, and to uphold it with justice
and with righteousness from this time forth and for
evermore (Is. 9:6–7).

The anticipated Messiah will come at his appointed time and, through his God-given charismatic ability as the ideal king, will lead the Jewish nation-kingdom into permanent uncontested sovereignty of the Jewish nation on earth. Under his leadership, all the other nations will fall into their place on earth, and Israel will stand permanently supreme.

Behold my servant, whom I uphold, my chosen, in
whom my soul delights; I have put my Spirit upon
him, he will bring forth justice to the nations. He will
not cry or lift up his voice, or make it heard in the
street; a bruised reed he will not break, and a dimly
burning wick he will not quench; he will faithfully
bring forth justice. He will not fail or be discouraged
till he has established justice in the earth; and the
coastlands wait for his law (Is. 42:1–4).

The term *messiah* is Hebrew for "anointed." *Christ* is Greek for "anointed," so *Messiah*, *Christ*, and *Anointed One* are the same. When we call Him Jesus Christ, we are affirming that Jesus of Nazareth is the Messiah.

Is He the Messiah? In the story of the Samaritan woman at the well, it says,

The woman said to him, "I know that Messiah is
coming (he who is called Christ); when he comes, he
will show us all things." Jesus said to her, "I who
speak to you am he" (John 4:25–26).

Jesus said He is the Messiah. Thereby all the Biblical prophecies about the Messiah must come true in Jesus.

Of course, Judaism in Jesus' day did not receive Him as the Messiah. This rejection was for two general reasons. The first was that in the view of the Jewish leadership, Jesus did not fulfill the prophesied messianic expectations. He was both beneath them and above them. Jesus was beneath them in that He failed to meet their expectations, because He did not come from an esteemed pedigree. He did not win the favor of Jerusalem's religious and political leadership, and He was executed. He was above their expectations because He had power that far exceeded any man's ability and talked of bringing a kingdom into existence, but not one in this world. Moreover, His power was steered not toward military and political accomplishments but the poor, the lame, the blind, the outcasts, and the sick.

The second reason the Jewish leadership did not receive Him as the Messiah was because He was not through: He rose from the dead, ascended, and has yet a second coming to fulfill the prophetic vision.

Had the Jewish leadership in Jerusalem not been blinded by jealousy over His popularity, perhaps they could have come to faith, as indeed some of them did. And had they been able to see through their misguided perception of the Messiah and into the deeper things revealed by the prophets, they would have then seen Jesus for who He is — the Messiah.

Almost every element in Old Testament scripture can be shown to have its own value. There is one passage that remains in Judaism a mystery: what does this mean? Who is it about? This same passage was frequently relied up by the early Christians to prove that Jesus is the Messiah. It is referred to as the "Song of the Suffering Servant," and it is in Isaiah.

As an example, we are given this story. An angel of God spoke to Philip and sent him to the desert road leading from Jerusalem to Gaza. Philip was one of the seven men appointed and ordained to serve the church community in Jerusalem — the first "deacons." Philip encountered there an Ethiopian who served in the court of Candace, queen of Ethiopia. He was reading in Isaiah the Song of the Suffering Servant and was perplexed who the passage referenced. Philip, hearing him, asked if he understood what he was reading. "How could I, unless someone guides me?" Philip was invited to join the man in the chariot and, beginning with this passage, preached to him about Jesus. The result is that the Ethiopian court official believed all that Philip taught him and halted his journey to get baptized. The unique passage in Isaiah tells of an idealized, charismatic figure with many messianic qualities, but who was rejected by the people and was killed. The Song of the Suffering Servant:

Behold, my servant shall prosper, he shall be exalted and lifted up, and shall be very high. As many were astonished at him — his appearance was so marred, beyond human semblance, and his form beyond that of the sons of men — so shall he startle many nations; kings shall shut their mouths because of him; for that which has not been told them they shall see, and that which they have not heard they shall understand. Who has believed what we have heard? And to whom has the arm of the LORD been revealed? For he grew up before him like a young plant, and like a root out of dry ground; he had no form or comeliness that we should look at him, and no beauty that we should desire him. He was despised and rejected by men; a man of sorrows, and acquainted with grief; and as one from whom men hide their faces he was despised, and we esteemed him not. Surely he has borne our griefs and carried our sorrows; yet we esteemed him stricken, smitten by God, and afflicted. But he was wounded for our transgressions, he was bruised for our iniquities; upon him was the chastisement that made us whole, and with his stripes we are healed. All we like sheep have gone astray; we have turned every one to his own way; and the LORD has laid on him the iniquity of us all. He was oppressed, and he was afflicted, yet he opened not his mouth; like a lamb that is led to the slaughter, and like a sheep that before its shearers is dumb, so he opened not his mouth. By oppression and judgment he was taken away; and as for his generation, who considered that he was cut off out of the land of the living, stricken for the transgression of my people? And they made his grave with the wicked and with a rich man in his death, although he had done no violence, and there was no deceit in his mouth. Yet it was the will of the LORD to bruise him; he has put him to grief; when he makes himself an offering for sin, he shall see his offspring, he shall prolong his days; the will of the LORD shall prosper in his hand; he shall see the fruit of the travail of his soul and be satisfied; by his knowledge shall the righteous one, my servant, make many to be accounted righteous; and he shall bear their iniquities. Therefore I will divide him a portion with the great, and he shall divide the spoil with the strong; because he poured out his soul to death, and was numbered with the transgressors; yet he bore the sin of many, and made intercession for the transgressors (Is. 52:13—53:12).

The New Testament church embraced this passage thoroughly. It was not possible to point to any other figure in history as the fulfillment of this prophecy, and yet Jesus fulfilled it completely.

187

Jesus, in fact, identified Himself as the fulfillment of this prophetic servant (See Luke 22:37.) It described a strangely mysterious person. It was the will of the Lord God, Yahweh, to bruise this servant and put him to grief, to wound him for our sins, and to lay upon him the iniquity of us all. He was despised and rejected by men; He was killed and was buried, even though he was innocent. Yet, by what he did, many will be made righteous, and Yahweh, his God, shall prosper him because of what he had accomplished and will reward him among the great.

To this day, Judaism has never successfully assigned this prophecy to any person. The Jewish faith continues unable to see an answer to the Suffering Servant it in Jesus of Nazareth.

There is in the Old Testament another remarkable testimony to the necessity of Jesus Christ to salvation. This testimony must not be underestimated, for its impact is quite significant. It has to do with Moses and why he is barred from entering the Promised Land.

Why Moses Was Denied Entrance into the Promised Land
It had been a vexing problem to many scholars, because Moses — the great and humble Moses — was not permitted by God to enter into the Promised Land. He sinned in what seems to be the smallest of matters. Along with the Israelites, whom he brought to the Promised Land, and especially in light of all he had been through to get them there, he was nevertheless denied entrance. The vexing problem was the seemingly insignificant event when he struck twice the rock at the waters of Meribah, causing water to come forth for the thirsty Israelites. Perplexed about this, one biblical commentary refers to this, as an example, as a "puzzling incident,"[45] puzzling

---

[45] *The Jerome Biblical Commentary* (Englewood Cliffs, Prentice Hall, Inc., 1968) p.93.

188

because God suddenly becomes angry with Moses and Aaron. "How did they offend God?" Some commentators suggest that relevant biblical material had gone missing. Others suggest a "certain lack of faith" on the part of Moses and Aaron. None of these answers was adequate. The intention here was to show the real reason why Moses was prohibited from entering and further how this may be considered the most powerful witness for Christianity in the entire Hebrew Bible.

Moses Had a Unique Standing with God
We shall begin with a good look at Moses. The Bible describes Moses in glowing terms; he is unique in quality and character. Numbers 12:3 states unequivocally, "Now the man Moses was very humble, more than any man who was on the face of the earth." Deuteronomy 34:10 states, "Since then no prophet has risen in Israel like Moses, whom the Lord knew face to face." And Exodus 33:11 adds, "Yahweh used to speak to Moses face to face, just as a man speaks to his friend."

Moses' Sin
All the magnificence of Moses' persona stands in startling contrast to his punishment. What is his sin? The following passage from the Book of Numbers explains the event.

> *And there was no water for the congregation; and they assembled themselves against Moses and Aaron. The people thus contended with Moses and spoke, saying, "If only we had perished when our brothers perished before the Lord! Why then have you brought the Lord's assembly into this wilderness, for us and our beasts to die here? And why have you made us come up from Egypt, to bring us to this wretched place? It is not a place of grain or figs or vines or pomegranates, nor is there water*

to drink." Then Moses and Aaron came in from the presence of the assembly to the doorway of the tent of meeting, and fell on their faces. Then the glory of the LORD appeared to them; and the LORD spoke to Moses, saying, "Take the rod; and you and your brother Aaron assemble the congregation and speak to the rock before their eyes, that it may yield its water. You shall thus bring forth water for them out of the rock and let the congregation and their beasts drink." So Moses took the rod from before the LORD, just as he had commanded him; and Moses and Aaron gathered the assembly before the rock. And he said to them, "Listen now, you rebels; shall we bring forth water for you out of this rock?" Then Moses lifted up his hand and struck the rock twice with his rod; and water came forth abundantly, and the congregation and their beasts drank. But the LORD said to Moses and Aaron, "Because you have not believed me, to treat Me as holy in the sight of the people of Israel, therefore you shall not bring this assembly into the land which I have given them" (Num. 20:2–12).

God commanded Moses to speak to the rock, and instead, he struck it. (Whether God told him to speak to the rock, and Moses disobeyed by striking it, or in the parallel section in Exodus 17 where God said to strike the rock and Moses disobeyed by striking it a second time, is not clear. The point remains the same.) The consequence is that Aaron dies, and Moses is denied entrance into the coveted land of promise.

Aaron's punishment is described in the latter part of Numbers 20.

And they journeyed from Kadesh, and the people of Israel, the whole congregation, came to Mount Hor. And the LORD said to Moses and Aaron at Mount Hor, on the border of the land of Edom, "Aaron shall be gathered to his people; for he shall not enter the land which I have given to the people of Israel, because you rebelled against my command at the waters of Meribah. Take Aaron and Eleazar his son, and bring them up to Mount Hor; and strip Aaron of his garments, and put them upon Eleazar his son; and Aaron shall be gathered to his people, and shall die there." Moses did as the LORD commanded; and they went up Mount Hor in the sight of all the congregation. And Moses stripped Aaron of his garments, and put them upon Eleazar his son; and Aaron died there on the top of the mountain. Then Moses and Eleazar came down from the mountain. And when all the congregation saw that Aaron was dead, all the house of Israel wept for Aaron thirty days (22–29).

The Book of Deuteronomy records events some years later when the Israelites are finally ready to cross over the Jordan River into the Promised Land. Deuteronomy as a book is Moses' summarization of the wilderness events up to this point and a reminder to the people of God's promise to bless them. Moses' words serve as a warning, as well, of what God shall do should they prove themselves unfaithful. The event at the waters of Meribah is described again by Moses with these words.

And I besought the LORD at that time, saying, "O Lord GOD, thou hast only begun to show thy servant thy greatness and thy mighty hand; for what god is there in heaven or on earth who can do such works *and mighty acts as thine? Let me go over, I pray, and see the good land beyond the Jordan, that goodly hill country, and Lebanon."* But the LORD *was angry with me on your account, and would not hearken to me; and the* LORD *said to me, "Let it suffice you; speak no more to me of this matter.* Go up to the top of Pisgah, and lift up your eyes westward and northward and southward and eastward, and behold it with your eyes; for you shall not go over this Jordan. But charge Joshua, and encourage and strengthen him; for he shall go over at the head of this people, and he shall put them in possession of the land which you shall see" (3:23–28).*

The pain of Moses' punishment is great, and apparently, an appeal to God has been heard once too often from Moses' lips. "Enough! Speak no more to Me of this matter," is God's response.

At the end of the Book of Deuteronomy, now 30 to 40 years after his sin, Moses dies on the mountain. God says to him, "Then die on the mountain which you ascend, and be gathered to your people, as Aaron your brother died in Mount Hor and was gathered to his people; because you broke faith with me in the midst of the people of Israel at the waters of Meribath Kadesh, in the wilderness of Zin; because you did not revere me as holy in the midst of the people of Israel" (32:50–51).

Why Joshua?
The answer to the vexing question begins with Joshua. Why Joshua? Why is he able to lead the people in the land of promise while Moses is not? Is Joshua a better man? Was he sinless? Is he more humble, holy, or, for whatever reason, more favored by God? The answer is "no, he is not." Then why?

What is the Promised Land? What does it represent? It represents heaven. The Israelites are entrapped in Egypt. As we said earlier, this represents the state of sin into which all humans are born. We are sinful, separated from God, and have not the power to deliver ourselves. The people are "saved," rescued from the bondage of slavery in Egypt under the pharaoh, by God's power through Moses and Aaron. Then they are "baptized" in the waters of the Red Sea, washing away the past to give them new life. The many years in the wilderness represent the wanderings in this lifetime, learning to be faithful and trusting of God, learning to love and obey Him. Finally, God's people enter the Promised Land, and this represents the Kingdom of Heaven.

What does Moses represent? He represents the law. It is essential to understand the deep identification between Moses and the law. Phrases from New Testament books imply the same, "Moses commanded you ... Moses permitted you ... According to the law of Moses ... If they do not listen to Moses and the prophets ..." All these show that, biblically, Moses and the law are the same. Moses is mentioned in nearly half the New Testament books, representing the law, signifying the law. He is the personification, the representative, and the figurehead of God's law as revealed in the Old Testament.

Should Moses have been permitted into the Promised Land, it would have been a significant statement. It would have signified that an individual who keeps the law well enough will get to enter heaven. But this is not the case, and it never was. In the New Testament Book of Hebrews, it is expressed,

> *For the law, since it has only a shadow of the good things to come instead of the true form of these realities, can never, by the same sacrifices which are continually offered year after year, make perfect those who draw near. Otherwise, would they not*

have ceased to be offered? If the worshipers had once been cleansed, they would no longer have any consciousness of sin. But in these sacrifices there is a reminder of sin year after year. For it is impossible that the blood of bulls and goats should take away sins (10:1–4).

The law is incapable of eliminating sin and delivering a soul to heaven. Moreover, the law itself states that "whoever keeps the whole law and yet stumbles in one point, he has become guilty of all" (James 2:10). James 2:10 references Deuteronomy 27:26, "Cursed be he who does not confirm (all) the words of this law by doing them." If Moses is the personification of the law, indeed, he must abide by what it says. He broke the law at one point; he disobeyed God in one instance. No matter how small the failing may seem to be, nor how long ago it took place, disobedience and irreverence are just that. "You rebelled against my command at the waters of Meribah." Keeping the law cannot save a person; he must be saved by a means external to himself.

The point is that the denied entrance is not about Moses as a person; it is all about what Moses represents. We know that Moses is indeed a good person; we know that he is "saved." He appears with Elijah on the Mount of Transfiguration. But the law itself cannot save anyone, and Moses, its personification, because he stumbles "in one point," cannot enter the earthly symbol of heaven.

Let's turn back to Joshua. Why can he enter and lead the people into the promised land? It is because he, too, represents something significant, something beyond himself, and something powerful. Joshua is not a better man than Moses, but his name is "Joshua." The Hebrew name *Joshua* (*Yeshua*) means "Savior." There is only one other significant individual in the Bible with the name "Yeshua," and that is Jesus. They have the same name, and Jesus is the ultimate Savior. Joshua is a foreshadowing of Jesus.

And now we can understand why Moses was denied entrance into the Promised Land. It is because God wanted to show the world the limits of man's ability. "But Jesus looked at them and said to them, 'With men this is impossible, but with God all things are possible.'" (Matt. 19:26). Moses disobeys in one instance. If Moses cannot achieve entrance into heaven — the man who "was very humble, more than any man who was on the face of the earth" — no other human can accomplish it either. The human race needs a savior, and there is only one true Savior: Jesus.

It seems strange that in all the Old Testament teachings about purity, holiness, and moral perfection, that written into the very heart of the law (the Torah) is a story — hidden for the ages until the time is right — of the inevitable failure of the law to save, and the inherent need for all humanity to seek and find the One true Savior. Humanity will never achieve God's holiness, but Jesus alone accomplishes the one thing that the law attempts but fails to attain: salvation.

The Ultimate Salvation of Israel
Judaism, with its law and worship, was not a man-made religion; God created it. The Jewish leadership of His day rejected Jesus Christ as their Messiah, Lord, and Savior. This rejection happened almost 2,000 years ago. But Judaism as a religion was the foundation upon which Christianity was formed and the root upon which it had grown. At dinner one evening in Colorado with friends, one of them asked me point blank, "Will the Jews be saved?" "Yes," I answered, "if we are reading Paul correctly, the Jews will be saved. But in order to be saved, they will have to believe in Jesus Christ." There is no path to salvation other than through Jesus.

Paul, a Jew, explained to the Gentile Christians in Rome that they were the beneficiaries of what happened to the Jews. "A partial hardening has happened to Israel until the fulness of the Gentiles has come in; and thus, Israel will be saved" (Rom. 11:25). The "partial hardening" occurred when Christ and Christianity were rejected. The persecution that followed caused the followers of Christ to disperse all over the world, bringing the message of the Gospel to the whole world. It was momentous to discover that, while Jews throughout the Mediterranean region continued to reject the Gospel, Gentiles were accepting it readily, and it was spreading fast.

At some point, the "times of the Gentiles" (Luke 21:24) will be fulfilled, and, at that time, many Jews will return to Christ, like the Prodigal Son coming home.

> *From the standpoint of the gospel they (the Jews) are enemies of God, for your sake; but as regards election they are beloved for the sake of their forefathers. For the gifts and the call of God are irrevocable (Rom. 11:28–29).*

Probably the most amazing testimony to this is the miraculous repatriation of the Jews into their homeland of Israel in 1948. It is astonishing that they are allowed back into Israel and are granted sovereignty of their land. Even more phenomenal is that they as a race still exist.

In A.D. 70, the Jews were expelled by the Roman Empire from their land. The Jewish temple of Herod in Jerusalem was torn apart stone from stone and has never been reconstructed. It was the nature of human nationalities that when the whole of a tribe, nation, or ethnic group was expelled from their land, forced to live among others, and had the exercise of their religion barred from them, within a generation or two, they disappeared.

Myriads of examples of this pattern exist. Anyone reading the Bible could ask, "Where are the Hittites today?" Or the Canaanites,

Jebusites, Babylonians, Hivites, and so on? Even in the United States, articles are written about the disappearance of the Anasazi native Americans who dwelt in great tribes in the four-corners region of the Southwest. Force a nation of people to expatriate their land, and soon they cease to exist. They begin dwelling among other people, intermarry, and, within generations, their unique identity is lost.

It is for this reason that the repatriation of a particular ethnic group of people who retain their identity for over 1900 years and then resume living in their original land has been referred to as "a phenomenon unprecedented in human history."[46] It is nothing short of miraculous that this has happened and attests firmly that God continues to have His hand upon the Jews for the fulfilling of His greater salvation-historical purposes. And Jesus is their Lord and Messiah.

Jesus Is Not Compatible with This World

Jesus came into the world to save it, but He was incompatible with it. *Incompatible* is defined as "incapable of harmonious coexistence." He did not "harmoniously coexist" with the world; the world hated Jesus, and it destroyed Him. Of course, He knew it would. One might say the world and Jesus were like oil and water; they cannot dissolve one into the other. This dubious condition Jesus passed on to His followers. He warned His apostles the night before He died that as the people hated Him, the people will likewise hate them.

> *You did not choose me, but I chose you and appointed you that you should go and bear fruit and that your fruit should abide; so that whatever you ask the Father in my name, he may give it to you. This I*

---

[46] Unknown encyclopedia entry

command you, to love one another. If the world hates
you, know that it has hated me before it hated you. If
you were of the world, the world would love its own;
but because you are not of the world, but I chose you
out of the world, therefore the world hates you (John
15:16–19).

It only makes sense; Jesus' proper place is at the right hand of His
Father in heaven. It is from there that He came, and it is to this same
place that He has returned. All of His disciples, ourselves included,
are from this world originally and are probably more or less
compatible with it. But when Jesus chooses us and chooses to reveal
Himself to us, He planted within us His Holy Spirit, and we began
living a different kind of life. Now we also find ourselves different
from this world, and we are taught, in fact, not to be conformed to it
in any way, but to complete the transformation through the renewing
of our mind (Rom. 12:2).

God the Father sends Jesus into the world; now Jesus sends us into
the world. The night before He dies, Jesus prays over His disciples
— a prayer for them that extends to us.

While I was with them, I kept them in thy name, which
thou hast given me; I have guarded them, and none
of them is lost but the son of perdition, that the
scripture might be fulfilled. But now I am coming to
thee; and these things I speak in the world, that they
may have my joy fulfilled in themselves. I have given
them thy word; and the world has hated them
because they are not of the world, even as I am not
of the world. I do not pray that thou shouldst take
them out of the world, but that thou shouldst keep
them from the evil one. They are not of the world,
even as I am not of the world. Sanctify them in the

truth; thy word is truth. As thou didst send me into the world, so I have sent them into the world (John 17:12–18).

This passage depicts our situation in life. As believing Christians, we are no longer *of* the world, just as Jesus was not of the world. We are *in* the world because we are "sent" by Jesus to be here. The simple words *of* and *in* bear great importance; they tell us where we belong. Our homeland is no longer here on earth, but up in heaven. We are born again. We are born from above (See John 3:3–7.). We belong above. Indeed we are citizens now of a new place. "Our citizenship is in heaven," Paul writes (Phil. 3:20).

And when we arrive there someday in the future, we will realize in a marvelous way that we have come home!

This observation begs the question: What are we doing here if we belong elsewhere? We have been sent. We are servants of our Lord Jesus Christ, and He has sent us here. We have already explained why: He is the light of the world (John 8:12). Now that He is ascended, He has sent us to take His place.

You are the light of the world. Let your light so shine before men, that they may see your good works and give glory to your Father who is in heaven (Matt. 5:14,16).

This verse explains what we are doing here. Since Jesus is in us, we are His light in a dark place. We live here. By our thoughts, words, behavior, and demeanor, the light of Jesus shines through us. In fact, the world is being saved through us. Therefore, in this time, God is accomplishing a great work through us. Our work is not over until we are called to heaven.

It helps that Paul explains that we are here as ambassadors.

All this is from God, who through Christ reconciled us to himself and gave us the ministry of reconciliation; that is, in Christ God was reconciling the world to himself, not counting their trespasses against them, and entrusting to us the message of reconciliation. So we are ambassadors for Christ, God making his appeal through us. We beseech you on behalf of Christ, be reconciled to God (II Cor. 5:17–20).

This role of ambassador is a good analogy. A lot is said here. Jesus has reconciled the world to God; now we are here doing the same, with Christ working through us. Reconciling the world to God is our work of bringing Jesus Christ to the many lost souls who live here. It is helpful to see ourselves and our role here on earth, as Paul says, as ambassadors.

Ambassadors are citizens *of* one country who live *in* another. They remain citizens of their home country, but are sent to the other. They find a place to live and become acquainted with the life, the language, and the citizenry of the new one. They live, work, and play among the new people, but they represent the country from which they came. Therefore, as ambassadors from heaven, in all we think, do, and say, we want to see ourselves as representatives of heaven, doing here the work of Christ.

I once had a manager in work I did as an engineer. He was very good. He not only told me what he needed me to do, but went to the trouble to explain his entire reasoning. This approach was a highly productive way of managing, because I could fully understand what was intended and fully apply myself to the project. Jesus did this for us: He taught us everything He was here seeking to accomplish and explained it to us so that we can fully apply ourselves to accomplishing all that He wanted. Jesus said to His disciples, "all things that I have heard from My Father I have made known to you" (John 15:15).

Therefore, we must remember we are no longer "of" this society; the world is not our place anymore. We are to live among its people but not to conform to its ways, because its ways are influenced by the darkness of Satan and the desires of self-love. It is not just the people subjected to corruption, but all of creation.

> *For the creation waits with eager longing for the revealing of the sons of God; for the creation was subjected to futility, not of its own will but by the will of him who subjected it in hope; because the creation itself will be set free from its bondage to decay and obtain the glorious liberty of the children of God. We know that the whole creation has been groaning in travail together until now; and not only the creation, but we ourselves, who have the first fruits of the Spirit, groan inwardly as we wait for adoption as sons, the redemption of our bodies (Rom. 8:19–23).*

All of creation falls into suffering and corruption at the Fall when Adam and Eve sinned. If you cannot see it clearly, go to the wilderness areas of Africa, where all one sees are hordes of exotic animals striving for survival day in and day out. Many are stressed by the threat of being eaten by one of the many carnivores on any given day. Others are stressed with the constant need to find food and water. All of creation awaits the redemption of humanity, for not only will he be set free, but even the lion and the lamb will lay down side by side. This peaceful picture is the imagery offered by our scriptures as we await the great day of the Lord. In the meantime, we who have Jesus in our hearts live here as ambassadors of heaven, bringing His light — the truth of the Gospel — to this darkened world.

Returning to the word *hate*, Jesus uses this term to express the severity of the conflicting natures between God and society. The world "hated Me."

However, Jesus was loved by many people here. He had multitudes of people following Him, loving Him, praising Him, and yearning to be close to Him. If the world "hates" Him, how can this be? And how will it be for those of us who follow Him? The answer is *agape*. Jesus is *agape*.

Jesus came with *agape*, loving the world even though the world rejected Him. "While we were yet sinners, Jesus Christ died for us." He gave His life for us, sacrificial love at its highest. *Agape* had the power to enter a foreign territory and break through the resistant hardness, sinfulness, and darkness. *Agape* had the power to penetrate a person's heart as no other force can. Jesus came and proved His love. He cared for a people who had no care for Him. Jesus and the world were oil and water, but Jesus did not come as oil, seeking compatibility with the water. He came to save the "water." Had He not come with the force of *agape* love, it would not have been possible. Had He not come with the force of *agape*, he would not have been able to forgive, as He forgave even those crucifying Him. Jesus came into this world by love, and to demonstrate love showing the people and giving the people a new way of life. And the hordes of people loved Him for doing so. "God so loved the world that He gave His only begotten Son." Had He not loved the world in this way, Jesus Christ would never have happened. But because of *agape*, He did; and because of His *agape* love for us, He commissioned us to do the same.

Jesus Is the Lamb of God

John the Baptist — the last of the Old Testament-style prophets — introduced the idea of Jesus being the Lamb of God.

The next day he saw Jesus coming toward him, and said, "Behold, the Lamb of God, who takes away the sin of the world!" (John 1:29).

Jesus is often referred to as the Lamb of God, especially in the Book of Revelation, where the Lamb takes a prominent role: "Worthy is the Lamb that was slain ..." (Rev. 5:12).

I want first to broach the question, "Why a lamb?" With a myriad of animals available, why would God choose a lamb to represent His Son? I must believe, as it seems, there is one particular characteristic that stands unique in a lamb. It is the only defenseless animal in existence! In other words, a lamb is chosen because of its inherent humility. No other animal I can think of is without some defensive capability entirely. Some animals are strong like an elephant, ferocious like a lion, fast like an antelope, have protective armor like an armadillo, can stab like an elk, sting like a bee, bite like a dog, claw like a cat, stink like a skunk, fly like a bird, hide like a reptile, or camouflage like a moth. All of these animals and more have a great variety of defensive protection, weapons, or strategies except the lamb.

He was oppressed, and he was afflicted, yet he opened not his mouth; like a lamb that is led to the slaughter, and like a sheep that before its shearers is dumb, so he opened not his mouth (Is. 53:7).

The helplessness of the defenseless and humble lamb made it the perfect representation of the way Jesus offered Himself as a sacrifice to the world. He was given to the world and did nothing to resist it.

Throughout the Old Testament, lambs and goats were the classical sacrificial animal. Lambs were put to death repeatedly as a substitute for the sins of humans. When John the Baptist identified Jesus as the Lamb of God, his reference implied that he would be sacrificed.

Thus, Jesus is the Lamb of God, but which lamb? Is He the Passover Lamb, sacrificed to ward off the plague of death in Egypt? Is He the one that purchased their release from Egypt? The early fathers of Roman Catholicism would say so. Is He the "ram caught in the thicket by his horns," sacrificed in place of Abraham's son Isaac in Genesis 22? This ram caught up in the thicket symbolized Jesus caught up on the cross. Is He the "scapegoat" in Leviticus 16, upon whom the hands of Aaron conferred all the iniquities of the sons of Israel? This annual sacrifice sending the scapegoat to die in the desert delivers the people from their sins. Is He the lamb to which we referred in the verse above — the lamb "led to the slaughter" in the Song of the Suffering Servant? The early fathers of the Greek Orthodox church say so. Or is the Lamb of God identified by John the Baptist all of the above? Indeed, Jesus accomplishes in His death the same deliverance of sin once and for all, represented by the sacrifice of each of these lambs and goats. Such would stand to reason.

Jesus Is the Perfect Man

Psalm 143:2 says, "For in Thy sight no man living is righteous." No man has walked upon this earth that is righteous. Some are better than others, but at least at one point, everyone has broken the law of God, and, by this, everyone has broken the covenant. Romans 3:23 provides the New Testament version of this, "All have sinned and fall short of the glory of God."

Because everyone had failed to keep the covenant except Jesus Christ, He came and lived and brought salvation to the world. But He also successfully "closed" the covenant God made with Moses, which contains the bulk of the law as found in the Old Testament. Jesus did not close it by revoking it; the covenant was irrevocable. He closed it by fulfilling its demands; He alone did what it said to do. The law, the covenant of Moses, made a demand upon humanity that no one could fulfill. It took one man to do it — one man to keep the law perfectly — and Jesus was that man. Jesus was the only man without sin. Jesus said,

> Think not that I have come to abolish the law and the prophets; I have come not to abolish them but to fulfil them. For truly, I say to you, till heaven and earth pass away, not an iota, not a dot, will pass from the law until all is accomplished (Matt. 5:17–18).

By His perfect keeping of the law, the covenant's demand upon humanity was fulfilled, and the covenant was closed.

We still read the law, of course, because it has great value to us: it enlightens us on the will of God and guides us in moral responsibility. We recall that even Jesus' faithful parents made certain on His behalf that all the stipulations governing a newborn boy were kept precisely according to the law: His circumcision on the eighth day and presentation in the temple on the fortieth.

Jesus is, therefore, our perfect model. The suggestion that "we do what Jesus would do" when faced with moral choices is an excellent word of guidance. Act like Jesus, love like Jesus, forgive like Jesus, and give yourself to God like Jesus.

Jesus Is the Word of God

> In the beginning was the Word, and the Word was with God, and the Word was God. He was in the beginning with God (John 1:1–2).

It is curious that John, the Gospel writer, chose to describe Jesus this way, as the word. What is meant by this? We certainly know that words are used for communication. This word is no different.

First of all, let us understand some differences between our thinking and God's thinking. For one, I cannot multitask very well. At my age, I don't even want to. I do my best thinking one subject at a time, dealing with it, and then go to the next. Some people think that multitasking is an esteemed and highly marketable professional skill. They can keep several tasks going at once and get a lot of things done in a hurry. They may be correct, but multi-tasking is not for me. If I have a problem to solve, I have to process it. If it is not complicated, I may conclude in a short time. If it is complicated, it may take me a while, even several days.

God is not like this. He is omniscient. All thoughts and all ideas, all solutions and conclusions are all in the front of His "mind" immediately. He is infinite; He holds before Himself all thoughts at one time. He never has to "think through" or process anything. The word *thinking* does not even fit Him.

Secondly, let us consider *Word.* "Word" to us is generally one individual word. This sentence is composed of eight individual words. We usually use "word" in this way. Occasionally we may use it differently. Someone may ask, "May I have a word with you?" If they do, I know they have more than one word in mind; it will be a conversation. The Greek for "word" is *logos,* representing a concept, an idea, a message of advice, a sermon, or even more. In John 1, it means more. If God were to take all He had to say to us, every thought to express, every concept to ponder, every goal to which He aspires, every revelation about Himself, every expression of His love and passion that He wishes to communicate, could He say it? He could. The Word is the complete communication of all the things God wants to say to us. The Word existed with Him in the beginning, and then, at the chosen time, He spoke it to us: "And the Word became flesh and dwelt among us" (John 1:14).

Jesus, as the Word, was God's communication to us.[47] He chose to speak, not with written words, art, or pictures, but with a real being. God made flesh, who lived, prayed, taught, wept, rejoiced, felt anger, expressed love, healed, delivered, and died on a cross as an innocent, self-giving, sacrificial Lamb! All of this was what God wanted to say. And He said it. What God the Father chose to say to us is "Jesus."

Jesus Was Tempted as We Are

This segment could have been entitled *We Are Not Alone.* Jesus understands our struggles, all of them. And He wants to help us get through them.

> *Therefore he (Jesus) had to be made like his brethren in every respect, so that he might become a merciful and faithful high priest in the service of God, to make expiation for the sins of the people. For because he himself has suffered and been tempted, he is able to help those who are tempted. (Heb. 2:17–18).*

> *Since then we have a great high priest who has passed through the heavens, Jesus, the Son of God, let us hold fast our confession. For we have not a high priest who is unable to sympathize with our weaknesses, but one who in every respect has been tempted as we are, yet without sin. Let us then with confidence draw near to the throne of grace, that we may receive mercy and find grace to help in time of need (Heb. 4:14–16).*

It is profound to think that the very God who created the universe and all that was in it, this same Holy God, of His own choosing,

---

[47]Fr Homer Rogers is credited with introducing this concept through his writings.

became a man like us. We were sinful and altogether unholy by nature, and He chose to empty Himself of His place in the divine and become one among us. He took upon Himself not only our own human body and mind, but allowed Himself to become vulnerable to the same temptations. He was "tempted as we are," yet did not give in to these temptations. In the Torah, the first five books of the Old Testament, it was established that the high priest must offer up sin offerings for the nation of Israel and himself as well. This sacrifice was a required action that reminded the high priest that he, too, was a sinner needing forgiveness (Lev. 9:7).

By allowing Himself to be vulnerable to sin, Jesus wants us to remember always that we are not alone in facing our struggles against sin. He knows what we go through. While it is difficult to believe He was faced with the same temptations as we, we should realize that He was faced with the same categories of sin and temptation and understands us entirely. He knows that He will prevail, and He knows that many times we will not prevail. He understands us, and the last thing He would want is for us to flee from Him because of our sin and darkness. We can sympathize with the words of Peter, "Depart from me, for I am a sinful man, O Lord!" (Luke 5:8). The Lord was never going to depart from Peter. However, we may identify with Peter's sentiment. We must never flee from the Lord when we are faced with the darkness of our sinfulness. Instead, we should flee to Him and "draw near to the throne of grace" whenever we are in sin. We approach Him "with confidence," meaning trusting in His grace.

Jesus Supplants the Established Institutions of Judaism

In the 2004 film, "The Passion of the Christ,"[48] Jesus struggles to carry His cross up the hill to Calvary. Beaten, bloody, and dirty, He falls to his grieving mother and finds the strength to comfort her, saying, "See, mother, I make all things new."

This verse is a most moving proclamation from Revelation 21:5, where it is spoken by God the Father from His great white throne at the height of glory in the Kingdom of Heaven. To have Jesus proclaim it in the film as He struggles up to Calvary requires a significant degree of editorial license. But cleverly, I will say, nothing is lost. Jesus is in the very moment making all things new! One must understand that Jesus knew the good He was accomplishing. It says in Hebrews, "Who for the joy set before Him endured the cross" (12:2). Accordingly, what enables Him to get through the passion and suffering is that He knows He is accomplishing an extraordinarily wonderful deliverance for the people He loves. He knows He is making all things new!

We want to see this now as it applies to all the relevant institutions of ancient Judaism. In Jesus, the very order of priesthood is changed. Aaron and all the Levitical priests are priests of the order of Aaron whom God called into priesthood under Moses. But Jesus is now a priest under a new order, the order of Melchizedek. Melchizedek preceded Aaron by many years and is a rather enigmatic, almost mythical figure from the days of Abraham. While Aaron was born at some point in time and died at a known time, Melchizedek is described as following,

> *He is without father or mother or genealogy, and has neither beginning of days nor end of life, but*

---

[48] The Passion of the Christ, produced and directed by Mel Gibson, Newmarket Films, 2004.

resembling the Son of God he continues a priest for ever (Heb. 7:3).

He is eternal, and Jesus remains a priest of this order perpetually, as well. Unlike priests of the order of Aaron, who must offer up sacrifices for sins daily, Jesus offers up a sacrifice "once for all" when He offered up Himself (Heb. 7:27).

The text goes on to say that "when the priesthood is changed, of necessity there takes place a change of law also" (Heb. 7:12). Jesus repeatedly takes precedence over the law when He says, "You have heard that it was said ... but I say to you..." referring to statements in the law of Moses (Matt. 5). Then He adds a new commandment, "That you love one another even as I have loved you, that you also love one another" (John 13:34). Under Moses's covenant, the ethical system is described as "prescriptive," meaning righteousness is accomplished by the exact obedience to dictated rules. The ethical system under the new covenant with Jesus is "relational," meaning righteousness is accomplished by engaging in whatever produces the highest good for others with whom we relate:

Beloved, if God so loved us, we also ought to love one another (I John 4:11). God is love, and he who abides in love abides in God, and God abides in him (I John 4:16). There is no fear in love, but perfect love casts out fear. For fear has to do with punishment, and he who fears is not perfected in love (I John 4:18). Beloved, if God so loved us, we also ought to love one another (Gal. 5:14).

The law of the new covenant is summed up in one word, love. For example, it does not matter now as Christians whether or not we eat shrimp (an unclean food under Moses). What matters is whether we forgive, love, and serve our neighbors. We can eat meat that was once sacrificed to an idol, but not if it weakens our neighbor's faith.

(See I Cor. 8.) Whether one has kept the law of the new covenant is a question of whether one acted in genuine love.

Jesus institutes a new covenant with God — "a better covenant" (7:22), for indeed it was prophesied in Jeremiah,

> *"Behold, the days are coming," declares the LORD, "when I will make a new covenant with the house of Israel and the house of Judah, not like the covenant which I made with their fathers in the day I took them by the hand to bring them out of the land of Egypt ...*
>
> *"I will put My law within them, and on their heart I will write it; and I will be their God and they shall be my people. And no longer shall each man teach his neighbor and each his brother, saying, `Know the LORD,' for they shall all know me, from the least of them to the greatest, says the LORD; for I will forgive their iniquity, and I will remember their sin no more"* (Jer. 31:31–34).

Jesus, having fulfilled the Mosaic Covenant in Himself — by His perfect obedience to God — now institutes a new covenant where God is not "outside" His people looking in, but is "in their heart." They "know the Lord" internally.

I attended a presentation a few years ago where a local Jewish rabbi was allowed to describe "what was wrong with Christians." Among other things that he listed, he complained that Christians say they "know God." They are wrong in saying this, he insisted, for no one can know God. I wanted so intensely to interrupt and remind him that Judaism's prophets prophesied this very thing: there would come a time when the Lord's people would have a new covenant, and they would indeed in "their heart" "know God." Indeed, Christians can say this. Unfortunately, we were not given the opportunity to rebut his presentation. At any rate, the new covenant had come into being through Jesus, just as the prophet Jeremiah predicted.

Covenants with God are not "free." They are costly.

> *For where a covenant is involved, there must of necessity be the death of the one who made it. For a covenant is valid only at death, since it is not in force as long as the one who made it is alive (Heb. 9:16–17).*

When the covenant of Moses was proclaimed to the people, he took the blood of calves and goats with water and sprinkled the book of the covenant itself with it. The new covenant was, of course, ratified through the blood of Jesus once for all, and remembered in the covenant by communion in His body and blood.

The statement that Jesus "made all things new" is hardly an overstatement. He initiated a new order of priesthood under the order of Melchizedek. He initiated a new covenant, with a completely new relationship with God where we now "know God" in our hearts. The new covenant has an entirely new system of law (relational), which is fulfilled in a completely new way (love). The new covenant was initiated with a new and perfect sacrifice of blood, which brings forgiveness of sin now once and for all. Jesus even asserted His supremacy over the temple in Jerusalem and the Sabbath day (Matt. 12:6,8). It is little wonder that he endured the cross for the joy that was set before Him. For indeed, He was making "all things new!"

Jesus Is the Exact Re-Presentation of the Nature of God

The first thing we must understand is nature. What is nature? Nature is "the inherent basic constitution of a person or thing."[49] It is out of the nature of a person that he thinks, acts, says, and does. If there is a singular nature in a person, then everything he thinks, says, and does represents that nature. Obviously, we can learn a great deal about the nature of a person by assessing all the choices of their behavior. In contending with the current overemphasis on dietary laws, this is the reason Jesus said,

> *It is not what enters into the mouth that defiles the man, but what proceeds out of the mouth, this defiles the man ... For the things that proceed out of the mouth come from the heart, and those defile the man (Matt. 15:11,18).*

The heart is considered the seat of one's nature and the core of his constitution. Man is defiled by what comes forth from his *eros-*driven nature, his self-love.

Consider Jesus' exchange with the apostle Philip the night before Jesus dies. Jesus explains to the apostles that He must leave and return to the Father; He must go and prepare a place for them in the Father's kingdom. Philip then asks Jesus, "Lord, show us the Father, and it is enough for us." I can visualize Jesus rolling His eyes at Philip in exasperation and saying,

> *Have I been with you so long, and yet you do not know me, Philip? He who has seen Me has seen the Father; how can you say, "Show us the Father"? Do*

---

[49] *Webster's Tenth New Collegiate Dictionary* (Springfield, MA, Merriam-Webster, Inc., 1996) "Nature"

you not believe that I am in the Father and the Father in Me? (John 14:8–10).

"He who has seen Me has seen the Father!" What does Jesus mean by this? What is it that Philip is supposed to see in Jesus that mirrors the Father? Is he supposed to see that God the Father is five-foot-eleven, with long brown hair and brown, slightly hazel eyes? Medium weight, strong shoulders, and favors the use of His right hand? Of course not. "He who has seen Me, has seen the Father" means that if you have seen Me and My nature, you have seen the nature of God the Father, and that is all you need to see. It is all one needs to know about God, His nature.

Thus, when we learn what Jesus thinks about vendors buying and selling in the temple in Jerusalem, we are learning exactly what the Father thinks about this as well. When we see what Jesus does, how He acts, and what makes Him glad or sad or angry, we know exactly what pleases God the Father and what makes Him glad, sad, or angry. Hebrews 1:3 says,

Jesus is ... the exact representation of (the Father's) nature.

Jesus does nothing on His own. John 5:19 says, "Jesus said to them, Truly, truly, I say to you, the Son can do nothing of his own accord, but only what he sees the Father doing; for whatever He does, that the Son does likewise." Jesus performs an exact replication of what God the Father chooses to do. It is not that Jesus has to see what the Father does before He knows what to do, He simply works out of His own nature, and it is the exact same thing. Jesus "sees" that His nature and that of His Father are the same. In this last verse, He tells us He is not out on His own; He is not doing His own thing, taking every encounter as an opportunity for self-expression and finding His place in history. He is every minute of every day acting as an exact reflection of the mind, heart, and nature of His Father in heaven.

As a child, I used to be fascinated with my Uncle Bob's tricks at the kitchen table. One trick was that he mysteriously made a paperclip move around the tabletop without touching it. First, it slid slowly toward me, then to the right or left, and then back to Uncle Bob. How did he do that? Later I learned, of course, that Uncle Bob was sliding surreptitiously with his hidden right hand, a magnet under the table. Had I known his secret, I would have known that by following the paperclip, which I could see, exactly where under the table the magnet was, which I could not see.

Similarly, Jesus is revealing everything we need to know about God. We cannot see God, but we know now a great deal about what makes Him angry, sad, glad, and rejoicing by watching Jesus, whom we can see. We know by listening to Jesus and watching Him what God thinks about the abuse of His temple and the poor, blind, and lame. We know what He thinks about children: "Permit the children to come to Me; do not hinder them; for the kingdom of God belongs to such as these" (Mark 10:14). We know He established the law, but we also know now how the law is to be applied to people and their needs. We know that loving each other is chief and that loving God and our neighbor sum up the entire purpose of the law: "On these two commandments depend the whole Law and the Prophets" (Matt. 22:40). We know that God gives His Spirit to the world and considers this His precious gift: "If you then, who are evil, know how to give good gifts to your children, how much more will the heavenly Father give the Holy Spirit to those who ask him!" (Luke 11:13).

Everything we need to know about God the Father — into whose kingdom we seek entrance — is fully expressed in Jesus Christ. For

Jesus, exactly and precisely, is a mirror reflection of the nature of God. "Show us the Father," urged Philip.

Philip, "He who has seen Me has seen the Father!"

One can easily understand why salvation cannot come any way other than through Jesus Christ. If anyone does not like Jesus Christ, he will not like God the Father into whose kingdom he seeks to enter. Salvation can be defined as coming to live in the kingdom of God the Father. Entrance into this kingdom where *agape* love is the entire mode of operation cannot happen if one cannot or will not love God. Jesus is the door through whom all must pass into salvation because He is the One, sole representation of who God is. "I am the door; if anyone enters through Me, he shall be saved" (John 10:9). Those who reject Jesus reject God the Father; those who receive Jesus are receiving God the Father (Matt. 10:40; Luke 10:16).

Furthermore, Jesus is cautious about revealing His full identity, probably for the exact reason that encountering Jesus is dangerous. Coming to know Jesus and receiving Him is the wonderful path to true eternal love and salvation. But if one comes to know Him and chooses not to receive Him, their prospects for salvation are grievously jeopardized. Out of love for all people, Jesus is cautious, therefore, about how and to whom He reveals Himself, hoping that only at the most opportune moment will they be given that choice. As an example, when Jesus met the woman at the well, the Samaritan woman in John 4, He is willing to tell her clearly that He is the Messiah, because He can see she has a heart to receive Him. She does, and she invites many other Samaritans who likewise are willing to become His followers. In contrast, when He encounters the hard-hearted chief priests, scribes, and elders in Luke 20, He says to these who refused to admit John the Baptist had come with God's authority, "Neither will I tell you by what authority I am doing these things" (vv. 1–8).

Human beings are not easy to figure out. There are all sorts of behavior, character, and attitudes coming forth from ourselves — both good and bad — all the time. How can we fully figure someone out? Sometimes, we can just barely understand ourselves. This problem is not just because we have different God-given personalities, but more so because we have more than one nature operating inside of us — at least Christians do. We have the nature of God (*agape*) imbued in us by the Holy Spirit, but we still have the old *eros* alive and operating in us.

For this reason, Paul spoke of the "war" that goes on in him all the time — the war between these two natures, which he calls the flesh and the Spirit (Rom. 7:19,23; Gal. 5:17). Jesus had a singular nature. From Him, we "learned" God because He singularly, clearly, and without failure mirrored the one, singular nature of God the Father. Therefore, Jesus' best advice was, "Follow Me."

Why Did Jesus Come to Us?

Rather than merely suggest that the reason Jesus came into the world should be evident to all of us, let us look more carefully at exactly what He says. When Zacchaeus of Jericho stands in his house, confesses, and repents, Jesus exclaims, "Today salvation has come to this house ... for the Son of Man has come to seek and to save that which was lost" (Luke 19:10). Two verbs are used here to express why Jesus has come into the world: "to seek" and "to save." He comes to seek the lost. I think this makes it easy to understand why, as we said earlier, that if we seek Him, "He will be found by us" (Jer. 29:13–14). He is out there looking for us! Naturally, He can promise that if we seek Him with "all our heart," we will find Him. When it says He comes to save the lost, He finds them by drawing them to Him and dying for their sins as the perfect and final act of atonement.

217

"Upward Call"

In Mark 2, Jesus says something more that helps define His purpose in being here.

> And the scribes of the Pharisees, when they saw that he was eating with sinners and tax collectors, said to his disciples, "Why does he eat with tax collectors and sinners?" And when Jesus heard it, he said to them, "Those who are well have no need of a physician, but those who are sick; I came not to call the righteous, but sinners" (Mark 2:16–17).

Of course, those that considered themselves "righteous" are "sicker" than the average "sinner." But Jesus leaves that matter hanging before these scribes, hoping perhaps that it will sink in that they are not so "righteous" that they are beyond the need of help. The "sick" are those that are spiritually sick, yet realize their need for help and are willing to accept it. Jesus here is announcing his purpose in coming to earth: to call sinners to Himself and bring them salvation.

Indeed it can be said that all of us who have come to salvation in Jesus did so because, in one way or another, we felt the drawing to Him as if something in our heart was calling or drawing us to Him. And those that find Him have found Him to be all we could have hoped for. Jesus' use of the word *physician* here may have been summoning the phrase from the Song of the Suffering Servant,

> But He was wounded for our transgressions, He was crushed for our iniquities; the chastening for our well-being fell upon Him, and by His scourging we are healed (Is. 53:5).

218

Looking further at the matter of why Jesus came to earth, I want to share an enlightening story written by David Manuel Jr.[50] I have shared this in many Christmas sermons.

He regretted the words the moment they were out of his mouth. No, maybe it was better to let her know exactly why he wasn't coming with her. Not that she'd nagged him; his wife had only mentioned the Christmas eve service once all evening. But he could feel her hope.

He'd explained to her often enough how he felt, that this Jesus, whom she loved so in her quiet way, had indeed been a great man, perhaps the greatest who had ever lived. But to say that he was the Son of God — or God himself, adopting human form — that was too much! He would not hurt her for the world, but he could not go against all reason.

"I'm sorry," he said more softly when he'd come in from lifting the garage door for her, "but I cannot be a hypocrite. If you could show me just once why God would ever want to become a man, I'd gladly come with you, but ...." There was nothing more to say. The few times she'd tried, in her soft-spoken way, to persuade him, she'd failed. As she left, he tried not to notice the tears in her eyes.

The house seemed very quiet after she'd gone. He wandered into the den, turned on the television, turned it off again, and went into the dining room. Outside the picture window, the wind was picking

[50] David Manuel Jr., *Christmas Story*, Logos Journal, Nov–Dec 1975. Reprinted with permission from his daughter.

up, whipping fresh snow laterally across his path of vision, till he could hardly make out the bird feeder. Caught in the illumination of the backyard floodlight, it was a cold, forbidding snow, and he shuddered and turned to go into the kitchen to make some hot cocoa.

But something made him turn back, and there, out of the corner of his eye, he caught a movement that wasn't snow. It was a lone sparrow, being buffeted by the wind as it foraged for food on the rapidly whitening ground.

If there was one thing that got to him, it was birds. They were so beautiful, so graceful and fragile, such a joy to watch ... even sparrows. But this one gave him concern; it was having trouble.

Even as he watched, the wind steadily increased till it was practically a full gale. And he saw that there wasn't just one sparrow — a whole flock of them had gotten disoriented in the snowstorm and were down on the ground, searching for food. He knew what could happen if they didn't find it.

Going quickly to the back hall closet, he pulled on boots, parka, and gloves and headed for the garage where the covered pail of birdseed was kept. There was a small plastic bowl he used as a scoop, and this he filled to the brim and headed out into the night.

Slowly, so as not to startle them, he worked his way upwind of the birds and cast the contents of the bowl into the air, so the seed fell among them. A few sparrows were able to find the kernels, but fresh-driven snow-covered it almost immediately.

Back he went for more, this time bringing the whole pail. He flung fistful after fistful into the driving snow, but to no avail. Finally, he stopped and straightened. His body shook with fatigue and the frustration at being powerless to help. "I know!" he exclaimed aloud, "I'll put the seed on the floor of the garage and turn the light on!"

He went back to the garage, turned on the light, and scattered the remaining contents of the pail all over the floor. It would be quite a mess to clean up, but it was worth it. And he went inside, holding the garage door open a crack, to see what would happen.

But the birds did not seem to get the idea. There was food and shelter in plain sight, yet they stayed out in the backyard. He swore and ran into the kitchen, going out the back door to come up behind them and try to shoo them towards the garage. He only succeeded in scaring them away — off the ground and into the trees.

When he returned to the house, they flittered from the trees back to the ground. They seemed to sense there was help there, somewhere, but when he went out again, they only flew away. He stood there at the edge of the pool of light, shaking his head, tears springing to his eyes.

"Oh, God, why won't they understand? Everything they need is right there, but they won't see it. If only there were some way I could show them. If only I

were a bird myself, I could lead them to the garage
...."

He turned. A sliver of yellow light from the garage
door reflected across a white aspen tree in the yard,
forming a cross.

Oh, my God!

The Crucifixion Opens Our Hearts to God

We struggle to understand why the sacrifice of the Lamb of God was
necessary for the atonement of the human race. It is beyond us to
know why exactly blood had to be shed for our sins to be forgiven
and why the sacrificial victim had to be completely sinless. These
are matters requiring a deeper understanding than has been revealed
to us. But there is something we can understand that happened at
the crucifixion that has a rather profound impact on the human mind
and softens even the hardest of hearts. That understanding relates
to the injustice of the innocent suffering.

On April 19, 1995, a bombing in Oklahoma City destroyed the
Alfred P. Murrah Federal Building. The bombing took place during
the workday and killed several government workers and their
children — at least 168 persons. It remains one of the deadliest acts
of domestic terrorism in American history.[51]

There was an impromptu photograph taken in the immediate
aftermath of the bombing. It won the Pulitzer Prize. It was taken by
a man named Charles Porter, and it was of a fireman, climbing out
of the rubble, carrying in his arms a dying child. Her name was
Baylee Almun. The explosion killed her. What was it about the
photograph that warranted such a prize? Was it the lighting, the

---

[51] Wikipedia, *Oklahoma City Bombing*, 2017.

setting, the staging? No, it was that it had such a powerful impact on the human heart.

The photo remains the most moving, memorable, and heart-rending image of the tragedy. It deeply enkindles the pity, anger, and tears of those that see the photo. Why? Because it is a riveting image of innocent suffering. The author of the book, *The Shack* said it so well, "Something in the hearts of most human beings simply cannot abide pain inflicted on the innocent, especially children."[52] How true. God has planted in the human heart a sense of irreconcilable horror at the injustice of innocent suffering. As for the Oklahoma bombing photograph, it is the child. The child does not deserve this; it should not have happened, yet we live in a world where it can. Had the wounded been an adult, we would not have been so moved, but a child in our thinking is innocent and undeserving of punishment — vulnerable and unable to care for herself. The human heart simply cannot abide such a thing, without being torn, without feeling deep, irreconcilable pain.

What did the centurion attending the crucifixion say the moment Jesus breathed His last?

> *Now when the centurion saw what had taken place, he praised God, and said, "Certainly this man was innocent!"* (Luke 23:47).

Realizing that Jesus suffered and died this way and realizing that He was entirely innocent moves even the heart of a calloused Roman soldier. Likewise, while one of the two criminals being crucified with Jesus hurled abuse at Him, the other rebuked him, saying,

> *"Do you not fear God, since you are under the same sentence of condemnation? And we indeed justly; for*

---

[52] William P. Young, *The Shack* (Windblown Media, 2007).

we are receiving the due reward of our deeds; but this man has done nothing wrong." And he said, "Jesus, remember me when you come into your kingdom" (Luke 23:40–42).

The cause of this thief's repentance was watching Jesus, a man who had "done nothing wrong," dying. His torture was real, His pain was real, and His suffering and death were all very real. Gazing at this travesty, especially in that it was for the cause of humanity that He did this, began a powerful impact on many souls.

This realization caused a kind of sadness that opened hardened hearts and brought about repentance as few other things could. Jesus was innocent and did not deserve this. And the only way to cope with this and abide the pain was to turn to Him, admitting we desperately needed this sacrifice but were not worthy of it. The crucifixion caused the curtain in the nearby temple to be torn from top to bottom. But it can be said that His death did not impact the temple made of stones in Jerusalem as much as it did the temple that was in the soul of every believer. The real rending turned a "heart of stone" into a softened and repented heart of flesh, now willing to believe. As the prophet Ezekiel expressed,

A new heart I will give you, and a new spirit I will put within you; and I will take out of your flesh the heart of stone and give you a heart of flesh. And I will put my spirit within you, and cause you to walk in my statutes and be careful to observe my ordinances (36:26–27).

This result is what the crucifixion of Jesus Christ does to human beings. The crucifixion itself had the cosmological impact that put the prophet's words into effect. This effect is also why the martyrdom of the Lord's followers has accomplished so much throughout Christian history to bring non-believers to faith. Every time a Christian is martyred for his faith, he imitates before the eyes of his abusers the same sacrifice of Jesus. This sacrifice is what makes his faith so powerful that this Christian would surrender his life when, in fact, he was innocent of any evil. The innocent death changed hardened hearts to God and won them for Christ.

God's Ultimate Plan for Us

This last portion of the book is about God's ultimate intention for those of us whom He has brought into being and has called into salvation with Him forever. What an unimaginably glorious future we have waiting for us.

As I have said many times, it is helpful to see everything we can from God's perspective. In other words, we wish to gain as best as we can a clear sense of what He is up to in our lives. Knowing this, we can then join with Him in fulfilling His intentions.

I mentioned earlier that I had a good manager in an engineering company I once worked for. He would tell me not just what he wanted me to do but would explain why and paint a clear picture of all that was to be achieved. His approach was good: If I thoroughly understood the ultimate goal that needed to be accomplished, I would be able to do my part in making it happen with little further guidance.

In this instance, it is learning what God intends to accomplish in us. And although He is the ultimate artist and the inimitable sculptor of our souls, my cooperation is an offering of love to God and a willing abandonment that I may be for Him like softened clay in His hands ready to be shaped as He wills.

God through Jesus Christ, the Holy Spirit, and scripture has made known to us what He intends for us. Investigating His ultimate goal for us from several points of view is the intent of this last portion of the book.

Our Holiness

Paul writes in his epistle to the Romans,

"Upward Call"

We know that in everything God works for good with those who love him, who are called according to His purpose (Rom. 8:28).

To many, this is a very familiar verse. I wish to look at the last phrase. We "are called according to" a purpose, that is, "we are called with a specific purpose in mind." "Purpose," for which the Greek word *prosthesis* is understood as the fulfillment of an "eternal plan." This verse tells us then that God masterfully works through everything in our lives, not to make life pleasant and easy for us now, but for the fulfillment of a much higher, eternal purpose. The purpose is our holiness, and as long as we do not adamantly resist Him, He will accomplish it.

His purpose is that we shall become holy people. The root word for *holy* in Hebrew is a little lost to us in its etymology, but it is generally thought to mean "cut off" or "set apart," in this instance, for God. Quoting a reference work on Biblical Hebrew words,

A basic element of Israelite religion was the maintenance of an inviolable distinction between the spheres of the sacred and the common or profane. ... Man was made in the image of God and capable of reflecting the Divine likeness. And as God reveals Himself as holy, He calls men to a holiness resembling His own.[53]

The ultimate purpose for the whole community of God's people we find therefore in Leviticus 19:1-2.

---

[53] Harris, Archer, Waltke, *Theological Wordbook of the Old Testament* (Chicago, Moody Press, 1980) Vol. II, p.787.

"Upward Call"

And the LORD said to Moses, "Say to all the congregation of the people of Israel, You shall be holy; for I the LORD your God am holy."

God is not satisfied we finish up this lifetime as "common" or "profane." We are made in His image, and there is nothing common or profane about Him; God is working day and night to form us into holy people just as He is holy. Our perfection is His purpose. How many people give up on God because He does not do what they want. "I prayed and prayed for God to get me that job, and I did not get it; I never get what I ask for." God is not a concession machine. He may seek to win our hearts by occasionally granting the things that please us in our everyday life, but He has a much loftier goal for every one of us, and His greater plan and purpose is to achieve it.

Holy means set apart for God and being so filled with His love and Spirit that we radiate His nature and accomplish His purposes, even while hardly noticing it. This result is what we are about.

Holy also means being fully possessed by God. We are His own; He has purchased us. As a shepherd owns a sheep and may do with it as He wishes, so God owns us and is entitled to do with us as He wishes.

For the grace of God has appeared for the salvation of all men, training us to deny ungodliness and worldly desires, and to live sensibly, righteously, and godly lives in this world, awaiting our blessed hope, the appearing of the glory of our great God and Savior Jesus Christ, who gave himself for us to redeem us from all iniquity and to purify for Himself a people for His own possession who are zealous for good deeds (Titus 2:1–14).

228

The New Testament holds for the same cause of holiness, but uses a different word; it is the Greek word *telos*. The word is not easy to translate into English, so it appears in several forms. Its root is closely associated with "destiny," but the word gets translated as "completed," "mature," "fulfilled," "finished," and "perfect." The idea is that when something has accomplished its purpose and has fulfilled what it is created to be, it has reached its *telos*.

When Jesus was on the cross, He said, "It is finished," and He died (John 19:30). The word "finished" is *tetelestai*, the perfect passive of the verb form of *telos*. It was His way of saying that in dying, He had now accomplished the purpose for which He came to earth. He did not end or finish His existence (See Matt. 28:20, "I am with you always"), but in dying on the cross, He had accomplished (*telos*) His essential purpose in coming to earth. The New Testament used *telos* also when Jesus repeated the classic verse from Leviticus:

> *Therefore you are to be perfect, as your heavenly Father is perfect* (*telos*) *(Matt. 5:48).*

Jesus repeats God's intention that we become holy as He is. What we gain from exploring the use of the Greek word, *telos*, is that it is not as if God has chosen us out of the common and profane to make us holy, but it emphasizes that when we were created, we were made for the express purpose of holiness, and, therefore, becoming "perfect" is our destiny; we were created to become holy!

So, knowing this, how do we do it? Everything listed in this book comprise the recipe for the journey to holiness:

- repenting,
- seeking God,
- surrendering to God,
- obeying God,
- confessing our sins,

- learning to pray,
- studying the word,
- living in Christian fellowship,
- partaking of the gifts of Baptism and Communion,
- growing in faith,
- growing in humility,
- practicing true love,
- preserving His temple within us,
- learning to listen to God,
- sharing the good news with others, and
- coming to know Jesus Christ for all He is.

Becoming Holy Is the Work God Accomplishes in Us
This holy work is our discipline for drawing closer to God. However, it is important to realize that applying all this positive discipline to our lives does nothing to make us more holy! We are supposed to become holy, but accomplishing true holiness is beyond us. I cannot make myself any more holy than I can fly from Los Angeles to Chicago without an airplane! To make that journey requires something much bigger, greater, more powerful than I. It is impossible for me to do it. What I can do, though, is make preparations for the flight. I can drive myself to the airport. I can even get myself to the gate. But the flight itself requires something more, a great deal more.

All these things listed above are what we do to present ourselves to God, to learn about Him, to draw close to Him, and make ourselves available to Him — all for the very greatest of reasons, His kingdom is eternity. But holiness itself is a transformation of the heart on the deepest level. It is an internal matter where eros dies out at the core of our being, and *agape* gains preeminence.

Holiness is an act of God. We die to Jesus; He raises us back up with Him to God in holiness. The good news is that most likely, the process of transformation has already begun, for it is most unlikely that you would have read this far into this book had He not planted within you a deep desire for Him. So, while we cannot make ourselves holy, we can look within us for the various signs that God is making us holier.

The work of God the Holy Spirit is a lot like the parable of the sheep and the goats discussed earlier. The sheep were told, "Come ... inherit the kingdom prepared for you from the foundation of the world." And the sheep who had unconsciously adopted the character of Christ within them asked when they had done the good things He said they did. They had been acting Christlike while not realizing His character had been built in them. Similarly, we can only look at ourselves retrospectively to ascertain that God had been making us in His holy likeness.

What are some of these signs? Do we find ourselves experiencing any of the following more often?

- Do I, from time to time, find myself yearning for God? "As the deer longs for the water brooks, so longs my soul for You, O God" (Ps. 42:1). Do I hunger and thirst for God?
- Do I desire to please Him?
- Do I find myself increasingly grateful to Jesus?
- Do I want others to come to know this same God?
- Do I find myself conscious of God more often?
- Do I increasingly look at myself and my actions with a degree of disdain, as Paul did when he wrote, "For that which I am doing, I do not understand; for I am not practicing what I would like to do, but I am doing the very thing I hate" (Rom. 7:15).

231

- Am I growing more and more disagreeable with my sinfulness; am I seeing my sins more clearly?
- As I pray, do I often run out of words even though the thoughts I wish to convey to God still seem not fully expressed?
- Do I more often find myself thinking that I am different from the rest of the world, but closer to God?
- Do I find rest in His silence? "For God alone my soul in silence waits" (Ps. 62:1).
- Do I have more confidence in God and less in myself? Solomon's prayer: "I am but a little child: I do not know how to go out or come in" (I Kings 3:7).

These signs are indications that God is accomplishing the soul's transformation into His holiness, His own likeness. It is a given that anyone who continues seeking the Lord, through the work of the Holy Spirit, may be certain that it happens. This holiness indeed is what He does!

> *I am confident of this very thing, that He who began a good work in you will perfect it until the day of Christ Jesus (Phil. 1:6).*

> *And we all, with unveiled face, beholding the glory of the Lord, are being changed into his likeness from one degree of glory to another; for this comes from the Lord who is the Spirit (II Cor. 3:18).*

Domesticating Us for Heaven

I had never been very good at domesticating or training our house pets. I was particularly fond of Labrador pups, and as soon as we acquired one, we would run around the house with him, play with him, feed him, etc. This 4-pound pup soon became a 20-pound pup and was still of the mindset that being rambunctious was the thing to do. While my house could handle a happy little pup, it could not handle 20 pounds of rambunctiousness. So, I insisted that he spends more time outdoors and cast him out into the backyard. He did not like it, and I soon heard a strange, grating sound out back. I found him lying down at the outside corner of the bedroom, happily eating my house.

Similarly, we have had a variety of cats. They had to be housebroken and taught what they may and may not do in our house. Cats may not sharpen their claws on our furniture. They may not bring their food into the den or bedrooms. They may not meow at all times of the night and, for that matter, may not meow persistently at any time. One cat would not stop climbing the drapes, and it had to be de-clawed, a decision for which our cat-loving friends were abhorred. It had come down to either de-clawing or giving away. There were rules and behavior stipulations required for living in our house. But the benefits were wonderful. These animals from the pound, now lived in a warm house day and night. They were well-fed, had a cozy place to sleep at night, and were protected from predators and other wild animals of the darkness. We took good care of them, got them inoculated to stay healthy, and bought them toys they enjoyed playing with. Best of all, they sat in our laps or beside us on the couch by the fireplace in winter. Everyone was happy together. If house pets can enjoy love, as it seems they do, they were in pet heaven.

In contrast, many animals spend their lives surviving in the outer darkness. In the piney woods of East Texas, there once was a pack of wild dogs. We were warned about them. They were never domesticated; they grew up in the wild, and they were dangerous. They worked as a pack and lived off whatever they found. A lone pet or even child caught by them could quickly be killed. Traps were set around the county, and many of the dogs were finally caught and eliminated. I often wondered if it were possible whether some of them could have been caught and ultimately domesticated.

Human beings are not altogether different. Families are the perfect place for a child to be reared because, in the family context, the young child is greatly loved and provided for, but is also taught what kind of behaviors are accepted for continued existence in the loving home.

It is a good thing, whether I have done well or poorly, that I have had the experience of schooling a pet to live in my home. I now have a better idea of what God is doing to all of us, myself included. God is domesticating me for living in the Kingdom of Heaven. I am not a wild man, like the demoniac that lived in the hills of the Gerasenes in Mark 5, who was not of his right mind and was dangerous to himself and others. At least, I do not think I am. However, I am born in this world and have been "of" this world in many ways through many years. I operated by the self-love in me, and I acted, talked, and behaved like any average person in our society. Jesus came teaching about the Kingdom of God and drew the contrast through many explanations and symbols of how different it is in heaven from the way it is here. "The last shall be first, and the first last" (Matt. 20:16). "Truly, I say to you, unless you turn and become like children, you will never enter the kingdom of heaven" (Matt. 18:3). It is not the rich and aggressive who shall inherit the earth, but the meek. Paul, from his own revelation, could say, "The sufferings of this present time are not worthy to be compared with the glory that is to be revealed" (Rom. 8:18).

The Kingdom of love is inexpressibly better than life on earth; it is "like heaven" in the best sense of that expression. I am not ready for it; I am not worthy of it. At least, this is my self-assessment. God knows when I will be ready or not, and He is busy day and night shaping and forming me into His holiness and into perfect *agape*.

For a Christian, our life on earth is our "Saint Obedience School." Heaven is our destiny and our home — the "mansion" He has prepared. He is getting us ready to be welcomed with loving arms into a domicile of incomparable love. Thanks be to God for all He is doing to shape, transform, and domesticate us to fit well in heaven.

Meeting Our True Self

I suppose there is a true me out there somewhere — or in here — somewhere. Maybe he is just a gleam in my Father's eye. I do not know. John wrote,

> *See what love the Father has given us, that we should be called children of God; and so we are. The reason why the world does not know us is that it did not know Him. Beloved, we are God's children now; it does not yet appear what we shall be, but we know that when He appears we shall be like Him, for we shall see Him as He is. And every one who thus hopes in Him purifies himself as he is pure (I John 3:1–3).*

We are now children of God. We are His, we belong to Him, and we are being watched over and reared in accordance with His will and strength. He is our loving Father, and He disciplines us like His own. (See Heb. 12:5–13.) We see in these verses both the present reality of our sonship in God and, on a much higher level, a fulfillment (*telos*) of what this means in the time yet to come. "We are God's children now ... but we know ... we shall be like Him." We see in this the glorious promise that if we maintain this hope, we shall be purified "as He is pure."

Paul seemed to speak of this true self and referred to him as the "inner man." The outer man is "decaying" (the flesh?), but the "inner man is being renewed day by day" (II Cor. 4:16). The law of God resides in the inner man (Rom. 7:22) and stands opposed to the flesh.

God made us to have an authentic self. I do not know much about my true self, but this much I do know. For one, the true self will be all truth and have no falseness. Said more poetically (or biblically), there will be all light and no darkness in him at all. (See Matt. 6:22–23.) Darkness, falsehood, and duplicity are character faults born out of the *eros* self-love within us, driven by what we want to believe about ourselves or what we want other people to believe. Most of our troubles on this front begin or gain ground when we are in our teens. It is then that we leave the relative innocence of childhood, pass through puberty, and begin the intense process of self-discovery: who am I? If we are not very secure in who we are, we begin innocently experimenting with personalities and behaviors that match up with the peer group we want to join or contrast with the peer group of which we do not want to be part. At any rate, many teens stumble into the bad habit of trying to be someone they are not. It leaves them confused and depressed, and they usually do not even know why.

At a teenage and young adult conference in Massachusetts, I told the story about a bright and shiny Mr. Apple who classmates considered a cool kid. The girls liked him, and the guys admired and were envious of him. He had "cool" answers to teachers, never appeared afraid, walked with a bit of a strut, and was admired by several. Mr. Banana decided he wanted to be "cool" too, so he began trying in every way to look like, talk like, and act like Mr. Apple. To show what I meant, I squeezed Mr. Banana up into a ball and, with a felt-tipped marker, covered him all in red. After a time, Mr. Banana realized he was very unhappy with himself. He was confused, depressed, and, worst of all, had lost touch with who he really was. The story ended well because Mr. Banana showed up at a Christian conference like this one, made his confession (confessing he has been living a false self), and learned how to walk after Christ (rather than after Mr. Apple). Then Mr. Banana was forgiven; he understood God had not made him an apple nor wanted him to become an apple. God had made him a banana and a good one at that. Lastly, he learned that despite efforts to be otherwise, he would never be good at anything except being the Mr. Banana he was created to be.

Unconsciously or consciously, *eros* drives us to want to be something we are not. Even the twelve disciples of Jesus argue over which of them is the greatest (Luke 9:46). Humility is the weapon against this form of pride and self-deception. God in His Spirit humbles us and purifies us until there remains no falsehood in us, and this characterizes our true self.

The other characteristic I know my true self will have is holiness. My true self will be one with God; his holiness will resemble that of his Father in heaven. Paul wrote,

> *Since we have these promises, beloved, let us cleanse ourselves from all defilement of flesh and spirit, perfecting holiness in the fear of God (II Cor. 7:1).*

True holiness is formed within us by the gift of God. Perhaps one other image can help us see what true holiness looks like. The first of the Ten Commandments is "I am Yahweh your God, Who brought you out of the land of Egypt, out of the house of slavery (out of sin and darkness). You shall have no other gods before Me" (Ex. 20:2–3). There is no authority, guide, or leader influencing a holy person other than His Father in heaven. He is focused on this God. His only dream is to please His God. He loves this God above all. No one else, including pride and self-love itself, has any significant influence over him. He lives a relatively detached, singular, and peaceful life, resting in His God and Father.

"Upward Call"

1979, I moved to Pittsburgh, Pennsylvania, to work for the
iscopal Diocese of Pittsburgh. For those new to the diocese, a
ries of short workshops was provided to acquaint us with its
frastructure. We met several administrators and ministry leaders
d learned about insurance, pensions, and diocesan finances.

1e day, however, they brought into our group a nun from a local
man Catholic convent who gave us some guidance in the conduct
our spiritual lives. She wanted to teach us about scriptural
editation and then led us through a meditation on Zacchaeus of
ticho (Luke 19). She read the story of Zacchaeus slowly, then
vited us for a period of silence to meditate on the passage,
entifying with a person of our choosing in the story. I was willing,
I tried. With my eyes closed, I put myself in place of Zacchaeus.
othing worked. I sensed nothing. Then I tried taking on the
rceptions of Jesus' disciples in the story. Again, nothing. Next, I
ed the disdaining townspeople who objected to Jesus staying with
is tax collector. Still empty. Lastly, and desperately, I tried
entifying with the thoughts of Jesus Himself. Nothing there. I
member feeling disappointment and frustration, saying to myself
at this was not working and that I might as well just go home.

, with my eyes still closed and still in a mode of meditation, I went
my "home" in the center of my heart. There was all of a sudden,
door there. I opened it and had a vision. I call it a vision, but it
obably was not a vision. It was like an image in a flash. There was
room in the middle of my heart, and in it were three chairs. The
rst was a large, over-stuffed, richly upholstered chair. Next to it
as a richly carved, straight-backed, dining room-style chair. The
ird was an ordinary desk chair. In the oversized, overstuffed chair
t God Himself. In the dining room-styled chair sat my true self.
nd the third desk chair was empty; it was mine. As I entered, God
d my true self immediately stood to welcome me and, smiling,

said, "We've been waiting for you." Their welcome was loving and gracious. There the image ends.

The truly memorable part of this "vision" was the clear and perfect sense of union between God and my true self. They were comfortable together and enjoyed being in each other's presence. My true self looked a lot like me, but was taller and completely unflawed spiritually and physically. He was entirely satisfied, peaceful, full of life, but content. He had the character of Christ within him. He was perfectly one with God; he was my future me.

Whether this vision was of my imagination or a gift from God, I do not know. In seeing my true self, I know that it gave me a very believable hope in the promises set before me. He was the person I will be when I am completed, my true self. He was the eschatological fulfillment referenced in I John above: "When Jesus appears we shall be like Him, for we shall see Him as He is."

The Four Loves of St Bernard of Clairvaux

Loving Self for Self's Sake

St Bernard of Clairvaux writes about four degrees or progressions of love as we draw closer to God.[54] The first progression of love is where we all naturally begin — it is the love we are born with — it is the love of self (*eros*). "No one has ever hated his own flesh," writes Paul (Eph. 5:29). As we have said before, we may sometimes not like ourselves very much, but since we remain our primary matter of concern, we clearly still love ourselves. The first progression of love is "loving self for self's sake."

Any one of several things might nudge us beyond this first progression of love: a sense of emptiness, that the God-shaped void in our heart begins to ache for relief, the pressing needs of those

---

[54] St. Bernard of Clairvaux, *On Loving God*

about us, or simple shame or guilt over our selfishness. Preferably, our departure from this first progression occurs when a good thing happens: when we begin reading the Gospels or hear the Christian message and when we begin hearing God's call upon our lives. We are not made to live solely for ourselves; God's word makes this abundantly clear.

Loving God for Self's Sake

Indeed, when God came into my life, my love for Him was born. He was no longer the past figure of historical fame; He had just become a living God who knew me personally and was calling me to be with Him now and forever. Treating me much like a child newly adopted out of an orphanage, God began saying yes to many of my prayers. There were many concerns in my life involving people, academics, responsibilities, and work I needed to do. So, totally unlike ever before, now I had a God who promised if I prayed and believed, it would be done for me. (See Matt. 17:20.) So many things I prayed about in those first days came out well. More than anything, I had become fully conscious of Him. He had won my heart. My God was mine. My sins were forgiven, and my name was written in His book. I loved Him for all the good things He did for me.

There are thousands of books on the Christian life, and many more are being written every day. Most of them have something to teach the followers of Jesus how to better walk following God's will and derive the benefits of doing so. Growing in our love of God is the greatest endeavor one can undergo in this lifetime. This lifetime was created for the Christian believer to journey through the wilderness of light and darkness to the ultimate Light, which is God. We love Jesus, and we love God the Father for all He does for us — for our self's sake.

"Upward Call"

Loving God for God's Sake

I remember a few years ago carefully reading through the Gospel of John, chapter 14, preparing for something; whether it was a sermon or a presentation for a retreat, I do not remember. John 14 is one of several chapters narrating the activities and the teachings of Jesus the night before His death. At this point in the narration, the washing of the feet is finished, and Jesus, seated with His disciples, delivers to them what is called His "farewell discourse." He explains once more that it is time for Him to leave them. He promises, though, that the Helper, the "Spirit of Truth," will be sent to comfort and assist them through their days to come. He must have known their sadness and fear, for He promises, "I will not leave you as orphans; I will come to you" (John 14:18). "Let not your heart be troubled, nor let it be fearful" (John 14:27). All of these comments reflect the fear and sadness, which must have hovered over the disciples. He has been with them day and night for three years and, though a lot of it had been rough, He has been excellent at answering all the criticisms brilliantly and performing with power all the miracles that made their incomparable journey a wonderful and powerful experience. He has been their protective Guardian and Father, and now He is leaving. The heaviness of their heart is palpable.

Then I read a verse that hit me like a ton of bricks. While the disciples are lamenting the impending loss of their friend and protector, Jesus says to them,

> *You heard me say to you, "I go away, and I will come to you." If you loved me, you would have rejoiced, because I go to the Father (John 14:28).*

We should pause to reflect on this. If the disciples love Jesus, they would be thinking of Him instead of thinking about their condition and being absorbed in their grief. Instead of navel-gazing at their lamentable circumstance, they should be congratulating Him on His impending graduation. In their *eros* love, they think only of themselves; had they embraced *agape* love, their thoughts would be for Him. Since He is now, after many punishing years, getting to do what everyone wishes to do — go to the Father in heaven — they should be rejoicing for His sake. I do not think it ever struck them for even a second that they should be glad for Him!

Naturally, while reading the passage, I resonated with their concerns; I, too, was not thinking of Him.

In fact, I began realizing I seldom just think about pleasing the Lord. I may often try to do what would please Him, but this was ultimately so that I can be found in His favor. When did I think, do, or say something exclusively to please God no matter the cost? In other words, when did I make Him the sole object of my love — *agape* for God?

If, for example, I get stuck on an elevator (a cause of great fear for claustrophobics like me), am I going to be at my wit's end engrossed in my rescue, or calmly call for assistance and then sit patiently on the floor meditating on how wonderful God is, knowing He is sitting there with me? What a show of love and faith that would be; what a way of telling God I love Him above all by taking this dead time and using it simply to please Him. I am not suggesting I would have the courage to act that bravely. I am saying I would find it most honorable if I did!

Naturally, we look to our amazing God as the resource of all our needs. When do we return the favor, asking for nothing, just praising Him because He deserves it? Indeed, a Christian on the pathway to union with God has just rounded a most significant corner in the journey when he learns to occupy himself not with getting from God but giving to God. St Bernard writes, "No longer do we love God because of our necessity, but because we have tasted and seen how gracious the Lord is." He adds, "Once (loving God for His sake) is recognized, it will not be hard to fulfill the commandment touching love to our neighbors; for whosoever loves God aright loves all God's creatures." Lastly, St Bernard seems to summarize with this, "Whosoever praises God for His essential goodness, and not merely because of the benefits He has bestowed, does really love God for His sake."[55]

Loving Self for God's Sake

There is a last progression of love, learning to love ourselves for God's sake. This progression of love seems beyond consideration to one such as myself who is much more inclined toward Paul's vision of himself: "Wretched man that I am, who will set me free from the body of this death?" (Rom. 7:24). Yet St Bernard sees learning to love oneself as the fourth progression in Christian love.

It is not correct to say we "learn" to do this; it is a gift from God. St Bernard writes,

> *I would count him blessed and holy to whom such rapture has been granted as a favor in this mortal life, for even an instant to lose yourself, as if you were emptied and lost and swallowed up in God, is no human love; it is celestial.*[56]

"Emptied, lost, and swallowed up in God" — these words say that we have died thoroughly to self, the empire *eros* has long claimed over our heart has been conquered. *Agape* alone rules within us. The nature of Jesus, His character, has become one with ours, and *agape* love has taken over the throne of our heart. We love God with the same love that God loves us. We love Jesus with the same love Jesus

---

[55] St Bernard of Clairvaux, *On Loving God*, Ch. 9.

[56] St Bernard of Clairvaux, *On Loving God*. Ch. 10.

loves us. We love our neighbor with the same love Jesus loved the world. Lost in this love, we love even ourselves.

All this sublimity probably seems far beyond imagination. Indeed, St Bernard speaks of a divine gift, a rapturous act which, if granted, may last only for a moment in time. If it does happen, its value is instilled in our conscious a vision of heaven, and such a vision would define the hope that remains in us until we die.

Hope is a virtue. I remember an event my earthly father had in the last years of his life: He had reached the point in aging that he could hardly remember anyone's name. He did not remember even what he did the day before. He pointed out that he remembers my sisters and me, but beyond Mom and us, he was not sure. One event, though, embedded itself in his memory bank, and he did not forget, for he mentioned it many times in his last years on earth. He woke up one morning and believed he had died. His death was wonderful news to him, because he was looking forward to heaven, and rightly so, for his life was secure in Christ. He woke up, and, believing he had died, he felt this incredible joy. The memorable part was that heaven was joy. He felt that and talked about that joy for many days to come. Of course, that morning, when the fog of waking up cleared, he realized he had not died, that he was still here. He was very disappointed and got out of bed. But, again, while he could not remember yesterday, he remembered that joy, and I emphasized to him this was a gift from God to help him get through his last days.

There is not much reason to get excited about a spiritual experience that is unlikely to happen. I am speaking now of the one that St Bernard mentions. If I find myself loving self for God's sake, as he describes, well and good; it's just that I am not going to look for it. But that it is out there and that it most probably is true, like my father's memory of joy, warrants our aiming in that direction even now. What I mean by this is that if we one day genuinely love ourselves for God's sake, then this is good reason to begin practicing it now!

I share my vision of my "true self," the "inner man" of whom Paul speaks. Now I am even more convinced that the true self, which *is* one with God, wrapped up in His love, is indeed a lovable person. And what makes him that way is God's love. Anyone knows that an excellent way to love a parent is to love his children. There is a union there; loving the child and being good to him is a love felt in the parent's heart. If God loves my neighbor, then I will love him, too, for God's sake. And if I am my Father's son, then I shall learn to love him because he is God's son, and by this, I love God as well.

So, while the fourth progression of love may or may not occur to any of us in this lifetime, the fact that it is part of our ultimate future enables us to incorporate the concept into our thoughts now.

The bottom line is to love yourself. God does; He considers it the thing to do. So, join with Him and with His *agape* love, love God, love Jesus, love your neighbor, and love even yourself. With all this powerful love circling our thoughts, surely we must be experiencing the upward call of God in Christ Jesus!

APPENDIX

A Recommended Office of Morning Prayer:[57]

Lord, open our lips, and our mouth shall proclaim your praise.

Glory to the Father, and to the Son, and to the Holy Spirit: as it was in the beginning, is now, and will be forever. Amen.

Psalm 100

O be joyful in the Lord all ye lands; serve the Lord with gladness and come before his presence with a song.

Be ye sure that the Lord he is God; it is he that hath made us and not we ourselves; we are his people and the sheep of his pasture.

O go your way into his gates with thanksgiving and into his courts with praise; be thankful unto him and speak good of his Name.

For the Lord is gracious; his mercy is everlasting; and his truth endureth from generation to generation.

or Psalm 143

Hear my prayer, O LORD; give ear to my supplications! In thy faithfulness answer me, in thy righteousness!

Enter not into judgment with thy servant; for no man living is righteous before thee. For the enemy has pursued me; he has crushed my life to the ground; he has made me sit in darkness like those long dead.

---

[57] Adapted from *The Book of Common Prayer*, 1979 (Kingsport, Kingsport Press, 1977) "The Morning Office, Rite II.

"Upward Call"

Therefore my spirit faints within me; my heart within me is appalled. I remember the days of old, I meditate on all that thou hast done; I muse on what thy hands have wrought.

I stretch out my hands to thee; my soul thirsts for thee like a parched land. Make haste to answer me, O LORD! My spirit fails! Hide not thy face from me, lest I be like those who go down to the Pit.

Let me hear in the morning of thy steadfast love, for in thee I put my trust. Teach me the way I should go, for to thee I lift up my soul.

Deliver me, O LORD, from my enemies! I have fled to thee for refuge!

Teach me to do thy will, for thou art my God! Let thy good spirit lead me on a level path! For thy name's sake, O LORD, preserve my life! In thy righteousness bring me out of trouble!

And in thy steadfast love cut off my enemies, and destroy all my adversaries, for I am thy servant.

The Readings. (It is recommended that you read a Psalm or a portion of a Psalm followed by a chapter from one of the other books of the Bible — Old or New Testament — as a time for prayerful thought, not study.)

A Psalm is read.

A passage of scripture is read.

Either of the following passages from Isaiah is now read.

Surely, it is God who saves me; I will trust in him and not be afraid. For the Lord is my stronghold and my sure defense, and he will be my Savior. Therefore you shall draw water with rejoicing from the springs of salvation. And on that day you shall say, give thanks to the Lord and call upon his Name; make his deeds known among the peoples; see that they remember that his Name is exalted. Sing the praises of the Lord, for he has done great things, and this is known in all the world. Cry aloud, inhabitants of Zion, ring out your joy, for the great one in the midst of you is the Holy One of Israel (Is. 12:2–6).

or

Seek the Lord while he wills to be found; call upon him when he draws near. Let the wicked forsake their ways and the evil ones their thoughts; and let them turn to the Lord, and he will have compassion, and to our God, for he will richly pardon.

For my thoughts are not your thoughts, nor your ways my ways, says the Lord. For as the heavens are higher than the earth, so are my ways higher than your ways, and my thoughts than your thoughts. For as rain and snow fall from the heavens and return not again, but water the earth, bringing forth life and giving growth, seed for sowing and bread for eating, so is my word that goes forth from my mouth; it will not return to me empty; but it will accomplish that which I have purposed, and prosper in that for which I sent it (Is. 55:6–11).

The Lord's Prayer

Our Father, who art in heaven, hallowed be thy Name, thy kingdom come, thy will be done, on earth as it is in heaven. Give us this day our daily bread. And forgive us our trespasses, as we forgive those who trespass against us. And lead us not into temptation, but deliver us from evil. For thine is the kingdom, and the power, and the glory, for ever and ever. Amen.

"Upward Call"

One or more of the following prayers are said.

A Prayer for the Renewal of Life

O God, the King eternal, whose light divides the day from the night and turns the shadow of death into the morning: Drive far from us all wrong desires, incline our hearts to keep your law, and guide our feet into the way of peace; that, having done your will with cheerfulness during the day, we may, when night comes, rejoice to give you thanks; through Jesus Christ our Lord. Amen.

A Prayer for Peace

O God, the author of peace and lover of concord, to know you is eternal life and to serve you is perfect freedom: Defend us, your humble servants, in all assaults of our enemies; that we, surely trusting in your defense, may not fear the power of any adversaries; through the might of Jesus Christ our Lord. Amen.

A Prayer for Grace

Lord God, almighty and everlasting Father, you have brought us in safety to this new day: Preserve us with your mighty power, that we may not fall into sin, nor be overcome by adversity; and in all we do, direct us to the fulfilling of your purpose; through Jesus Christ our Lord. Amen.

A Prayer for Guidance

Heavenly Father, in you we live and move and have our being: We humbly pray you so to guide and govern us by your Holy Spirit, that in all the cares and occupations of our life we may not forget you, but may remember that we are ever walking in your sight; through Jesus Christ our Lord. Amen.

A Prayer for Mission

Lord Jesus Christ, you stretched out your arms of love on the hard wood of the cross that everyone might come within the reach of your saving embrace: So clothe us in your Spirit that we, reaching forth our hands in love, may bring those who do not know you to the knowledge and love of you; for the honor of your Name. Amen.

In the space below, intercessions for others are offered, as well as petitions for ourselves.

The Office of Morning Prayer may be closed with the following.

The General Thanksgiving

Almighty God, Father of all mercies, we your unworthy servants give you humble thanks for all your goodness and loving-kindness to us and to all whom you have made. We bless you for our creation, preservation, and all the blessings of this life; but above all for your immeasurable love in the redemption of the world by our Lord Jesus Christ; for the means of grace, and for the hope of glory.

And, we pray, give us such an awareness of your mercies, that with truly thankful hearts we may show forth your praise, not only with our lips, but in our lives, by giving up our selves to your service, and by walking before you in holiness and righteousness all our days; through Jesus Christ our Lord, to whom, with you and the Holy Spirit, be honor and glory throughout all ages. Amen.

Then may be said

Let us bless the Lord. Thanks be to God.

The grace of our Lord Jesus Christ, and the love of God, and the fellowship of the Holy Spirit, be with us all evermore. Amen. *(II Cor. 13:14)*

"Upward Call"

It is a joy to recommend to you Father Scott Wilson's inspirational new book entitled *Upward Call.* It is intended for all who seek a closer relationship with God, whether they are new believers or seasoned pilgrims in the Christian walk. In a collection of anecdotes, illustrations, and sound Biblical teachings, Fr. Wilson puts before us basic principles for spiritual growth and inspires us to press onward and upward in our daily response to God's call to us in Jesus Christ. As an experienced pastor, priest, and spiritual guide, he shares with us his wisdom and insights, gained from decades of leading others to a closer walk with the Living Lord.

The Rt. Rev. Jack Leo Iker, SSC, DD
Third Bishop of Fort Worth (retired)

Upward Call, How to Draw Closer to God, is a well written, practical, inspirational book that will give the reader a detailed guide to deepen their Christian faith. I first met Canon Wilson in the Diocese of Dallas through the Renewal Center that did programs such as Cursillo and one for High School students called Happening in the early 1970's. Many of the references in his book are in regard to those early years of renewal in the Church. Canon Wilson was a Spiritual Director on many of those renewal weekends and has first-hand experience of guiding lay men and women and youth in a closer relationship to God Almighty and especially His Son, Jesus Christ. Being in love for the first time is a special gift. Being in love with our Lord Jesus Christ is an extra special gift that connects our spiritual heart to our mind. When the heart and mind are connected by the Almighty, wonderful blessings are realized by that person and those who are blessed to know them. A must read for those seeking to develop their spiritual life.

Canon H.W. Sandy Herrmann, SSC
Co-founder of the Happening Movement

Upward Call: How to Draw Closer to God

I am delighted to be among the people to review the book. I have known Canon Scott Wilson since 1999 when I visited the United States the first time. After Happening we had a reunion in his parish along with all Happeners at St. Matthias. Since then, we have shared each other's ministry path. We were part of the launching of the Cursillo in the Diocese Northern Malawi in the year 2000. Canon Scott has conducted a number of retreats for our clergy and the nuns, and has led a good number of mission trips to our Diocese since I became Bishop of this Diocese. He has been a companion for my work as a Bishop, something that is seen in this book, as a true reflection of his own devotion to the work of the Lord.

Reading through the book from the perspective of a student of Missiology, I found it useful as it presents the truth of the call by God in inviting us to participate in His mission. The Canon has presented a Biblical perspective of the mission of God which engages us in His plan for our salvation. The Father sent the Son and the Son, by the power of the Holy Spirit, is sending us into the work. By this book we know that we are ambassadors of the Kingdom of God. We are here to participate in the mission of God as the Canon has ably encouraged each Baptized Christian to engage in the mission of God.

I have been challenged on the point of listening to God and being obedient to his will. I do remember very well how Canon Scott listened to what God said to him when the Diocese of Northern Malawi called him to be our third Bishop. We settled on Canon Scott as our sole candidate where he had all the chances to be elected at the provincial electoral synod. He came to Malawi for a familiarization tour as his final step to discern his call. We only heard a few days later that he had heard God not to come and be the Bishop, and that a bishop should come from among the clergy of the

Diocese of Northern Malawi. I was one of the people who could not see any of us taking over in those early days of the diocese. I was one of the people who was seeing him as the person we need for a Bishop.

When I was reading the book under the topic *"Why Moses Was Denied Entrance into the Promised Land" I* came to understand more how Canon Scott reached the conclusion to obey God when He spoke to him of not coming to be our bishop here in Northern Malawi.

Indeed, we only give what we have been given. I have observed that Canon Scott truly has given us in his book what he has been given to share on his deep insight in the love of God and our participation into the mission of God. We indeed need to hear God's upward call to join everyone as participants in His greater mission as we draw closer to Him.

Yours in our Most Blessed Lord

+FanuEL Northern Malawi
The Rt. Rev. Dr. FanuEL Emmanuel Magangani,
Anglican Diocese of Northern Malawi,